Gender Concepts of Swedish and American Youth

Gender Concepts of Swedish and American Youth

Margaret Jean Intons-Peterson
Indiana University

LEA LAWRENCE ERLBAUM ASSOCIATES, PUBLISHERS
1988   Hillsdale, New Jersey   Hove and London

Lawrence Erlbaum Associates, Inc., Publishers
365 Broadway
Hillsdale, New Jersey 07642

Library of Congress Cataloging in Publication Data
Intons-Peterson, Margaret Jean.
   Gender concepts of Swedish and American youth.

   Bibliography: p.
   Includes index.
   1.Youth—United States. 2. Youth—Sweden. 3. Sex
role—United States. 4. Sex role—Sweden. 5. Sweden—
Social policy. I. Title.
HQ796.I55   1988   305.2′35′09   87-33174
   ISBN 0-8058-0173-1

Printed in the United States of America
10 9 8 7 6 5 4 3 2 1

This book is fondly and gratefully dedicated to
Inga-Lena Matthews
and to
the young women and men who served as respondents

CONTENTS

7

PERSONAL GENDER CONCEPTS: RATINGS OF CURRENT AND IDEAL SELF/119

8

THE CHANGE-SEX STORY/147

9

LIFESTYLES THAT 18-YEAR-OLDS EXPECT FOR THEMSELVES IN 10 YEARS' TIME/161

10

CONCLUSIONS AND DISCUSSION/171

PREFACE

Imagine a United States whose policies simultaneously strengthen the family and foster equality of the sexes, two goals often considered incompatible. Imagine further that these policies could become effective in less than a generation. Fantasy? Not at all, Sweden tells us. In about 16 years, Sweden has done the seemingly impossible: Its futuristic plan for the equality of the sexes has the family as a central component.

In 1968, Sweden astonished the world with its startlingly revolutionary plan to establish equality between the sexes. This goal, the proposal explained, would benefit both sexes. It would also alter the lives of both women and men, affecting the family, the workplace, education, and many other aspects of society. Now it is time to assess the Swedish experiment. It is time to examine the changes and their underlying philosophies, to evaluate the benefits and costs of the new practices. It is time to ask what can be learned from Sweden's remarkable experience. Most interesting of all, it is time to ask about changes in attitudes, in the expectations for and about the two sexes. These are some of the concerns that drew me to Sweden in August 1983, as part of a sabbatical leave research project.

The project grew out of my long-standing interest in Sweden, a curiosity originally instigated by the experiences of my parents-in-law, both of whom immigrated from Sweden to the United States as children. This curiosity led to a most memorable visit to Sweden in 1971. Relatives we had never met before gave us a wonderfully warm welcome.

The professional roots of the project date back to 1973 when I first taught a class entitled "Women: A Psychological Prospective." Sweden was included as part of its cross-cultural section. I have continued to gather information throughout the years, both to keep the class current and to watch the progress of Sweden's efforts. This process culminated in the 1983–1984 sabbatical leave project spent at the Department of Psychology, University of Stockholm and the Center for Women Scholars and Research on Women at the University of Uppsala, as a guest scholar of the Swedish Institute.

ACKNOWLEDGMENTS

I am greatly indebted to many people and many organizations. So many, in fact, that I am hesitant to name them, for fear of inadvertently omitting some of the people. Let me begin by expressing my gratitude to the many individuals in the United States and in Sweden who served as advisers and counselors, sometimes unbeknownst to them, as they responded to my plans. I was particularly impressed by the openness of Swedish politicians and business people. Many of these people graciously agreed to see me, and they were invariably helpful, informative, and straightforward. They had given considerable thought to the merits and demerits of their country's policies and practices and were willing to share their views with an outsider. I am most appreciative.

My quest for information was guided in part by the vast collection of papers published by The Swedish Institute. These papers are a wealthy resource for all people interested in Sweden, and they play an almost ambassadorial role for Sweden. My friends at the Swedish Institute often identified individuals who had contributed to the research, and it was the Swedish Institute that made my stay in Sweden financially feasible. I give all of these individuals and the Swedish Institute my warmest thanks.

The Department of Psychology at the University of Stockholm served as my base of operations during the project. Professor David Magnusson, then chairing the department, introduced me to a number of people in the department, who helped me in numerous ways. Through frequent conversations with these people I learned about Sweden; about research in Sweden (including "thou shalts" and "thou shalt nots"); about cooperative school districts that met the criteria I had set forth; about Swedish educational, political, and value systems. Their friendship and assistance sustained me. To all of the people in the Department of Psychology, I convey my grateful appreciation.

The Center for Women Scholars and Research on Women at the University of Uppsala, was a haven and a source of counsel and support. Its director, Dr. Mona Eliasson, first bid me welcome as we sat in the hospital where she had recently given birth to her second baby. It was my only opportunity to visit a Swedish hospital. Almost every Tuesday I traveled to Uppsala to consult with Dr. Eliasson, with Dr. Marianne Carlsson, Birgitta Paget, and others who made the castle (the location of the Center) hum. Dr. Eliasson not only made possible my visit to a hospital, but she was responsible for my receiving a key to the castle, a rare experience for an American!

Most of all, I am indebted to Inga-Lena Matthews, my assistant in Sweden. She did all of the original translations, helped me work out the logistics of the research, contacted the schools, shepherded me from place to place, rescued me as I floundered in my halting Swedish, and completed the project when I had to return to the United States due to a family emergency. In recognition of her many contributions, I dedicate this book to Inga-Lena and to the young people who were our respondents. One young person served as a different kind of respondent—Christopher Matthews, Inga-Lena's son. Thirteen years old at the time we began the work, he was an ideal pilot subject, and we asked many questions of him.

I had some outstanding assistants in the United States, as well. These responsibilities were shared more widely than in Sweden, where Inga-Lena and I gathered all of the data. In the United States, Greg Brown, Chris Davis, Maria Howard, Ruth Hughes, Debbie Smith, and Jeffrey West provided dedicated service.

Needless to say, without the cooperation and assistance of the principals (rektors) and teachers of the schools in the United States and Sweden, no data would have been gathered. I hope that these magnanimous people and their students will find some benefit from the research. Professor Linda Haas also played a highly significant role. Her editorial comments were extremely useful, as were our conversations about the two countries.

It is easy to overlook the contributions of one's colleagues, of the people to whom one confides one's experimental woes, the pains of experimental design, the difficulties of instantiating that design, of authorship, and the multitude of other complaints that we heap on commiserating, supportive colleagues. I do not want to commit that error. Hence, it is with great pride in the camaraderie, in the friendly, challenging, intellectually intense atmosphere of the Department of Psychology at Indiana University, that I publicly proclaim how greatly I have benefited from being part of their enterprise.

Perhaps the greatest impetus for concern about a gender-equal society has come from my own family. In many ways, they have influenced my thinking about problems, and they have tolerated my absences with graciousness. I am particularly grateful to my husband, whose heart problems were not helped by being a "bachelor" for the time I was in Sweden. For his sake and for the sake of our children, I hope the world will offer increasing acknowledgment and approbation of the humanity and talents of both sexes.

Finally, my most profound indebtedness is to the young people who served as respondents. They represent the future. They seemed to enjoy participation, but they deserve more. They deserve true gender equality, an equality that will permit each of them to live life to the fullest. We older people owe it to them.

1

The Problem

If you woke up tomorrow and discovered that you were a *girl*, how would your life be different?" "Terrible . . . ," "a catastrophe . . . ," "I would immediately commit suicide . . . ," wrote some astonished and horrified boys. When asked about becoming a boy, some delighted and enthusiastic girls offered, "Great . . . ," "now I can do what I want . . . ," "now I can be happy . . ." These are comments of American children responding to the "Change-sex question" tested by Alice Baumgartner (see Tavris with Baumgartner, 1983). Although not rejecting female roles, the girls often described advantages of male roles. In contrast, boys were dubious about female roles, infrequently noting advantages; they firmly espoused male roles. Thus, girls, but rarely boys, wrote positive stories about changing gender. Moreover, this asymmetry spanned Grades 3 through 12.

Why should girls find the male role appealing and boys find the female role unappealing? The stories written in reaction to the cue just given, along with responses to other measures, suggest that even recently, after more than a decade of sporadic efforts in the United States to promote equality of the sexes, the female role still is considered restrictive by females themselves, their parents, peers, employers, and society in general. It is a devalued role, commanding less esteem and prestige than its male counterpart. By contrast, the male role is perceived as much freer of these restrictions. It is the more influential, respected role.

These results are startling, because they indicate that even third graders held traditional conceptions about gender in 1983. The results also are dismaying, for some statements inaccurately exaggerate attributes assigned to the sexes. Taken in their entirety, the data suggest that the subjects had mental constellations or schemata about the two sexes, which were applied in a general fashion to assess the roles of the two sexes.

Why, we wondered, are such views still held? Because the United States has not adopted a concerted, organized policy of promoting equality of the sexes? Because attitudes have not kept pace with legally mandated affirmative action plans and equal opportunity practices? Because attitudes perpetuate gender stereotypes, which continue to foster the development of asymmetric gender concepts? If these explanations are accurate, children growing up in a society that has systematically encouraged equality of the sexes throughout the lifetimes of the youths, such as Sweden, should exhibit different gender concepts. Specifically, these children should show fewer gender-stereotypic and fewer asymmetric gender views than children from a society with a less systematic commitment to equality, such as the United States. Sweden's equality efforts officially date to 1968 when its policy of holding both parents responsible for the emotional as well as the financial well-being of the family was announced. Ever since, it has been formulating laws and practices to bolster its goals. The central purpose of the current research is to explore these possibilities by comparing components of gender concepts in Sweden with those in the United States.

This purpose entails a comparison of the contents and development of gender concepts in Swedish and American youth. The project presupposes that people form mental structures (concepts, constellations, schemata) about gender. That is, gender-related information such as typical occupations, personality traits, and physical attributes associated with each sex constitute a cohesive mental concept. Presumably, all people form gender concepts about both sexes in their culture. These concepts are important, because they influence our views of the world. Like other schematic concepts, the attitudes, expectations, and beliefs about gender function as filters or channels through which we perceive our environment.[1] Moreover, our concepts about gender guide our behavior toward and our interactions with others. Knowledge of the contents and development of gender concepts provide a window to the operation of the human mind. Hence, the pursuit of this knowledge is the primary goal of the current research.

---

[1] Williams and Best (1982) prefer the concept of "sex stereotypes," which they define as:

> belief systems containing generalizations about the characteristics of groups of persons. . . . Sex stereo-types . . . have to do with general *beliefs* about men and women that operate at two levels: *sex-role stereotypes*, which consist of beliefs concerning the general appropriateness of various roles and activities for men and for women, and *sex-trait stereotypes*, which consist of the psychological characteristics or behavioral traits that are believed to characterize men with much greater (or lesser) frequency that they characterize women. (p. 16)

This definition implies a recognition that both sexes may manifest sex-trait stereotypes even though one sex may be thought to possess any particular trait to a greater extent than the other sex. This view seems reasonable, for most people appear to manifest most traits or attributes to at least some extent under appropriate circumstances. Unfortunately, the measures used by Williams and Best do not recognize this situation. As discussed in chapter 2, their measures require subjects to associate one and only one sex with a particular trait. We found that even young children (Intons-Peterson, in press) recognized that both sexes possessed many traits, although sometimes to a different extent.

There are other reasons for studying the components of gender concepts. These components are not necessarily accurate, but without specification of the components, we have no way to assess their accuracy. Two illustrations are the beliefs about women's "emotional frailty" and men's "inability to nurture," beliefs that are widely held despite substantial disconfirming objective evidence. Another reason for studying the components of gender concepts is that the components of these concepts may be generalized to most females or to most males, regardless of the accuracy of the components. Such overgeneralization might not even be recognized by the individual. It follows, therefore, that the identity and validity of these components is singularly important. Accordingly, the first aim of this research is to identify the contents of gender concepts.

The contents of gender concepts appear to change with age (Intons-Peterson, in press; Williams & Best, 1982). For example, our ideas about most girls almost certainly change as we grow up, just as our ideas about most boys, most women, and most men may change. Consequently, to understand the development of gender concepts, we need to assess their contents at different ages, the second goal of this research.

As important as the first two goals are, our understanding of gender concepts would be incomplete without an assessment of how culture shapes these concepts. Hence, our third goal is to examine the effects of cultural influences on the contents of gender concepts. We assume that the contents of these constellations are culturally determined to a substantial extent. One strategy for testing this assumption is to contrast views about gender in markedly different countries. Such a comparison would not be particularly interesting, however, because the results would be trivially predictable. More challenging is the possibility of comparing gender concepts from two countries that are quite similar in many respects but that differ in terms of their commitments to equality between the sexes. Sweden and the United States are two countries that afford this kind of comparison.

Sweden has actively pursued a policy of equality of opportunity for the sexes during the lifetime of our Swedish participants (see chapter 2), whereas the United States has followed a less formal, extra-constitutional, nonsystematic course. These cultural differences led us to predict that Swedish gender concepts would be less asymmetric than the American counterparts.

CULTURAL AND PERSONAL GENDER CONCEPTS

We assume that these cultural differences influence the components encoded in gender concepts. The first type of gender concepts, *cultural* gender concepts, is that previously described. We propose that cultural gender concepts contain components that are generally and typically attributed to each sex by the women and men of the culture (e.g., Spence, Helmreich, & Stapp, 1975). Thus, both women and men have similar concepts for women and similar concepts for men, although the components of the two constellations differ. In addition, individuals have a *personal* or self-concept. This concept contains information relevant to the self, including some gender-related items. Note that the components of a person's personal concept are not necessarily identical to those of their cultural gender concept for that person's own sex. For example, a woman may think that most women are gentle but that she, as an individual, is not. Similarly, a man may think that most men are competitive but that he is not. Both types of concepts are important, for personal concepts index the individual's beliefs about herself or himself, whereas the cultural gender concepts reflect stereotypic views of the two sexes in the country.

Most research has focused on cultural gender concepts. This evidence suggests that, in the United States, the two sexes are assigned different personality attributes. For example, a number of researchers (e.g., Bem, 1981; Deaux, 1984; Spence, Helmreich, & Holahan, 1979) have shown that women are often characterized as warm, gentle, affectionate, selfless, and kind—traits that often are described as "expressive," and "communal." Men often are assigned "instrumental" or "agentic" traits such as having leadership qualities, making decisions easily, not giving up easily, being self-confident, being self-sufficient, standing up well under pressure, and having strong personalities. Typically, both sexes agree about these attributes, suggesting that these attributes may be components of cultural gender concepts for women and men in the United States. We cannot be sure that these components were truly representative of the gender concepts, however, because the subjects in the aforementioned experiments rated "women" and "men," rather than "most women" and "most men." They might have used only a few or even a single woman or man as the model(s) they described when answering the questions. Clearly, when assessing cultural gender concepts, we want to identify the characteristics that are assigned routinely, customarily, and consensually to one sex or the other. It follows, therefore, that the referent, say "most women" or "most men," should be unambiguously identified and that less clear designations, such as "women" or "men" should be avoided. In our experiments in the United States and Sweden, participants were specifically instructed to rate most women or most men. Our results corroborated and extended those previously described.

The other type of gender concept, the personal concept, is assessed through participants' self-ratings. Although most previous work has not obtained both cultural and personal gender ratings from the same subjects (excepting research by Spence et al., 1975, which did not specifically instruct subjects to rate *most* women and *most* men), our preliminary evidence indicated that the two were not identical. Therefore, in the current research, we obtained self-ratings in addition to ratings of most men and most women in both countries.

SUMMARY OF THE PROJECT

To summarize more fully, our goals were to map the development of both cultural and personal gender concepts in Swedish and American youth. This is an awesome task, for it is difficult to be sure that the measures actually assess significant facets of the gender concepts. Consider the problem of selecting traits or attributes, for example. While selecting traits to test, an experimenter may unintentionally exclude some important characteristics. It has been customary to assess personality traits, but other factors such as strength, height, activities, occupations (Deaux, 1984; Deaux & Lewis, 1984), and even hair or eye color (Carlsson, personal communication; Intons-Peterson, in press) also may be important gender differentiators. In recently completed research in our laboratory, we found that females are thought to have longer, lighter, and curlier hair than males, despite the unreliability of these differentiators (Intons-Peterson, in press). The subjects in this experiment were American, but Carlsson (personal communication) has found similar results with Swedish children: They think that girls have curlier, longer hair, and even are more likely to have blue eyes than boys. Neither study found any evidence that the preschool subjects use genital or secondary sex characteristics to identify the two sexes. These results suggest that the measures of gender concepts should allow for the inclusion of new gender-salient cues, in addition to already recognized ones. Accordingly, we used a number of different types of measures, in the hope that we would obtain sensitive, converging—and therefore, compelling—results.

The specific measures were the following. First, we obtained unrestricted descriptions of attributes considered desirable in all people, regardless of sex. These reports should index attributes particularly valued by both sexes in each of the countries. We also asked for written descriptions of four stimulus groups: most girls, most boys, most women, and most men. This measure has a number of advantages. The respondents were not "led" or biased toward specific kinds of attributes. They were free to respond with whatever occurred to them, thus allowing for the possibility of identifying some unexpected and new gender cues. The measure assumes that the subjects will record the most salient characteristics for each sex and age, a distinct advantage, but it also has some disadvantages. The informants may not write as fast as they think, and some attributes may be forgotten as others are being written (output interference). In addition, the pressures of testing or their opinions about what the investigator is seeking may result in failures to list some attributes that the respondents actually consider important. For example, they might ignore activities or occupational interests, if they happen to start with other types of attributes, such as personality traits. Also, the measure does not access the relative importance of each attribute to the gender concept, an aspect that may be particularly sensitive to cross-cultural differences.

Consequently, a second approach was used to identify the relative importance of various gender components already known to be important in one or the other country, plus some attributes that seemed likely to be important. These measures of cultural gender concepts consisted of ratings of how important the subjects thought it was for each of the four stimulus groups to possess the described characteristics. The same procedure was used to obtain estimates of personal gender concepts. In these cases, the respondents were asked to rate themselves on the traits, from the perspective of both how they are now and how they would like to be. These measures used 7-point rating scales that ranged from extremely unimportant to extremely important.

The aforementioned measures are susceptible to social desirability factors. That is, informants may record responses that they think are socially desirable, correct, or appropriate. They may record what they think the experimenter wants them to say, rather than what they really believe. Another measure was used to at least partially circumvent these problems. The respondents were asked to imagine that, when they awaken the next morning, they discover that they have become the other sex. They were to write a brief story describing what their lives would be like after this change. Note that this task permits the subjects to state that no changes would occur, whereas Baumgartner's (see Tavris with Baumgartner, 1983) final line—"how would your life be different?"—precludes that option.

Each of these measures should yield information about the contents of gender concepts. These measures were used to test children and youths at three ages: 11, 14, and 18 years. These ages were selected so that the youngest group would be prepubescent, the middle group would be pubescent and starting to make educational and occupational choices, and the third group would be entering adulthood. In addition, all respondents would be literate. The oldest group would already have made some educational and occupational choices.

Our contentions that one's culture and experiences lead to the development of both cultural and personal gender concepts yield the following general predictions: (a) the components of the concepts would differ somewhat for the two sexes, (b) the components of the gender concepts would change with age, (c) cultural and personal gender concepts would differ on at least some components, and (d) differences between the concepts for the two sexes would be less pronounced in Sweden than in the United States.

This latter prediction rests on the assumption that Sweden's systematic policy of equal opportunity has effectively moderated stereotypic gender differences. The practices followed by Sweden since 1968 have been directed toward providing equality of opportunity; the question is whether these efforts have modified attitudes, as well. Although earlier gender concepts have not been assessed, the very traditional and stereotypic gender roles of Swedish society in the 1950s strongly suggest that the Swedes held markedly different expectations for the two sexes. In the 1950s, for example, less than 30% of married women worked outside the home. Within a generation, that figure skyrocketed to 85%. What had Sweden done? Chapter 2 presents a brief description of Sweden's practices since 1969.

Following the description of contemporary Swedish efforts to secure equal opportunity for the two sexes in Chapter 2, we turn to a consideration of cross-cultural research, in general, and the results of cross-cultural explorations of gender concepts, in particular (chapter 3), to the methodology of our project (chapter 4), the results (chapters 5-9), and a discussion of the implications (chapter 10). Readers may wish to skip ahead to chapters that are of particular interest to them.

2

Sweden's Equal Opportunity Policies and Practices

In 1968, Sweden startled the world with its progressive plan to establish equality between the sexes. This equality, the plan said, required fundamental changes in the lives of both women and men, changes that would involve the family, the workplace, the school, and other aspects of society. I know of no other country that has embarked on such an ambitious program. Perhaps its most unusual, most salient feature is its insistence on the sharing of familial responsibilities by both sexes. Its provision for the joint participation of both sexes in the workplace also is important, but this feature has been adopted by numerous countries. (Two Communist countries, the Soviet Union and the People's Republic of China, are frequently cited examples.) Not content with only a policy, even one backed up by government sanctions, Sweden has constructed an extensive array of social legislation designed to foster gender equality.

Because the extent of Sweden's commitment and the impressive implementation of its policy largely motivates the current research, I devote this chapter to a detailed examination of Sweden's plan, noting how the policies might be expected to influence gender concepts. In addition, the boldness and vision of Sweden's policies warrant scrutiny by all persons interested in the process of social change. There is still another reason for giving a detailed account of the provisions Sweden has made to undergird gender equality: Its assumption that a

> certain degree of basic security is required before sexual equality can be achieved, and this security . . . is derived from a wide variety of benefits. These include national health insurance, prenatal care for mothers, general child allowance, child care, free meals at school, housing subsidies, pensions and home-keep for elderly persons. (Equality between men and women in Sweden, *Fact Sheets on Sweden*, 1984)

The following description of contemporary Sweden draws heavily on Baude's (1979) chapter, Scott's (1982) *Sweden's Right To Be Human*, Wistrand's (1981) *Swedish Women on the Move*, and the Swedish Institute's rich collection of fact sheets and relevant articles, in addition to discussions with people in government, at universities, in industry, in the *Riksdag* (parliament), in politics, and in the media. These sources identified five areas as essential to Sweden's policies on equality: general policy and principles, the family, education, employment, and the mass media. In the rest of this chapter, I consider legislation and its results in each of the five areas.

SWEDEN'S POLICY OF EQUALITY
OF OPPORTUNITY: CHANGED SOCIAL
ROLES AND INDIVIDUAL INDEPENDENCE

In 1968, Sweden proclaimed its amazingly ambitious policy to the United Nations:

> The question of women's rights must be viewed as a function of the whole complex of roles and the division of labor imposed on both women and men by upbringing, tradition, and practice (and to a less extent by legislation). No decisive change in the distribution of function and status as between the sexes can be achieved if the duties of the male in society are assumed a priori to be unaltered. The division of functions as between the sexes must be changed in such a way that both the man and the woman in a family are afforded the same practical opportunities of participating in both active parenthood and gainful employment. If women are to attain a position in society outside the home which corresponds to their proportional membership in the citizen body, it follows that men must assume a greater share of responsibility for the upbringing of children and the care of the home. (Servan-Schreiber, 1973, pp. 89–90)

Thus, equality entails not only increased opportunities for women; it also ensures new opportunities for men, a view widely supported by the Swedish people. Both the policy and its acceptance are supplemented by three general principles. The first is the belief that each person is a unique and independent individual who should be self-sufficient, to every extent possible. Self-sufficiency is considered crucial to one's feelings of self-esteem and self-acceptance. Self-sufficiency betokens adult maturity. It epitomizes responsibility for one's self and one's dependents. The second principle that so firmly guides the general acceptance of equality is inherent in the Swedish word for equality, *jämställdhet*, a word that incorporates a sophisticated concept. *Jämställdhet* does not mean that all people are the same and therefore are equal. It does not deny individual differences. To the contrary, it recognizes that people differ—that women and men differ biologically, for example—but asserts that all people, regardless of their differences, are entitled to equal opportunities. This perceptive concept should not require modification due to new knowledge about the contributions of biology, culture, and social structure to the (increasingly similar) capabilities of the two sexes. The third principle is that true equality of opportunity necessarily involves changes in the traditional roles of men, in addition to those of women. Men, like women, have been shaped and molded by cultural expectations, some of which may be undesirable in the sense of depriving men of some fundamental human experiences. For example, the Swedes think that the lives of both sexes are enriched by close contact with children, as well as by work experiences.

The policy and the three general principles contribute to the legislation for the family, education, employment, and the mass media. For each of these areas, we explore the changes that have been made, the methods of implementation, the results, and the likely effects on perceptions of gender roles and on views about gender similarities and differences.

THE MANY COMPONENTS
OF FAMILY LEGISLATION

Foremost in Sweden's novel view of the desirability of gender equality is the assumption that both sexes will participate actively in parenthood and domestic maintenance. A companion, albeit internationally more common aspect of Sweden's vision of gender equality is the participation of both sexes in gainful employment. The achievement of these aims clearly called for legislation relating to the family that would foster the goals. But before describing this legislation, we need to know more about the Swedish family. Like families in most countries, Swedish families contain different numbers of adults and children, and these people have various relationships to each other. In September 1980, about one third (34%) of adults 20 years of age and older were single, divorced, widowed, or lived alone. The other two-thirds cohabited, as married or unmarried couples. Children often were part of both single and cohabiting households and were biologically related to none, one, or both of the adults. In brief, the Swedish "family" is as complex—and difficult to define—as families in the United States, where, according to the 1980 census, only 7% of the American families consisted of the so-called typical family of an employed father, a homemaker mother, and two or more dependent children living at home. Perhaps the two most distinctive aspects of the Swedish family are the widespread acceptance of unmarried cohabitation as the basis for a normal family life and the absence of the concept of illegitimate offspring. Unmarried cohabitation incurs no social disapproval; nevertheless, in 1982, about two-thirds of adults aged 25–64 were married or widowed. Illegitimacy was invalidated by the Swedish *Riksdag* in 1976 as a concept that unjustly penalized children of unmarried parents.

These characteristics of the Swedish family are incorporated in four provisions that governmental commissions decreed should be implemented in Swedish family legislation:

- Every adult, married or not, should be responsible for his or her own support.
- Marriage should be a voluntary form of cohabitation between independent people.
- No form of cohabitation is to be favored over any other.
- The emotional needs of children should be satisfied outside the family as well as within it.

Individual Taxation and Name Choice.   Swedish income tax law states that each adult's income is to be taxed individually. Thus, each adult files and pays tax on her or his own income, a system that implements the independence principle. Adults who do not have gainful employment are entitled to a deduction. This law does not differentiate between married and unmarried cohabitants, although the amount of the tax is affected by whether or not one is living alone and whether or not one has dependent children. In addition to boosting self-esteem, an incredible (to my American eyes) result of this system is that it does not penalize anyone for his or her marital status or for his or her choice to work outside the home. If anything, the progressive nature of the income tax makes it more advantageous to divide a family income between two adult wage earners than for a single person to earn the same income. Moreover, it eliminates the concepts of "head of the household" or "chief wage earner." Despite these psychological advantages, the Swedish tax system is at least as cumbersome and complicated as its American counterpart, and it elicits the same kinds of grumbles, complaints, and wails about strangling overtaxation as its American cousin. (These protestations are more valid in Sweden, whose overall tax burden, relative to its gross national product, was the highest of the 23 industrialized countries belonging to the Organization for Economic Development, as reported by the 1987, *Information Please Almanac.* In contrast, the United States was in the 20th position.) Simplifications and remedies to the complicated taxation systems are being sought in both countries. Another disadvantage of the Swedish tax system has implications for the financial and emotional welfare of the family. According to Lindblom (1986), the economic condition of families with children has worsened compared to that of families without children, in part because childrearing costs have not been offset by taxation relief and subsidies to families.

Also contributing to the independence principle is one of Sweden's most unusual legal changes: its new name law. This law, which took effect at the beginning of 1983, has two major provisions. One allows citizens to change their names easily, if they wish to do so. Such a provision is consistent with the concept of individual identity, of course, so it is not surprising that the passage of the legislation attracted relatively little attention. Nor is it surprising that preliminary information now available suggests that most people exercising this provision do so because they dislike their first or last name.

The second provision is that all infants will be given their mothers' surnames, unless a petition is made for another name within 3 months of the baby's birth. Scanty evidence suggests that relatively few people petition for a surname change for their infant.

Sweden's philosophy of independence for the individual undoubtedly fosters the development of individualized personal gender concepts in some specific ways. As defined in chapter 1, personal gender concepts contain attributes that the person considers to importantly define the self. The likely outcome of this emphasis on individual independence differs from what would be expected in the United States. As suggested earlier, Swedes view independence as a hallmark of self-sufficient, adult maturity. Independence is expected of adults of both sexes, in contrast to the United States, where even the tax forms still refer to the primary wage earner and spouse. The American system clearly fosters a differential sense of independence for the two sexes, with women assigned to a supporting, submissive, dependent role.

The Swedish view of independence has other consequences for gender concepts. As any visitor quickly learns, Swedes highly value a sense of belonging. They espouse an obligation to function as a contributing, cooperative member of a cohesive society. Thus, their view of independence eschews the blatant individualism, the drive to excel, the attempts to "be Number 1," that figure so prominently in an American view of independence (Lederer & Burdick, 1958; Peters & Austin, 1986; Ringer, 1977). Indeed, Swedish commitment to the well being of the group promotes an unease with being singled out, commended, praised, treated as an outstanding model. These considerations suggest that loyalty and similar attributes are more likely to be coupled with independence in Swedish personal concepts than in American ones.

Health Care: Prenatal Care, Family Planning, and Education.   Swedish family legislation provides other forms of familial assistance that contribute to their plan for equality, such as free health care, daycare and organized recreation for children, and some stipends. Particularly helpful to the family is excellent and routine prenatal care.

Another important element of the health-care system is family planning. Family planning in Sweden is based on two principles: Each individual has the right to decide freely on the number and spacing of children, and each child has the right to be wanted. Both principles promote the participation of women in the work force. These goals are implemented in a number of ways. First, the government subsidizes contraceptive advisory services. Advisors (social workers, nurses, and related personnel) discuss family planning with all persons seeking advice, and are authorized to dispense contraceptives. Specially trained midwives conduct many of these free consultations. School youth also may be counseled by school personnel, including doctors and nurses. Second, to reduce the cost of contraception, the charges for these devices are discounted, like other pharmaceuticals, in addition to the free distribution at the time of consultation. Third, an educational program was started in the late 1970s. This program, implemented by health and social service units in each municipality, is designed to coordinate and extend information about family planning through the schools, social service agencies, and other societal institutions. Fourth, the health-care provision also includes abortions and sterilizations. Abortion is viewed as an emergency measure, a resort to be used if contraception has failed. Up until the end of the 18th week of pregnancy, abortions are free on request of the mother, who must consult a doctor. The mother always has the right to a free consultation with a social worker about a potential abortion; this consultation becomes mandatory after the 12th week, in addition to the discussion with the doctor. These consultations are designed to give the woman facts pertaining to her situation and to support her during a difficult period. After the 18th week, the Board of Health and Welfare must approve an abortion. It rarely does so after the 24th week, because the fetus might be viable. Sterilization, like abortion, is free and voluntary. Only the individual involved may request her or his own sterilization. The Sterilization Act of 1976 states that any Swedish citizen or legal resident of Sweden at least 25 years of age may be sterilized at his or her own request. Persons between the ages of 18 and 24 may request sterilization for genetic reasons or, in the case of women, for medical reasons. All applicants must attend an information session with a doctor or social worker before the operation may occur. Both consequences of the operation and alternative birth control measures are explained during this session.

Before considering other kinds of family legislation, let us evaluate the effects of health care. The prenatal care undoubtedly contributes to Sweden's admirably low infant mortality rate—one of the lowest in the world. In 1983, for every 1,000 live births, Sweden had 7.0 deaths, whereas, in 1984, the United States reported 10.6 deaths, also for every 1,000 live births of each sex (*The World Factbook*, 1986). Sweden's low infant mortality rate is impressive. So is its decline in abortion: The 1982 rate of 19.0 abortions per 1,000 women aged 15–44 is the lowest since the law went into effect in 1975. Further, the rate for teenagers has declined each year since 1975.

Thus, family planning has reached an advanced state in Sweden, a state that should provide both for the individual determination of whether and when to have children and for children to be born to welcoming parents. These efforts have emancipated women from unwanted pregnancies, thus making it easier for them to participate more fully in their society.

Parental Education Programs.   To facilitate men's participation in child care, and to provide information to both sexes, the Swedish government also sponsors a program of parental education. This program includes information about prenatal care, birth, infant care, and the first year of a child's life. The education is explicitly designed for fathers as well as mothers, and many fathers attend, especially first-time fathers. A result is that most Swedish fathers now are present during the birth of their children.

This parenthood education plan was part of a more extensive proposal issued by a Child Care Commission (Sundström-Feigenberg) in 1975. The proposal called for a general parenthood education plan that would correspond to different phases of family life. The legislature decided to implement only the childbirth–first-year portion, although the more extensive need was recognized, according to Dr. Kajsa Sundström-Feigenberg, who chaired the committee.

The Comprehensive Parental Insurance Plan.   Also contributing to the support of the family is Sweden's Parental Insurance plan. Designed to encourage shared responsibility for children, this plan covers both childbirth and later child care. At the time of birth, fathers are entitled to 10 days' paid leave, along with the mother's coverage. In addition, all parents may divide between themselves 12 months' time for child care (including such activities as participation in parent education courses and helping other children adjust) after the birth of a baby. For the first 9 months, compensation is at 90% of the usual wages; for the last 3 months, it is a fixed allowance. An unemployed parent is entitled to the fixed allowance for the entire 1-year period. The last 6 months of the entitlement may be taken at any time until the child is 8 years of age. Parents also may take as many as 60 days' leave per year to care for sick children, and they may shorten their working day to 6 hours (with a proportionate decrease in income). These parental entitlements are unaffected by marital status.

The parental benefits reflect ameliorative legislation, the outgrowth of deliberate attempts to help "men become more complete human beings with more well-rounded personalities and wide-ranging abilities and interests" (Haas, 1982, p. 390). These benefits partially explain the increasing involvement of Swedish fathers in child care. Overall, however, more women than men claim these benefits, and "parental sharing" is disproportionately "maternal care." One example is that, in 1978, the Swedish government noted that only 11% of fathers requested leave to care for infants (Morgenthaler, 1979) and even in 1982, only one in five fathers requested parental leave during the child's first year (Hwang, 1987). Another study of parental sharing of child care found that only 34% of 71 Swedish couples interviewed in 1977 claimed that they shared these responsibilities equally, and no couple cited the man as the major caregiver (Haas, 1982). This figure rose to 41% when both spouses were employed in the workplace. The appearance of nearly equal child-care responsibilities among those who claimed it was challenged, however, by responses to questions about who bought the children's clothes, who recruited babysitters, who played with the children, and who stayed home with a sick child. In each of these cases, the woman was more likely to assume the responsibility. Indeed, the highest percentage of sharing was 38% for playing with children. These patterns were found for families with employed as well as with unemployed mothers.

Obviously, the aim of equally shared child-care responsibilities has not yet been reached.

Why? What are some factors that might inhibit men's use of child-care legislation and benefits? Haas (1982) tackled this problem, as well, asking about the effects of previous experience with children, age, education, and lack of flexibility of men's occupations, and the mother's more precarious economic status in the workplace. Maternal employment was the most important determinant of fathers' child-care participation. Specifically, child-care sharing increased when mothers were in the work force, when she worked more rather than fewer hours, and when she had a higher (than lower) income. Also instructive were the results that child-care sharing increased with increased attention to the gender-role debate in the mass media.

Haas's (1982) research tells us that, at least for a rather small sample of Swedish couples tested in 1977, a gap existed between the Swedish government's commitment to equal sharing of child care by the parents and actual practice. In addition, her work suggested that characteristics of maternal but not paternal employment were related to child-care sharing. The importance of the mother's employment status seems obvious. Women employed full time or almost full time, with substantial salaries, contribute in major ways to the financial welfare of the family, and the need for the fathers' domestic support is clearer than when mothers are not employed outside the home or are employed part time. But why weren't factors affecting the fathers' employment effective predictors of child-care sharing? If flexibility, occupational status, income, and even the father's early experience with child care do not predict his participation in child care, what does, beyond the mother's workplace involvement? The observation that sharing was affected by attention to discussions of gender role in the mass media offers an exploratory candidate: the adherence to traditional gender roles and beliefs. Fathers who ignored the media's discussions of gender role shared child care less than fathers who attended to these discussions. Ignoring the media's discussions may reflect a lack of interest in the subject or espousal of contradictory attitudes about gender roles. At the least, it means that these fathers are missing some of Sweden's efforts to promote gender equality. Are men resistent to changes that may increase their participation in domestic roles?

Some support for this view comes from another study (Trost, 1983). To explore men's own attitudes and their perceptions of others' opinions about paternal insurance provisions, Trost, Director of the Group for Family Research at the University of Uppsala, Sweden, surveyed 5,945 Swedish men, aged 21–60, in 1981. The men were asked about the numbers of days they had taken off work in 1980 due to the delivery of a baby by their domestic partner, and the numbers of days they had taken off work to care for a sick child. Of the 288 men whose partners gave birth in 1980, 75% had taken leaves of absence. Younger fathers were more likely than older men to use this entitlement. Fathers employed by the national government took these leaves more often (98%) than fathers who were employed by either local government (84%) or private industry (74%). Further, somewhat more unmarried fathers (87%) than married (71%) ones took these leaves. These remarkably high percentages declined somewhat when fathers were asked about using their child-care benefits. Of the 2,000 plus men with children under 12 in 1980, only one third took advantage of their rights to be paid for care of sick children, a rate that is slightly lower than that reported by Haas (1982) for her entire sample. As with childbirth leaves, younger men were more likely to claim the benefit than older men, although in the case of sick children, this relation is confounded with the ages and expected illness patterns of the children. That is, younger men may be more willing to take child-care leave than older men or, because their children are likely to be younger and in an age span of greater susceptibility to illness than the children of older men, younger men may have had greater need for child-care leave than older men. Last, the men were questioned about the attitudes of various people toward the parental entitlements. Over all respondents, 75% approved of a man's right to take time off due to childbirth and 67% approved of a man's right to child-care leave. In addition, men were more likely to claim their parental entitlements if their domestic partners, their work mates, and their employers approved of the policies than if these individuals disapproved. Generally, approval rates were higher among government and municipal employees than among private employers or employees.

Although most Swedish men support these parental benefits, the minority who disapprove is cause for concern. If one third of the men disagree with the policies, their attitudes may well discourage even supportive men from claiming the benefits. Although the managers cannot legally refuse to grant parental leave requests, they can express their disapproval in myriad ways. The managers control opportunities for advancements, salary increases, and the like, that could be construed as essential to the man's employment and, by extension, to the welfare of his family. Thus, the presence of these disapproving attitudes constitutes one of the unsolved problems facing Sweden in its fight for equality.

Women use parental insurance plans more than men. This pattern has several unfortunate effects. It reinforces traditional divisions of labor between the sexes. It forces women to be absent from work more than men, thereby fueling the view that women are unreliable workers. It limits women's opportunities for advancement and, as a consequence, threatens women's financial independence. These considerations imply that Swedish concepts of gender will still contain some traditional components—and that this tendency toward traditionalism will be more pronounced among Swedish men than among Swedish women.

Child-Care Programs. The next group of family laws involves nonparental child-care programs. Child-care programs enable children to have contact with other children and with adults other than their parents, two sources of social influence that Swedes consider important to the development of social maturity. (These beliefs reflect the results of a substantial amount of confirmatory research conducted in Sweden, the United States, and elsewhere.) Opportunities to interact with children and other adults have become increasingly less common as families became smaller and more nuclear in the industrial age. Accordingly, the Swedish government (and Sweden's other political parties) supported the child-care plan. The other rationale for the child-care programs was that they give both women and men the opportunity to work outside the home.

The 1982 Social Service Act defined the child-care programs, which were to be implemented by the municipalities. Some preschools are organized as part-time groups (children typically attend for less than 5 hours per day), others are day nurseries (children attend for 5 or more hours per day), and still others are family day nurseries (one or more children are tended in the home of a trained child-minder). Children may be enrolled when they are 6 months old, although most are older when they begin, in part because spaces are limited. In addition, the Act provides for care of children who have special needs of either a chronic or temporary nature. Finally, the Act covers recreational facilities for both preschool and older children.

The child-care centers have a varied curriculum that includes creative activities and common daily chores. The groups are small, with a very favorable child–adult ratio. On the average, the preschools have 4–5 children per adult, and the ratio in infant groups is even lower. The child-care programs are construed as experiences that aid and supplement the family, not as parental or family substitutes. Strong efforts are made to integrate families into the child-care systems through parental participation, parental involvement in decision making, parent–teacher conferences, and the like. Part of the cost of child care is publicly subsidized, one of the ways the government supports families. Other funds are derived from local taxes, payroll deductions, and parents' fees. The actual cost to the parents varies with their circumstances, with the average cost per child per year being 4,000 Swedish kronor[1] (about $500).

One problem with the child-care options is that not enough places are available. Although a 1976 decree of the Swedish *Riksdag* announced the aim of providing, by 1986, municipal child care to every preschool-age child whose parents were gainfully employed or studying and to each child with special needs, this goal was not achieved. In 1980, there were 219,300 children who had places in day nurseries or in family day nurseries. Without places, however, were 132,000 children, or over 35% of the children up to 6 years of age who met the previously stated requirements. In 1985, the total number of places was scheduled to increase to 301,600, but, because the number of eligible children also increased, 94,300 were expected to lack places. Until these places are available, some children will be deprived of the opportunity for extensive child

---

[1] One Swedish krona = 0.13 U.S. dollars in April 1984.

and adult interaction, and their parents will be deprived of the opportunity to participate fully in the Swedish vision.

Child Allowances. The most direct subsidy for families comes in the form of a child allowance. Under this plan, parents of children under 16 currently receive 3,000 Swedish kronor (about $275) per child per year. Families with more than two children receive an extra 750 Swedish kronor for the third child and 1,500 for each additional child. Should a child's parents separate, both parents are expected to continue to support the child. In the event that one parent does not contribute (a relatively rare occurrence), a child who lives with a single parent is guaranteed the minimal sum of 7,300 kronor per year. Youth who continue with their education in secondary schools receive study allowances of 2,250 kronor per year. University students receive study funds of 25,280 kronor per academic year, divided into two parts, a non-repayable grant of 2,178 kronor and a loan of 23,102 kronor. The loan is made at relatively low interest rates (usually pegged to the state's banking industry). All of these allowances, and the housing supplement discussed next, are granted without regard to the sex of the child or the marital status of the parents. This legal equality of the sexes should, by now, have nudged personal opinions of the two sexes toward greater similarity.

Housing Supplements. The government also addressed housing, assuming that each individual should be adequately housed. Consequently, housing supplements may be paid to families. These "means-tested" supplements increase with the number of children and decrease with additional income. A fact sheet published by the Swedish Institute states that in 1981 approximately one third of all families with children received housing supplements.

How successful are these equality-spawned family laws and practices? There can be no doubt that fathers are becoming more active participants in the lives of their children. Indeed, one of my most vivid impressions of Sweden was that fathers were everywhere. Fathers pushed baby carriages and strollers. They took children to school. They played with children in parks. They climbed mountains and grocery shopped with their children. In brief, Sweden's impressively innovative complex of laws and practices supporting the family has achieved an unusual melding of the financial and domestic roles of women and men. Nevertheless, research just cited and additional studies by Sweden's Center for Working Life show that practice is still short of the goal, for Swedish fathers assume less than an equal share of child care and household responsibilities. These discrepancies may well mirror persisting differences in attitudes toward gender roles, a possibility explored in our research.

EDUCATIONAL OPPORTUNITIES

The Swedish educational system incorporates a number of *jämställdhet*-enhancing characteristics. One is that discussion of social issues, such as democratic principles, the integrity of the individual, and the importance of equality of opportunity for the two sexes, is an official part of the educational curriculum. This last issue is further explained by the National Board of Education's statement about curriculum in the elementary and secondary schools: "The school should seek to implement equality between men and women, in the family, on the labor market and in social life in general. It should provide orientation in questions touching the life roles of the sexes and stimulate its pupils to discuss and question prevailing conditions." Another is that all courses, except for a few physical education classes in the upper grades, are open to both sexes. A third is that all students in Grades 8 and 9 take courses in home economics, child care, woodworking, metal working, textile work, and other technical skills. Fourth, in Grades 7–9, youth engage in practical work experience for a short period of time. The curriculum is designed to prepare both female and male students for jobs as well as to prepare them for additional education, if that is their choice.

After completing compulsory courses at about age 16, most students continue in "integrated upper secondary schools." The integrated upper secondary schools have programs in three main areas: arts and social subjects, economics and commercial subjects, and scientific and technical subjects. Each of these areas subsumes both 2-year programs that are strongly vocationally oriented and 3- or 4-year programs that are more theoretically oriented. All programs are open to both sexes, but more women than men choose the shorter, nonscientific, and nontechnical programs. Thus, girls are more likely to select secretarial and social service tracks, and boys are more likely to select scientific ones, thereby perpetuating traditional divisions of Sweden's (and most other countries') labor markets. After this pattern emerged, the National Board of Education, recognizing that these choices could reflect cultural expectations, a lack of knowledge about alternatives, and similar influences, adopted an action program in 1980. Youth now try different kinds of work experience in Grades 8 and 9 to gain exposure to more diverse occupations than were sampled previously. It is too soon to assess the effectiveness of these revisions, but a few indications of a continued preference for traditional sex-segregated occupations surfaced in some of my research. Early in 1984, I asked 14- and 18-year-old Swedish youth about their future plans. Most of the respondents thought that it was easier for boys than for girls to get jobs, a view that is supported by the larger percentage of men (93%) than women (53%) holding full-time positions in Sweden in 1982 (Swedish Central Statistics Bureau). My respondents thought it was more important for boys to train for positions in the currently "hot" areas of science and technology and for girls to train for the kinds of positions that can be easily practiced on a part-time basis, attitudes that have a traditionally sexist cast. These youth, then, have assimilated some pragmatic but equality-jeopardizing aspects of contemporary Swedish economic life, a situation that surely militates against full equality.

Of course, there is no reason why, if people could make truly free occupational choices, all would select certain occupations over others. The difficulty is that the choices are not entirely free: They are strongly influenced by societal expectations concerning "appropriate" vocations for the two sexes, by opportunistic considerations, by limited knowledge of vocational alternatives, and by the absence of like-sex role models in many areas. The persistence of sex-segregated occupational goals constitutes a major deterrent to the achievement of equality.

Sweden has moved on still another front: higher education. The universities and other institutions of higher education now consider life experience as one of the factors important to admission. For example, adults, aged over 25, with 4 years of work experience, including care of the home and children, receive points toward admission. Women now constitute 55% of the undergraduate body. Once at the universities, however, the students have tended to make sex-stereotypic academic selections.

Another unusual aspect of the Swedish educational system is the program for adult education. Some one third of Sweden's adult population pursues such studies, according to a report from the Swedish Institute. This pattern is encouraging, for it provides opportunities for life-long study to both sexes.

Strenuous efforts have been made to remove sexist treatments from books, but occasional complaints still are registered with the National Board of Education. Eliminating entrenched habits is a slow process!

LABOR FORCE PARTICIPATION OF SWEDISH AND AMERICAN WOMEN

Compared to their American counterparts, Swedish women hold an enviable position in Sweden's labor force. For the age range of highest labor force participation, 25 to 54 years, 85% of Swedish women were in the labor force in 1981, in contrast to 67% of American women. The extent of Swedish women's participation is made all the more impressive by the fact that only 30 years ago, in the 1950s, less than 30% of Swedish women were gainfully employed. These figures include both full- and part-time workers. Moreover, female–male discrepancies in wages are more pronounced in the United States than in Sweden. In Sweden, female white-collar workers make 87% of their male colleagues' salaries, whereas in the United States, women in comparable jobs make between 52%–75% of salaries of male white-collar workers. For blue-collar workers, Swedish women earn an overall 91% of what their male peers command; American women earn between 63%–81% of men's wages. All figures are from governmental reports in 1981.

Obviously, Swedish women participate more actively in the labor force than their American counterparts. Neither group, however, participates as fully as their male compatriots—probably for some of the same reasons. One reason is that women in both countries, more than men, are concentrated in lower paying, lower prestige, often service-related, female-dominated occupations. Put another way, for both countries, the higher paying positions are in male-dominated occupations. Other reasons may be the greater numbers of women than men in part-time positions and sex discrimination. The latter is supported by the fact that, in both countries, women make less money than men in the same positions. In brief, Swedish women are not yet sharing the same economic benefits as Swedish men, although the discrepancy is smaller than in the United States.

According to Swedish law, women and men performing the same job must receive equal pay. But this requirement is easily circumvented by defining jobs performed by women differently from similar jobs performed by men. Monitoring pay scales and other aspects of equal opportunity in employment is the responsibility of the Equal Opportunities Ombudsman (sic), an office created by the Act on Equality Between Women and Men at Work (July 1, 1980). The central purpose of the Act is to "promote equality between women and men in respect to employment, conditions of employment and opportunities for development in employment (equality at work)." It prohibits employment discrimination on the ground of sex, referring specifically to recruitment, promotion or training for promotion, conditions of work, terminations of employment contracts, layoffs, and transfers, when the differential treatment is based on the sex of the employee or job applicant. The Act also calls for active measures to promote equality, identifies routes of appeal and possible sanctions, and establishes the Equal Opportunity Commission whose task is to ensure compliance with the Act. An interesting aspect of the Act is that the burden of proving nondiscrimination is on the employer.

The substantial numbers of female part-time workers in the Swedish labor market deserves comment. In 1982, 47% of employed women were working part time (less than 40 hours per week). Part-time work is preferred by some women, such as new mothers and those who are entering the work force for the first time or are returning to it after an absence. For example, older women, who are reentering the labor force, sometimes after an absence of 30 years or more, occasionally find that part-time employment facilitates the transition. As one woman told me, "You can't imagine how fearful I was about going back to work. But I decided that I could handle 2 days a week. It's so exciting to be part of the 'real world' that now I want to work full time." Part-time employment also has hazards. Compared to full-time workers, part timers tend to make proportionately less money and often are not truly self-supporting. Their contributions to pensions are lower. Perhaps most important, they are taken less seriously by employers than full-time employees so their opportunities for advancement are accordingly limited. Large scale part-time employment thus constitutes a threat to the central principles of Sweden's equality efforts.

THE MASS MEDIA

What could account for the speed with which Sweden has effected its dramatic changes? One answer is that the Swedes are a relatively homogeneous people, who share many values and experiences. But that is a superficial explanation. A more substantive one would explain how, in a democracy, so many people hold similar views at any given time. For this kind of answer we must turn to the mass media. The media, more than other institutions, have the power to influence most of the population quickly and simultaneously. Indeed, I often heard that a few newspaper articles energized Sweden's quest for equality. Swedes avidly consume newspapers, periodicals, radio, and television. Newspaper and periodical readership is among the highest in the world. Television sets now reside in more than 90 of every 100 Swedish households, and even more have radios. On a typical Sunday, 82% of the Swedish population will watch television (one of two channels), and 66% will listen to the radio at some time during the day. On a typical weekday, 75% will listen to the radio and 74% will watch television. Thus, most Swedes watch and listen to a limited number of broadcast channels.

Sweden was one of the first countries to formally establish freedom of the press as part of its constitution when the *Riksdag* adopted a Freedom of the Press Act in 1766. Other versions have replaced the original one. Later, when electronic media became popular, a Radio Act was formulated to cover the broadcast media. The most recent version was adopted in 1978. These Acts guarantee the principles of freedom for all forms of the media, a commitment that Swedes treasure as being essential to a working democracy, to the active participation of its citizenry in public affairs, and to the development and maintenance of an advanced economy and lifestyle.

These Acts confer both rights and reponsibilities. Public censorship of the press and severe restrictions on publishing and distribution are forbidden. The identities of sources are protected. Various measures also are provided to guard against abuses of these rights. One of the most important measures is the appointment of a single individual to be personally liable and responsible for the contents of the medium. For radio and television, this person is the program supervisor, and for periodicals appearing four or more times a year, this person is the "responsible publisher." The relevant laws also cover exigencies, violations, prosecution, and litigation. Even more interesting to me than the preceding measures, which appear to work well, are the assumptions of responsible journalism on the part of the media. For example, the Radio Act of 1978 (which covers television as well) charges the broadcasting companies to "promote the basic principles of democratic government, the principles of the equality of Man, and the liberty and dignity of the individual." Among the violations of the Press Act are threats to or contempt for minority groups on the basis of race, color, creed, ethnic origin, and so forth!

The Radio Act of 1978 also stipulates that the government shall grant the rights to broadcast. Currently, these rights are held by the Swedish Broadcasting Corporation and its four subsidiaries, the Swedish Radio Company, the Swedish Television Company, the Swedish Local Radio Company (which is responsible for the local radio stations in Sweden), and the Swedish Educational Broadcasting Company. Because the Swedish Broadcasting Company has a monopoly on broadcasting, one might fear that it would abuse its rights. As a safeguard against such abuse, an independent Radio Council investigates complaints about programs and periodically examines programs itself to assess whether the programs comply with the mandates of the Radio Act. The Council's results must be publicized by the program-producing company. The Broadcast Liability Act further backs up this checks-and-balances control system.

What are the effects of these exhortations to foster equality? Substantial efforts are being made to include women journalists, news reporters, and analysts on the air. In addition, women are in various administrative positions. In the late 1970s, the Swedish Broadcasting Corporation produced a pamphlet describing its commitment to equality. The 69 measures designed to further equality are of two types, those that relate to personnel and those that deal with programs.

Personnel measures include seminars and study circles that examine attitudes about equality by giving information, discussing problems, and providing insight into the mechanisms that are used to avoid change or to further it. In addition, vacant positions must be advertised, and priority is given to the underrepresented sex. Salary inequities are being examined. The aim here is to have the same salary range and median salaries for women and men in the same occupation. Additionally, some opportunities to learn about other positions are available through job rotation and a few short courses. Other courses are designed to foster self-confidence, to give practice with public speaking, and to discuss work conditions, typing, and writing. On the program side, the Audience and Programme Research Department is exhorted to continue its research, and to participate in staff training in the field of equality. Moreover, the handbook reiterates the media's responsibility for equality, adding "that equality between the sexes is a fundamental aspect of the democratic values we are required to defend; that this equality includes respect for the value and dignity of the individual; that discrimination against any person by reason of sex is a grave injustice; and that the Corporation has a special responsibility with regard to the generation now growing towards adulthood, and the values it imparts to that generation." The numbers of women narrators and the training of program "leaders" are parts of the new program, as is the stipulation that "the debate on equality must be kept continuously alive at the news division." This latter reminder is intended to constantly refresh the commitment to equality in the minds of both journalists and the public.

Admirable as these efforts and ambitions are, they are not enough, as I discovered when I wanted to watch the women's slalom and cross-country skiing events during the 1984 Sarajevo Winter Olympics. These competitions were indeed broadcast, but only during nonprime daytime hours. By contrast, the counterpart events for men were broadcast during prime time. More scientifically, research conducted by the Corporation's Research Department showed a systematic tendency for more male than female main characters in programs, even in educational television. Women tend to be portrayed as trivial, incompetent, indecisive, or invisible (either not shown at all or present only as shadowy backdrops), whereas men appear as important, competent, decision makers who are involved in adventurous, exciting pursuits. Thus, the goals espoused by the Swedish Broadcasting Company still elude its grasp, but the fact that the Company itself is studying these problems is encouraging.

Now consider the print media, other powerful persuaders of the public. Similar laws prevail, with an added liaison between the public and the print media, the Press Ombudsman. This person, and the office of the Press Ombudsman, supervise adherence to ethical standards. Complaints from the public are investigated, and the office may initiate its own investigations. Serious complaints may be filed with the Press Council, which may then publish its findings in the newspaper concerned.

How effective have the print media been at treating the two sexes equivalently? To obtain a partial answer to this question, I examined articles on the most widely read pages of four newspapers—the front pages. My sample consisted of five consecutive Thursdays and Saturdays in February and March 1984, of two American newspapers, the *New York Times* and the *Washington Post*, and of the two largest Swedish newspapers, *Expressen*, an evening newspaper with an average daily circulation of 558,000 in January, 1984, and *Dagens Nyheter*, a morning newspaper with an average daily circulation of 387,000 at the same time. I tallied the articles on the front pages (or first two pages for the tabloid, *Expressen*) by the sex of the featured person or the sex of the person cited as the source of the information. Articles about women were fewer than I expected, 38% for *Expressen* and 26% for *Dagens Nyheter*. Lest one think that these percentages are very low, consider the same counts for the *New York Times* and the *Washington Post* for similar international news and feature articles on precisely the same days: 8% and 3%, respectively. Equality of coverage in these two Swedish newspapers may not equal the percentage of women in the population in Sweden, but it is much closer to such a reasonable ideal than two similar, and highly influential, American newspapers.

There are major differences between the structures of our media and those of Sweden, of course, despite the shared commitment to freedom of the press. But the possibility of having the American mass media take as their charge, "the promotion of the basic principles of democratic government, the principles of the equality of all persons, and the liberty and dignity of the individual" is very exciting. These are, after all, principles that are consistent with our own Constitution. They are fundamental tenets on which our country was founded. What a delight it would be to watch and to listen to programs or to read articles that did indeed celebrate the liberty and dignity of both women and men . . . and that took any form of sexist discrimination as a transgression of our democratic ideals.

Another major difference between the ways the media are handled in the two countries is the financial base. In Sweden, program production is financed from license revenues paid by all owners of television sets and by government subsidies. Swedish newspapers exist on sales, government subsidies, and income from advertising. The federal subsidies are considered important as ways to support democratic ideals. The costs have become so high, however, that various economy measures are being considered. The relative freedom from dictates of major advertisers is undoubtedly a strength of the Swedish system and a weakness of the American one, which heavily depends on income from selling advertisements. Another limiting aspect of the American media is their dependence on short-term evaluations by their listeners. American listeners have become accustomed to current types of programs. It is reasonable to expect new styles of programs, including those that minimize sexist treatment, to require time to develop a following, a situation that requires patience from the media—and from their financial backers. In my opinion, the benefits of these changes to the American people—and to the American nation—make the time and even temporary financial losses well worth the effort, but financial moguls may disagree.

GENDER-RELATED PRACTICES IN THE UNITED STATES

What is America's answer to the challenge of gender equality? Unfortunately, no simple response can be given to this question. Various American practices have been mentioned as contrasts with Swedish policies, but a more systematic rendition should set the stage for the predictions that gender concepts will show some cross-national differences. The most obvious difference between the two countries is the United States' failure to develop an integrated, government-espoused commitment to gender equality similar to the one in place in Sweden. Compare, for example, the Equal Rights Amendment with Sweden's 1968 statement cited at the beginning of the chapter. The ill-fated Equal Rights Amendment stated that:

Section 1. Equality of rights under the law shall not be denied or abridged by the United States or by any State on account of sex.

Section 2. The Congress shall have the power to enforce, by appropriate legislation, the provisions of this article.

Section 3. This amendment shall take effect two years after the date of ratification.

The Amendment barely failed to receive ratification by three-quarters of the states, as required to pass an amendment to the Constitution.

In contrast to Sweden's policy, this simple amendment makes no mention of financial or domestic responsibilities of either sex. It makes no pronouncement about favored domestic or work-place roles for either or both sexes. Like its Swedish correlate, it offers opportunities to both sexes, although the form of the opportunities is particularly vague in the American version.

Other gender-related laws exist at the federal level. The Equal Pay Act of 1963, as amended by the Education Amendments of 1972, prohibits discrimination in salaries on the basis of sex. Title VII of the Civil Rights Act of 1964, as amended by the Equal Employment Opportunity Act of 1972 and the Pregnancy Disability Act of 1978, extended the ban to all aspects of employment for all institutions with 15 or more employees. Pregnancy coverage is required only of employers who provide disability benefits. These provisions were bolstered by the Executive Order 11246 (October 1968), which prohibited discrimination in employment on the basis of race, color, religion, national origin, or sex for all institutions with federal contracts of over $10,000. Educational institutions receiving federal assistance were covered by Title IX of the Education Amendments of 1972 as amended by the Bayh Amendments of 1974 and the Education Amendments of 1976, and by Titles VII and VIII of the Public Health Service Act. The aforementioned legislation is undoubtedly helpful, but it also leaves much to be desired. Not all employers are covered. The scope of the policies is limited. Redress for transgressions is slow in coming, if it ever does (the backlog of the enforcing agencies, such as the Equal Opportunity Commission and the Office of Civil Rights, is notorious as one commentator, Basow, 1986, reports).

Abortion was legalized in the United States in 1973, when the Supreme Court barred the states from preventing abortion during the first trimester, given that the abortion was performed by a physician. States were granted the right to regulate abortion decisions "in ways that are reasonably related to maternal health" during the second trimester and to even proscribe abortion except when necessary "for the preservation of the life or health of the mother" during the third trimester. Both federal and state provisions for abortion have been under attack since the 1973 decision.

In addition to the mainly federal policies just described, individual states and municipalities have enacted provisions to foster equal opportunity in employment and education. These well-intentioned but necessarily haphazard approaches help and are welcome as efforts to afford gender equality. Like the federal approaches, these statues and provisions have come under attack and are often in jeopardy.

To date, no legislation provides for systematic health care, for sex education, or for child care. The national taxation system assumes that a man heads the household, as does the still outdated social security system. No discernible social-policy principles appear to govern the mass media of the United States; hence, the mass media seems unlikely to collectively advance the cause of gender equality or even to deliberately set forth a considered evaluation of the contents of gender concepts in the United States or elsewhere.

This rather bleak description of a largely uninformed gender conscience in the United States deals primarily with governmental agencies or legislation. It does not detail the many articles, books, lectures, and other attempts by interested parties to focus attention on the problem. Fruitful as these efforts have been, they do not command the weight, the power, and the instrumentality of legal and governmental policies. The result is that in the United States attitudes toward gender roles are formed by haphazard and diversified experiences in a heterogeneous country. Perhaps the most unifying aspect of the American model is an abiding belief in the sanctity and inviolability of the individual qua individual. To the extent that this view captures characteristics of American youth, we would expect them to have varied concepts of gender roles, to place a higher value on male than on female roles, and to emphasize individuality and personal gain/power rather than group loyalty. These attributes stand in marked contrast to predictions made for Swedish youth.

The central focus of this chapter has been on differences in the ways in which Sweden and the United States address the concept of the gender equality of opportunity and how these differences might affect concepts about gender. We need a broader perspective, however, because gender concepts also reflect general expectations for citizens of a culture. Hence, common expectations may exist for most Swedes, just as they exist for most Americans. To the extent that the countries differ, the expectations may emerge as cross-nationally different gender concepts. To the extent that the countries are similar, they may emerge as cross-nationally similar concepts. Indeed, the two countries share attributes. Both are industrialized, highly mechanized nations. Sweden, like the United States, heavily depends on contemporary, sophisticated technology. In fact, one Swedish newspaper proclaimed Sweden to be the most computerized country in the world. I was ready to believe the claim, because I had to keep a number of computer codes in mind, from the combination to my building to my number on the Department of Psychology's central processor. The two countries even share business management styles (Harbison & Myers, 1959; Hofstede, 1980). Both countries have extensive compulsory education; both subscribe to religious freedom and to freedom of expression. Both countries are democracies, despite some American erroneous beliefs that Sweden is exclusively socialistic. Political parties in Sweden conduct highly publicized campaigns, which elicit the same kinds of empassioned arguments among the populace that one hears in the United States. The acid test of the citizenry's commitment to a democracy, their willingness to participate in the democratic process, is passed with flying (perhaps I should say "soaring") colors in Sweden: Some 94% of the people voluntarily cast ballots in elections! Swedes are amazed and somewhat disapproving of the cavalier attitudes Americans take toward voting and their participation in the electoral process. Finally, the two countries enjoy among the highest standards of living in the world. In summary, the United States and Sweden share many attributes; they do not, however, have identical policies about gender equality.

To complete this chapter, it behooves us to comment on what has been achieved by Sweden's efforts, using the United States as a backdrop. Although Sweden has made conspicuous progress toward gender equality, it has not yet achieved its goal. What lessons can we learn about the role of gender concepts in this quest? Some reflections are in order.

REFLECTIONS

Jämställdhet is well advanced in Sweden. Both sexes are expected to nurture children; both are expected to work outside the home. Thus, from some perspectives, the goals that women and men will participate in both "active parenthood and gainful employment" are in sight in Sweden. Through the promulgation of sensible, clever, functional laws and through its social consciousness, Sweden had produced amazing societal changes in less than two decades. These policies are instructive models for other countries, particularly democracies.

Despite its progress, however, full *jämställdhet* has not yet emerged in Sweden. One reason is that the attitudes of some Swedes have not caught up with the political–legal–ideological principles embodied in the concept of *jämställdhet*. A correlate is that Sweden's push for equality has emphasized the advantages to both sexes; it has been reluctant to adopt practices for one sex that did not have a counterpart for the other sex. The result is that current, often subtle sex differences are not always recognized—and are not being addressed by the government. Some of my Swedish acquaintances did not know about or were apathetically resigned to the economic differences between the sexes. Some were unaware of or even accepted the unequal division of labor in the home. Puzzled, I asked if they were not concerned about these invidious influences that undermined their valiant attempts at equality. Most agreed that these are serious problems, for the perpetuation of sexist attitudes and practices reinforces such views in adults and instills them in youth. Discriminatory treatment deprives women of the personal benefits of self-acceptance and the self-esteem of knowing that one is a truly independent, mature, capable individual. These patterns contradict Swedish beliefs in the independence and dignity of the individual. Many Swedes do identify these problems and are trying to rectify them. Others recognize the problems but are taking a holiday from their efforts at social reform. (After all, the energy and the vigor required to maintain social activism is difficult to sustain over a long period of time.) A few simply did not recognize the problems.

Some efforts are being made to address remaining problems of sexism. One approach is to reduce the typical work day for all to 6 hours as a way to provide more family and recreational time. This approach might be a reasonable answer, if bolstered by guarantees that some people, men in particular, do not begin to work two jobs. Another approach appeals to me, although I have not heard it discussed in Sweden. This would be a full-scale attack on attitudes about the proper places of women and men. It would challenge the view that men do not belong in the home. It would debate the perspective that women, not men, should work shorter hours while the children are young. What I am advocating is a massive public education campaign to further strengthen the concepts of more equal sharing of parenthood and gainful employment than has existed heretofore. This campaign could be combined with other approaches, including a shortened work day. There is no reason why such a campaign would not be effective. Sweden already has a fine start; now she needs to complete the unfinished business.

Sweden is a relatively small, homogeneous country, whose advanced technology makes communication with almost all citizens reasonably easy to accomplish. A similar, extensive communication with its people is much harder for the United States. Even though the American citizenry watches television zealously, its people are heterogeneous and far more numerous, more television channels are available, and the media's messages are more diverse. What works in Sweden would not necessarily work in the United States. But America's current hodge-podge of laws, the absence of a coordinated policy, and the anarchy of the messages carried by the mass media all militate against significant modification of the status quo.

Highlighted in this brief comparison of Sweden and the United States are the differences in efforts to achieve equal opportunity for the two sexes. We turn to the psychological effects of these differences, focusing on concepts about gender in the two countries. We ask a number of questions, including the following: Do Swedes come to perceive the two sexes as more similar than Americans do? Do the gender concepts of the two nationalities differ? If so, do nationality differences appear in cultural gender concepts, personal gender concepts, or both? Unfortunately, answers to these questions are somewhat illusive, because cross-national differences in gender concepts might reflect the use of measuring instruments that are more appropriate for one country than for the other. The differences could manifest greater reluctance to disclose information about one's beliefs and attitudes in one country than in the other. In brief, attempts to answer these seemingly simple questions run headlong into myriad problems of cross-cultural research. Chapter 3 considers these problems and relevant research in the field.

3

Cross-Cultural Studies of Gender Roles

"What kind of a bird are you if you cannot fly?" chirped the bird. "What kind of a bird are you if you cannot swim?" replied the duck. As Sergei Prokofiev perspicuously queried in his "Peter and the Wolf," the questions we ask about others spring from our own experiences and self-awareness. Parallels exist in cross-cultural research. Perhaps the primary force motivating cross-cultural research is a desire to know whether other cultures have customs similar to our own. Cross-cultural investigations offer the promise of learning about human activities that transcend national boundaries and those that are nationally bound. In the absence of cross-cultural studies, our theories about human behavior risk the myopia of culturally circumscribed knowledge, for "what we know is constrained by interpretive frameworks which, of course, limit our thinking; what we *can* know will be determined by the kinds of questions we learn to ask" (Rosaldo, 1980, p. 390).

Cross-cultural comparisons offer a wealth of information not obtained by examining customs and practices within a single country or society. Such comparisons may illuminate how the environment shapes behavior, personality, attitudes, opinions, and other human characteristics in ways that might never be detected within a single nation. These approaches afford special opportunities for assessing the relative influence and interaction of biological and environmental variables in development. For example, these approaches may clarify the biological and cultural contributions to the development of gender concepts and gender roles. Rosaldo (1980) reminded us,

> Every social system uses facts of biological sex to organize and explain the roles and opportunities men and women may enjoy, just as all known human social

groups appeal to biologically based ties in the construction of "familial" groups and kinship bonds. . . . Sexual asymmetry, much like kinship, seems to exist everywhere, yet not without perpetual challenge or almost infinite variation in its contents and its forms. (p. 395)

The work of such eminent anthropologists as Ruth Benedict and Margaret Mead has made us aware of the importance of the culture in determining individual forms of behavior. Their work informs us that what appears to be the "natural order of things" in one society may be quite different in another, including traditional and expected gender-role behaviors for the two sexes. The purpose of our project is not to contrast gender roles in markedly different societies, but rather to make the more subtle (and, we think, more challenging) comparison between two countries that are quite similar in many respects but that differ in their commitment to and implementation of efforts to afford equal opportunity to the two sexes.

Comparisons of gender concepts in Sweden and the United States should delineate expectations for each sex by each sex. They should contrast self-concepts relating to gender in the two countries. But these comparisons offer still more possibilities. They should inform us about human capabilities and their malleability (i.e., the hows and whys of gender) as supplements to biological sex differentiation. They should provide insight into how different cultures cultivate, maintain, and perpetuate gender differences and gender similarities. Elaborating on these points, Ember (1981) noted that:

relatively little cross-cultural research has been designed to test theories about why there are sex differences. It is precisely because biologic sex and social factors are not always confounded in quite the same ways in different societies that cross-cultural research has tremendous potential for helping us to test theories about the etiology of sex differences. For example, if we want to test a particular socialization theory, we can compare societies that differ in the *degree* to which boys and girls are differently treated and see if the size of the supposed sex-difference effect varies as expected. (p. 532)

In a similar vein, Block (1973) contended that cross-cultural research can be used to answer questions about the effects of particular political systems on beliefs. For example, Bakan (1966) related *agency*, or an individual's self-protection, self-assertion, and self-expansion, to capitalism. The other fundamental set of characteristics that he ascribed to all living forms, *communion*, involves the sense of being at one with others. His model predicted not only that males will be particularly likely to possess agentic attributes and females, to possess communal attributes but also that citizens of capitalistic countries should manifest more agentic traits, regardless of sex, than should citizens of noncapitalistic states. Applied to our research, Bakan's model would predict that the typical gender patterns would be more pronounced in a strictly capitalist country, such as the

United States, than in a country that mixes capitalism and socialism, such as Sweden.

Cross-cultural research thus offers rich rewards. As is so often true, however, these rewards depend on successfully navigating the treacherous waters of cross-cultural research. Consequently, in this background chapter, we first consider some of the problems presented by cross-cultural comparisons and the methods used to try to solve them. We then review relevant literature about cross-cultrual gender roles. Readers who are not interested in this background material may wish to skip to chapter 4.

In what follows, we slip into the common practice of using the terms *cross-cultural* and *cross-national* interchangeably. Strictly speaking, cross-national refers to different nations that may or may not have distinctly separate cultures. Cross-cultural comparisons presumably involve different cultures that typically characterize two or more countries, although cultural comparisons also may be within the same country.

CROSS-CULTURAL RESEARCH
AND ITS PROBLEMS

A number of authors have written about the difficulties and hazards of cross-cultural work (e.g., Berry, 1969; Campbell, 1964; Cole, Gay, Glick, & Sharp, 1971; Ember, 1981; Frijda & Jahoda, 1966; Lonner, 1980; Osgood, May, & Miron, 1975; Price-Williams, 1975; Rosaldo, 1980; Strodtbeck, 1964; Williams & Best, 1982). They note many perils, including questions about the validity of cross-cultural comparisons, contacts with other countries, the potentially handicapping effects of the investigator's own cultural experiences, and methodological problems. Language difficulties often compound all of these problems.

The Validity of Cross-Cultural Comparisons

Is it possible to make valid cross-cultural comparisons? Malinkowski (1922) contended that such comparisons may be false because we are trying to compare incomparables. Every culture is considered unique and thus must be understood within its own customs. Although acknowledging the likely uniqueness of cultures in some respects, students of cultural comparisons have continued their quest for identifiable national/cultural similarities and differences. They seek universals while respecting the individual, a distinction captured by Pike's (1954) contrast between *emic* and *etic* approaches. Modeled on the linguistic distinction between phonemics and phonetics, emics refer to a particular nation, society, or group, whereas etics pertain to pancultural or culture-free aspects of the world.

According to Pike (1954), the emic approach studies behavior from within the system, examines only one culture, uses a structure discovered by the analyst, and utilizes criteria that are relative to internal characteristics. The etic approach studies behavior from a position outside the system, compares many cultures, uses a structure created by the analyst, and employs criteria that are considered absolute or universal. The importance of both approaches has been widely acknowledged (Berry, 1969; Price-Williams, 1975). We pursue a combination of the emic and etic approaches in our project.

Contacts with Other Countries

Nationalistic sensitivities and protectionism offer another challenge to the cross-national researcher.

National Pride and Sensitivity. As Williams and Best (1982) commented, the focus of cultural anthropology is on differences, rather than similarities, among societies. This emphasis may even be nurtured by political forces within a country, for it is often in the interests of politicians to foster nationalism and to cultivate a sense of national identity, dignity, and custom. This national self-interest may produce some resistance to and even resentment about cross-cultural research, particularly when the work purports to show similarities that might obscure politically useful national differences. Nonetheless, Lonner (1980) stated that "there is ample evidence that striking similarities, if not an avalanche of universals in human behavior, far outweigh substantive differences" (p. 147). Particularly relevant for our purposes, substantial similarities in gender stereotypes have been reported across cultures (e.g., Barry, Bacon, & Child, 1957; Block, 1973; Ember, 1981; Lonner, 1980; Munroe & Munroe, 1975; Williams & Best, 1982). The conduct of cross-cultural or cross-national research thus requires a sensitive balancing of scientific pursuits with respect for cultural and national integrity. Although the interests of science and international harmony dictate that cross-cultural or cross-national research should minimize entanglements in the sociopolitical matrices of the countries being studied, the very nature of this type of research requires at least some minimal involvement.

Exploitation versus Cooperation. Another problem, that of potential exploitation of studied cultures, is closely related to the potential for sociopolitical exploitation discussed previously. In most cases, cross-cultural research requires the active participation of knowledgeable people who are natives of the societies being studied. The resulting data should be shared so that each investigator has the opportunity to evaluate and interpret them. Such sharing has the additional advantage of facilitating independent, perhaps corroboratory assessments.

Cooperation also is needed to recruit consultants, translators, and subjects. For the current research, we made our initial contacts with people connected with universities, all of whom were helpful beyond our wildest hopes. These people then assisted us as we sought approval to use local schools, computer facilities, and other miscellany associated with a research project. In addition, because Sweden's government strongly believes in its obligation to its people, it operates in an amazingly open fashion. I was often able to make appointments with government officials who answered their own telephones!

We were particularly grateful to be briefed on the requirements for anonymity that are imposed by the state on research in Sweden. Without guidance, we might have suffered the fate of another researcher whose data were confiscated because some identifying information was inadvertently left on a test booklet! Our Swedish colleagues also steered us toward receptive school systems and away from over-tested, less receptive ones. In exchange, we have sent reports to all participating schools, universities, and funding agencies. Our data are open and may be used for any legitimate purpose.

Domestic versus Public Spheres. The cross-cultural researcher must be prepared to investigate both domestic and public spheres, particularly when the roles of the two sexes are at issue. Those roles assumed by one sex in the public domain, such as being dominant, decisive, and proscriptive, may have their parallels for the other sex in the private arena. Both realms must be investigated if we are to attain a reasonably comprehensive and minimally biased understanding of the gender-related customs of the societies.

Differences in Cultural Intangibles. Probably the most difficult problems to solve are those that represent *cultural intangibles.* The term may not be particularly apt, because with exposure to other cultures, the originally unsophisticated observer may become attuned to many of the nuances and subtle factors that contribute to, and even mold, behavior and attitudes in other cultures. At the outset, however, an investigator is likely to be somewhat ignorant of or insensitive to various practices in cultures other than her or his own. The literature is replete with horror stories of the mistakes that have been made because of differences in language, beliefs, practices, and so on. These seeming "intangibles" are ever present to trap even the most wary researchers, and they constitute serious hazards to any cross-cultural or cross-national research. Further, the more dissimilar the cultures, the more likely errors are to be made. Even with similar cultures and nations, the researcher must be constantly watchful for such errors. I tried to avoid this (and many other) intangible traps by having numerous discussions about the project with many and diverse Swedish people, about half of whom were not connected with a university.

Cultural Sensitivity and Insensitivity of the Investigator

Rosaldo's (1980) quotations given previously warn us about the effects of one's own cultural blinders. This problem occurs even with respect to the researcher's own culture, for we all share our culture's perspectives and may not be aware of our unknowing, uncritical acceptance of some cultural beliefs. The problem is what Bem and Bem (1976) called a "nonconscious ideology"—the inability to identify potential factors because one has never considered their influence. The now trite analogy for such a nonconscious ideology is the fish that does not know its environment is wet. Problems of nonconscious cultural ideologies include pervasive, yet often subtle expectations about gender.

Differential experiences of the two sexes pose at least two potential hazards. The first is that the unwary researcher may assume that the dissimilar experiences of the two sexes in one culture are paralleled in other cultures. The second hazard is that differential experiences of the two sexes may produce different performance, even though performance is equivalent for the two sexes when the experiences are equated (Stewart, 1973). For example, differences in male–female activities that appear to be due to biological effects may disappear when cultural experiences are equated.

One form of cultural sensitivity and insensitivity is a strong tendency for any researcher to treat his or her culture as the standard or norm against which other societies are judged. Not only is the investigator's own culture taken as the standard, it is also taken as the valued mode. This tendency is to be expected, of course, because the known and familiar obviously seem more understandable, more plausible, and even more rational than the unknown and unfamiliar. The consequence of these tendencies is unfortunate for many cross-cultural comparisons, for a substantial number of cross-cultural researchers are from Western countries. Hence, in these investigations, Western standards tend to be viewed as normative. Numerous examples could be cited, but, in the area of gender research, the work by Williams and Best (1982) documents this trend. Most of their derived analyses are based on scales constructed from American data. Hence, all of the derived analyses utilize American "filters," as the authors repeatedly state in their book. These authors caution the reader about such filters, but, because no alternatives are presented, it is difficult for the reader to envisage other perspectives. The best defense against such cultural biases would seem to be the offense of seeking the guidance of large numbers of Swedes and Americans about the research issues. Consequently, that is what I did.

Methodological Problems

Cross-cultural and cross-national research is difficult regardless of the basis of comparison, but it is particularly challenging when the purpose is to compare subtle subjective differences such as peoples' values, stereotypes, attitudes, feelings, meanings, opinions, and the like (Osgood et al., 1975) in other words, the kinds of things that were most interesting to me. Because these subjective differences encompass differences in both language and custom, they are highly vulnerable to error. The language and cultural barriers must be overcome or circumvented if the research is to yield meaningful results.

All phases of cross-cultural research are vulnerable to language problems.

Language encompasses, transmits, and is shaped by customs. It captures national uniqueness. In fact, one of the pervasive problems of all research involving translations is that some words either cannot be translated into other languages or lose some meaning through translation. These characteristics typically affect the adequacy of translation and the comparability (standardization) of the measures.

Planning Experiments

Like most cross-cultural research, our project had two primary purposes. The first was to gather information, and the second was to test hypotheses. The former is much more common. Its origins presumably spring from a desire to know, from curiosity (as expressed by Prokofiev's bird and duck). To test hypotheses, we need more structure. We need a rationale for testing specific countries and for not testing others. This approach is rare, (e.g., Osgood et al., 1975), but it is exactly the kind of approach that will satisfy Rosaldo's (1980) plea for learning to ask questions that may help to identify the factors that shape human development (Ember, 1981).

The perils of language translation affect all stages of cross-cultural research, but in no stage is it more important than in original planning. If research is poorly designed due to inadequate mastery of the languages and customs of the cultures involved, the outcomes are likely to be unpersuasive, unimpressive, and, at worst, uninterpretable. Obviously, the primary researcher does not need to be fluent in the native languages of the societies, but advisers or coinvestigators must be fluent unless language-free measures are used. Even in supposed language-free cases, the possiblity of differential interpretations of the task due to culturally varying customs should be considered in the planning stage.

One way of addressing this problem was to use only one language, most likely the senior investigator's native tongue. Thus, we might have used only English. This was feasible because Swedish children begin studying English in elementary school. But English tests would not necessarily capture the type of sensitive, highly personal views about gender that I sought. English tests might constrain written output simply because the participants were more concerned about their grammar, spelling, and vocabulary than in the content of their responses. Clearly, there was no choice: The testing instrument had to be written and administered in Swedish to Swedish participants and in English to American participants.

A common method for handling language problems is to devise language-equivalent instruments. Two techniques are often used to aid the development of linguistically similar forms of a task: committee translation and back translation. The use of a committee of multilingual persons simply increases the likelihood of obtaining agreement about the translations. Back translation documents the transitivity of the translations. I used both methods. Nonetheless, even if these precautions have been observed, some inadequacies of translation must be expected.

Sampling Problems

Sampling constitutes another troublesome area in cross-cultural experimentation. Decisions must be made about the countries/cultures to be examined, the subjects to be selected within each country, and the tasks to be used.

Sampling of Cultures. In practice, decisions about the nations and cultures to be studied have often been based on expediency (e.g., Williams & Best, 1982). Investigators choose certain countries because they have contacts in those countries. This approach informs our curiosity about practices and customs in different societies, but it does so in a rather haphazard fashion. It would be more desirable—and more consistent with cross-cultural hypothesis testing—to systematically select societies that vary on some principled basis and should, therefore, yield results that differ in predictable ways. In keeping with this tenet, we selected Sweden and the United States as our two target countries because they differed in the significant realm of systematic governmental support and implementation of equality while being fairly comparable in numerous other aspects, including standard of living.

Sampling of Subjects. Another concern is that of sampling subjects within each country. Ideally, the subjects would be comparable across countries. This situation is difficult to achieve, so most researchers settle for using subjects who have roughly similar socioeconomic backgrounds. Hence, subjects may be chosen who are "middle-class," "working-class," "have completed x years of education," and so on. We chose participants in both countries who are middle class. The same strategy applies to samples within each society. If different social strata are tested in one nation, the typical approach is to try to sample similar strata in the other countries. These precautions have not always been followed, probably because the simple availability of respondents was of paramount concern.

Sampling of Tasks. The choice of the task and of the materials also challenges the cross-cultural investigator. The task must be one that is easily described and understood to avoid the problem of lack of communication. Consultants from the target countries may prevent serious errors at this level of planning. Even they may underestimate the difficulty or the alienation of a task that was developed in some other nation. Piloting or pretesting the materials may avoid subsequent interpretational dangers.

In our selection of tasks, we sought tasks that would yield estimates of both cultural gender concepts and personal gender concepts. A number of considerations influenced our decisions, such as desires to maintain some comparability with previous related research, to use sensitive instruments, and to compare the results across a number of instruments. All of these considerations subsume our attempts to balance two divergent principles: naturalness and standardization (flexibility and comparability). Naturalness argues for the use of open-ended or nonproscriptive measures, such as Block's (1973) technique of asking respondents to describe the "kind of person I would most like to be." With open tasks, the participants have greater freedom to express their own individualities, including their cultural heritage, in a relatively unencumbered fashion. Open tasks probably encourage serendipity. They allow for unexpected responses. Natural measures maximize opportunities to discover unanticipated cross-national differences among the components of gender concepts and minimize the constraints inevitably imposed by preselecting a set of traits, behaviors, opinions, and the like, that are to be associated with the sexes. Natural measures also are likely to yield noncomparable and differing patterns across nations that may be difficult or even impossible to reconcile and to interpret.

Given satisfactory translations of the material, reconciliation does not appear to be a problem when all respondents perform a preselected task, such as deciding which sex more often manifests a particular trait adjective (e.g., Williams & Best, 1982). This approach presumably maximizes standardization of the task across the various nations, although the extent to which standardization is achieved heavily depends on the adequacy of the translations and the testing procedures. A major difficulty with standardization is the loss of naturalness—the loss of opportunities for unusual, personally, and societally idiosyncratic responses to emerge. This difficulty can be at least partly ameliorated by including a large number of traits, behaviors, opinions, and so on, that are assumed to be components of gender schemata in *each of the nations/cultures* to be surveyed.

We next considered the diverse tasks that have been used in cross-cultural gender research. Gender concepts have been probed using projective techniques (e.g., Block, 1973), adjective checklists, unidimensional masculinity–femininity scales, and bidimensional scales that contain a masculine (instrumental, agentic) dimension and a feminine (expressive, communal) dimension, among other methods.

Other commonly used methods are more likely to satisfy a standardization criterion than a naturalness one. For example, scales developed to assess gender differences should make it theoretically possible to present ostensibly the same test items, in appropriate translations, to all subjects. Thus, the English versions of measures such as the following could be translated into the to-be-tested languages: unidimensional scales of masculinity–femininity such as the Femininity Scale of the California Psychological Inventory (Gough, 1966; Levin & Karni, 1971) and bidimensional scales such as the Bem Sex Role Inventory (BSRI; Bem, 1974; Maloney, Wilkof, & Dambrot, 1981) and the Extended Personality Attributes Questionnaire (EPAQ; Runge, Frey, Gollwitzer, Helmreich, & Spence, 1981; Spence et al., 1979). These measures assess a fairly limited number of adjectives describing personality traits that may differentiate among gender concepts. The Femininity Scale of the California Psychological Inventory (Gough, 1966) contains 38 statements about topics such as interests, self-perceptions, feelings, and thoughts. Subjects indicate whether an item is true or false as it applies to them.

These tests have been standardized on American samples and are likely to carry some cultural bias. One obvious bias about gender concepts is the theoretical perspective of the instrument's developer toward gender roles. For example, some developers treat femininity and masculinity as bipolar opposites, as two ends of a single continuum. But what, exactly, does the continuum assess? How do we define the dimension that extends from masculinity at one end to femininity at the other? To date, this problem has not been satisfactorily resolved, perhaps because neither femininity nor masculinity has been defined in a noncircular manner. As Spence (1985) explains, even dictionary definitions refer back to the same concept: "Feminine is defined as 1. pertaining to a woman or girl: *feminine beauty*; *feminine dress*; 2. like a woman: weak; gentle. 3. effeminate, womanish; 4. belonging to the female sex, female." (p. 60). In her now-classical article, Constantinople (1973) concluded that the concepts—and definition of—femininity and masculinity are among the most elusive in psychology.

These problems of definition often have been evaded by simply selecting items that differentiated between the two sexes. The items could be quite diverse; the sole consideration was their ability to distinguish between the sexes. The conceptual difficulties with this approach are obvious: What do the scores mean? Even though the scale is unidimensional in construction, the underlying concepts may be complex and multidimensional. Consider intermediate scores, for example. Do these scores mean that a person has both "feminine" and "masculine" characteristics that almost balance each other, or is there some underlying, undefined, and as yet unspecified continuum that the person represents to only a moderate extent?

One response to the problems of unidimensional scales of femininity–masculinity has been the construction of separate scales for the two concepts (e.g., the BSRI and the EPAQ). This solution recognizes that all individuals may possess traits often associated with one sex or the other to a greater or lesser extent. Women, for example, may be warm and independent, just as men may be both competent and nurturant.

For example, the BSRI is composed of 60 adjectives that represent three 20-item scales: masculinity, femininity, and social desirability. Subjects respond, using a scale from 1 (never or almost never true) to 7 (always or almost always true), typically by describing themselves. The EPAQ contains 40 personality trait adjectives and their bipolar opposites (e.g., Very rough A . . . B . . . C . . . D . . . E Very gentle). The subject circles a letter to indicate his or her choice. The scales contain six subscales. One subscale contains eight traits judged to be socially desirable and expressive–communal in nature (the F+ scale). Another subscale contains eight traits judged to be socially desirable and instrumental–agentic in nature (the M+ scale). A third scale (M–F+) has eight items whose social desirability depends on the sex of persons with whom the item is usually associated. The fourth scale (M−) has eight items judged to be socially undesirable and instrumental–agentic. The last two scales, each with four items judged to be socially undesirable, tap items that are communal in nature (F_{C-}), and items that have a passive–aggressive nature (F_{VA-}).

The bidimensional approach also has problems. Rather than being bidimensional, factor analyses have shown the scales are multidimensional in many applications (e.g., Bem, 1974; Coffman & Levy, 1972; Helmreich, Spence, & Wilhelm, 1981; Major, Carnevale, & Deaux, 1981; Orlofsky, 1981; Pedhazur & Tetenbaum, 1979; Spence & Helmreich, 1978, 1980; Spence & Sawin, 1984; Taylor & Hall, 1982; Tellegen & Lubinski, 1983). These outcomes reveal the complexity of the concepts of femininity and masculinity; indeed, they could be interpreted as signals that the concepts of femininity and masculinity are so diverse and nonspecific as to be scientifically (and perhaps practically) questionable. Nevertheless, the bidimensional scales are widely used.

The bidimensional scales differ from the unidimensional in still other respects. The bidimensional scales have been used in conjunction with the concept of androgyny, the notion that people might manifest traits stereotypically assigned to both genders. Building on this notion, Bem (1974) and others suggested that individuals who are androgynous have the capabilities of being more flexible and adaptable than do less androgynous people, including those who manifest stereotypic gender traits. Like the definitions and conceptualizations of femininity and masculinity, the concept of androgyny has been controversial (e.g., Taylor & Hall, 1982; also see entire issue of the *Psychology of Women Quarterly*, edited by Kaplan, 1979), so much so that Bem (1985) has recanted in favor of a model of gender schemata. Many reasons contributed to this shift in emphasis, including research that found fairly high correlations between "masculinity" and androgyny (see Taylor & Hall, 1982, for a review).

Bem's (1981, 1982) gender-schema model shifted back into a unidimensional mode. In this model, a continuum of gender schematism extends from persons with strongly sex-stereotyped schemata about gender (masculine men and feminine women) to nonsex-typed persons (who identify with neither a feminine or masculine role). Thus, the continuum reaches from the strongly gender schematic to the gender aschematic. Other gender-schema models, such as those of Markus (Crane & Markus, 1982; Markus, Crane, Bernstein, & Siladi, 1982), Martin and Halverson (1981), and Spence (Spence, 1985; Spence & Helmreich, 1978), retain a two-factor, bidimensional conceptualization of femininity and masculinity. According to Markus, and similar to our model as presented in chapter 1, two gender schemata develop, one that captures characteristics associated with females and one that contains aspects associated with males. Martin and Halverson (1981) and Spence (1985) further assumed, as we do, that self-schemata may contain gender-related components. The schemata postulated by all of these models may include, but are not restricted to, the kinds of personality traits tested by both unidimensional and bidimensional scales of expressiveness (femininity) and instrumentality (masculinity).

This brief discussion of the relative merits of contemporary measures of femininity and masculinity highlights their conceptual and theoretical problems. One additional concern is that these scales contain only personality attributes. Hence their use restricts estimates of the components of gender schemata to personality aspects—and to only the personality attributes that happen to be tested. These restrictions are severe, because it seems likely that physical characteristics (e.g., Deaux, 1984; Deaux & Lewis, 1983, 1984), hair length, style, and color (e.g., Intons-Peterson, in press), eye color (Carlsson, personal communication), and activities and occupations (Deaux, 1984; Deaux & Lewis, 1983, 1984; Schau, Ein, & Tremaine, 1977; Tremaine, Schau, & Busch, 1982) also may function as important gender cues.

The many weaknesses of the standardized scales of femininity and masculinity and their restrictions to personality traits argued for the judicious selection of some personality attributes that have often distinguished between the sexes and of physical, occupational, and activity-related aspects that also appear likely to function as gender differentiators. Even after the careful and painstaking selection of items to be tested cross-nationally, the preparation of linguistically equivalent forms of these measures was difficult, because, as previously mentioned, translational problems are more acute with single words than with words in sentences or longer grammatical units. Additionally, not all words in one language have counterparts in other languages. Translational variations may jeopardize the standardization or comparability achieved across the countries.

These criticisms also apply to the Adjective Check List (ACL; Gough & Heilbrun, 1965, 1980), although its 300 personality-trait adjectives surely tap a great many aspects of personality. The technique also has been adapted for use with a child population. This version consists of brief stories that describe the essential meaning of each of 32 traits taken from the ACL. The children identify the sex of the person most often associated with each trait by pointing to a silhouette of a female or a male.

As it is commonly administered, the ACL and its story version are likely to constrain responses in another way. Subjects must choose whether a specific trait is frequently associated with either men or women. This forced-choice approach excludes the possibility of indicating that both sexes manifest the trait, or that neither sex manifests the trait, although this latter option was provided in some administrations (Williams & Bennett, 1975; Williams & Best, 1977). It also eliminates the option of quantifying the extent to which typical people are thought to exhibit the traits. Thus, a "female-rated" trait that might be perceived to be associated with 10% of the females and 8% of the males in a society would be weighted equally with another female-rated trait that is perceived to be found in 95% of the females and 5% of the males. This result of the forced-choice technique seriously reduces the method's usefulness, in our opinion. Williams and Best (1982) acknowledged these weaknesses, but they prefer their method because they consider it to be relative, as the respondents were told to select the sex more frequently associated with the trait. The problem with the forced-choice method is that, in fact, it yields absolute, not relative, indicators, despite the relative terms articulated in the instructions. Another rationale for using the forced-choice technique is that it avoids the uninformative "cannot say" response category. There are other ways to achieve both relative weightings of the traits for the two sexes and elimination of the "cannot say" category as described later.

The projective techniques offer naturalness whereas the scales and check-lists offer reasonable standardization, two desirable but often conflicting attributes for tasks in cross-national research. How can these attributes be reconciled? Our way was to use both kinds of measures. The use of both kinds of measures had another advantage—that of setting the stage for possible convergence of the results. Such convergence from quite different techniques would increase confidence in the stability of the gender concepts. Despite these advantages, the use of con-verging measures in cross-national research seems rare.

Part of the task selection process is the decision about the stimulus persons to be rated. The aforementioned scales and other measures can be used to rate the gender characteristics of various stimulus persons. The choice of stimulus person depends on the purposes of the experiment. When the purpose of the experiment is to assess the personality traits individuals claim for themselves or that they wish they had, the subjects are asked to rate "self" or "ideal self." These ratings could be interpreted as indices of personal gender schemata. To assess the personality traits associated with gender stereotypes of the nation in general, the stimulus persons should be "most women" and "most men" for adults and "most girls" and "most boys" for children. Unfortunately, most studies to date have used either more restrictive or vaguely specified stimulus persons, such as "a typical woman," or simply "women" (and the counterparts for men). These latter stimulus persons allow the subjects to describe a single person whom they consider representative of the group, or any number of persons up to the whole class. To gain more precision and to obtain judgments about a high proportion of members of the rated group when trying to estimate general cultural gender schemata, we consider it important to explicitly indicate that the group to be judged contains most members of that group (i.e., to rate "most women," for example). Additionally, to map developmental changes in gender schemata, younger stimulus persons should be rated in the same way by using "most girls" and "most boys."

We might ask what happens when methodologies are inadequate. At one ex-treme is the possibility that the results will be uninterpretable. Another possibility, according to Williams and Best (1982), is that methodological problems will produce spurious cross-cultural differences. This is a rather surprising and in-teresting view, because standard statistical principles would argue that method-ological problems are most likely to increase the variance that will, in turn, tend to obscure, rather than enhance, cross-cultural differences. Perhaps their view is predicated on the notion that design insufficiencies will induce different perceptions of the task in different societies and these different perceptions will yield differing results. This possibility is, of course, quite plausible. The decision about when differences or similarities are real, and not artifactual, is considered here.

Procedures and Task Administration

Not only is the selection of a task a problem, but the explanation of this task and whatever language is required for its execution are additional challenges. In short, the language barrier arises once again. Given the possibilities of inadequate communication about the task or of variations of meaning in the various translations of the material, it seems prudent for any cross-cultural researcher to (a) consult with knowledgeable representatives of each culture, (b) pretest the task and its materials, and (c) use different tasks or measures to test the possibility of convergence.

Finally, it is of utmost importance that participants be informed about the procedures before they begin the experiment and that they be given the opportunity to withdraw without penalty at any time. In addition to being sound practice, the scrupulous observation of these principles should help to maintain smooth political interactions with the participating nations. Wherever possible, confidentiality of the responses should also be guaranteed.

Data Collection and Analysis

In the actual collection of data, it is important for the experimenter or the observer to establish rapport with the subjects. This often means that different native speakers will serve as the experimenters or observers in different societies. These experimenters may develop idiosyncratic styles that influence the outcome. One way of trying to avoid the effects of individual idiosyncrasies is to train each of them to use a certain basic pattern, always recognizing that local custom may require some variation. At the least, these deviations should be noted and recorded. Another possibility is to supplement the training by having one investigator participate in all sessions along with an experimenter who is a native speaker. This was the method we used.

Perhaps the most serious hazard lurking in the analyses of cross-cultural data, other than such problems as unequal numbers of subjects in cells, unequal completion of tasks in some conditions, and the like, is that of imposing standards or techniques developed in the senior investigator's country on the results. For example, Williams and Best (1982) applied an affective meaning system, a transactional ego-state scoring system, and a needs assessment based on Murray's (1938) system to their data. All of these systems have American origins, and their appropriateness for other countries is not known.

Interpretation

Interpretation of the results of cross-cultural and cross-national research is in-extricably linked to the design of the projects. It follows, therefore, that all of the previously mentioned cautions must be observed. Clearly, one must always be alert to biological and cultural interpretations, as well as to the possibilities of interactions between the two.

Another problem is the possibility of confusing failures of communication with failures of actual perception or behavior (Campbell, 1964). Campbell argued for the importance of having a standard of similarity among cultures as a baseline against which to assess differences. That is, the similarities suggest, although they do not confirm, that both groups understand the task. Presumably, dif-ferences on other tasks may then be taken more seriously. Campbell contended that distinguishing differences of perception from those of failure of communica-tion are principal concerns of cross-cultural investigations.

A central focus of interpretation is to decide which variations are meaningful and which are random fluctuations. Appropriate statistics are vital, and they pro-vide one yardstick. Nevertheless, even a statistically significant difference might be so small that it lacks practical significance. A good example is the common result that females have somewhat higher scores than males on tests of verbal ability (e.g., Maccoby & Jacklin, 1974), and yet sex, per se, accounts for only 1% of the variance of the experiments surveyed by Maccoby and Jacklin (Hyde, 1981). Moreover, the difference is not statistically significant on national tests, such as the Scholastic Aptitude Test (SAT; Bieri, Bradburn, & Galinsky, 1958; Marks, 1968), and it is not found in England and West Germany, where reading is considered a masculine activity (Nash, 1979). Therefore, although it is ac-curate to note that the differences in verbal ability are found in some cir-cumstances, the differences seem too fragile to signal profound differences in underlying capacities.

One problem, then, is to decide when variations should be ignored and cultures thus considered the same and when the variations are important and the cultures considered different. Associated with these decisions are the con-comitant ones of deciding when different cultural practices yield similar results, and when similar results signal true similarities between the cultures. In brief, there are four questions, as Osgood et al. (1975) observed:

1. When is same really the same? "Given surface variations in language and culture [the demonstration of sameness] becomes a very difficult business" (Osgood et al., 1975, p. 31).

2. When is same really different? Insensitive measures, for example, may pro-duce variability in the responses that could camouflage true differences among cultures.

3. When is different really the same? Many factors may produce differing

results even though the cultures themselves do not really vary. The factors include different experimenters and varying perceptions of the task by participants in the different nations.

4. When is different really different? When are apparent cultural differences sufficiently robust and important to be recognized as real?

Some techniques are useful in trying to assess the significance of the results, in addition to statistical tests. None of the techniques is foolproof, however, and no single method guarantees a definitive answer. One alternative is to look for patterns of differences. If differences emerge on more than one theoretically related measure, the patterning lends credibility to the conclusion of differences (or, depending on the direction of the convergence, to the conclusion of sameness). This alternative requires advance preparation, because the design of the project must include potentially converging measures. A second alternative is to seek other corroboratory evidence. A third alternative is to use one's knowledge of the culture, usually bolstered by consultations with native coinvestigators or consultants. The fourth alternative is to evaluate the differences in light of the hypotheses. This alternative is tricky, for it may be self-serving. Uninvolved colleagues may be able to assist. If feasible, researchers may apply all four of the alternatives.

The evaluations of the reality of similarities and differences have direct implications for the extent to which universal behavior patterns are found among cultures. In addition to the questions just noted, definitional problems plague the concept of universality. Must a particular behavior pattern be found in all societies for it to be considered universal? Societies not exhibiting the pattern might have some factors that suppress its expression, even though such factors have not been recognized. Given this possibility, we might want to define universals in probabilistic terms, but such an approach simply raises a question about the probability level to use. Must 90% of the societies examined display the pattern or is 80% sufficient? What standard should be used to make this decision less arbitrary? How many societies should be examined?

The definition of a universal encounters other problems, for what appears to be a universal at one level of analysis (typically a broad, molar level) may break down at other (usually finer) levels of analysis. For example, what does it mean to assert that sexual asymmetry is universal? Simply that men and women perform different tasks? But they typically perform some similar or identical tasks, as well. In other words, what appears to be universal, at a very general level of analysis, such as the notion of male dominance, breaks down at finer levels of analysis. As Rosaldo (1980) noted:

> Male dominance . . . does not in actual behavioral terms assume a universal content or a universal shape. On the contrary, women typically have power and influence in political and economic life, display autonomy from men in their pur-

suits, and rarely find themselves confronted or constrained by what might seem to be the brute fact of male strength. For every case in which we see women confined, by powerful men or by the responsibilities of child care and the home, one can cite others which display female capacities to fight back, speak out in public, perform physically demanding tasks, and even subordinate the needs of infant children (in their homes or on their backs) to their desires for travel, labor, politics, love, or trade. (p. 394)

Indeed, the concept of universality may need to be defined with reference to specific tasks.

We turn next to a brief summary of the literature on cross-cultural variations in gender concepts.

CROSS-CULTURAL STUDIES
OF GENDER CONCEPTS

Because most anthropological research has considered both sexes, one could argue that it has investigated gender roles and concepts. However, many efforts have been devoted to simply describing the behaviors of the two sexes without attempting to probe the expectations and attitudes of each sex about other members of the same sex and about members of the other sex. Interesting as this work is, it is not as relevant to our project as research that has focused more directly on the *contents* of gender roles.

Cross-National Comparisons that Included
Sweden and the United States

We found only a few studies that compared Sweden and the United States. One project by Osgood et al. (1975) evaluated affective meaning of adjectival modifiers in 25 language/culture communities. Although gender concepts were not tested—in fact, only male high school students were tested—the results are useful because they suggest parallels between the affective meaning structures of the two languages in our study, Swedish and American English. The primary means of assessing affective aspects of language were Osgood's evaluative, activity, and potency scales. These three components were highly similar in many of the language/culture communities tested, including Sweden and the United States. The conclusions about affective parallels are severely limited, however, by the restricted sample.

More relevant is Block's (1973) work. She focused on gender concepts of both sexes, asking college students in Denmark, England, Finland, Norway, Sweden, and the United States to describe "the kind of person I would most like to be." This technique assumes that the responses would index "the culturally modal definition of the ideal male and the ideal female, . . . a projection of the values of that culture" (p. 519). She found substantial similarities in the feminine and masculine ideals that were expressed in the six countries. Despite the overall cross-national stability, some differences appeared. For example, the Swedish respondents reliably attributed (at the .05 level or beyond) only one trait more often to ideal males than to ideal females (practical/shrewd), whereas the American respondents reliably assigned seven traits more often to males than to females (practical/shrewd, assertive, dominating, competitive, critical, self-controlled, and rational/reasonable). Thus, on some traits, Swedes appeared to differentiate less between their conceptions of an ideal male and an ideal female than the Americans. The same pattern appeared for the traits assigned more often to ideal females than to ideal males. Swedish respondents thought that ideal females were reliably more likely than ideal males to be impulsive, generous, and vital/active, whereas American respondents accorded five traits more often to ideal females than to ideal males (loving/affectionate, impulsive, vital/active, sensitive, and reserved/shy). Similar comparisons of traits that differed at the .10 level yield the same general pattern: Americans differentiate between ideal persons of the two sexes on more adjectives than Swedes, although the gender-distinguished attributes tend to be cross-nationally similar.

These assessments must be regarded as tentative, for Block does not state the percentages of respondents assigning each trait to ideal females and to ideal males. Consequently, we cannot ascertain the frequencies—and the relative importance—of the trait-gender associations. Moreover, very little additional information is given about the responses.

Also relevant is Haas's (1986) comparison of wives' orientation toward employment outside the home in Sweden and the United States. This research does not probe the contents of gender concepts in a general way, but, rather, focuses on attitudes toward being a major producer of family income. Because the Swedish conception holds that both members of a couple share financial and domestic responsibilties but no such systematic view prevails in the United States, Haas reasoned that Swedish women would consider labor force participation as obligatory, whereas American women could consider it optional. To test these deductions, she tested full- and part-time women workers in both countries, asking them questions about the importance of a full sharing of the financial responsibilities, their beliefs that men should be the breadwinners, and other questions likely to be relevant to endorsement of fully shared financial responsibilities.

Recognizing that women work for assorted reasons that may or may not reflect their beliefs about the underlying importance of female–male sharing of financial responsibilities, Haas devised questions that led to a fourfold classification scheme. These questions asked about the extent of actual sharing of the bread-winner role and of the belief that men should be the primary breadwinners. Based on responses to these questions, Haas developed the following classification scheme. When women claimed that they believed that males should not be the primary breadwinners, they were classified as *willing breadwinners*. Women who did not share equally with their cohabitants in financial contributions, but who believed that men should not be primarily responsible for this role were considered *potential breadwinners*. The third category consisted of women who shared breadwinning equally with their cohabitants but did endorsed male financial responsibility. This category was labeled the *reluctant breadwinner*. The fourth category, called the *traditionalists*, consisted of individuals who neither shared breadwinning responsibilities with their spouses nor believed that they should.

Haas applied this classification scheme to 43 Swedish working women and to 242 American working women. More Swedish women (50%) than American women (23%) were working part time. Full- versus part-time work was an important distinction, as we see here.

Reflecting the Swedish national commitment to shared financial responsibility for the family and the absence of such a nationally endorsed commitment in the United States, Haas predicted that most Swedish working women would be willing or potential breadwinners and that more Swedish than American women would be willing or potential breadwinners. When full- plus part-time workers were considered, the results supported the second but not the first prediction. That is, reliably more Swedish than American women were classified as willing breadwinners (and more American than Swedish women were classified as traditionalists), but Swedish women were more likely to be classified as traditionalists (41%) than as willing breadwinners (26%). When only full-time workers were considered, however, more Swedish women were classified as willing breadwinners (46%) than as traditionalists (20%). The figures for Americans did not change much when they were restricted to only full-time workers, probably because 79% of the American sample were full-time workers. The change for Swedish respondents was not surprising because full-time workers are likely to have a greater commitment to a career than part timers.

These results suggest that the Swedish emphasis on the sharing of financial responsibilities has been partially, but not fully, incorporated into the philosophies of the women tested. Further, American, more than Swedish, women appear to view work force participation as optional.

Haas's research also probed the relation between various factors and the espousal of shared responsibility for financial support for the family. In general, she found that the endorsement of shared financial responsibilities increased, in both countries, with education, younger age (the differences were greater in Sweden than in the United States), exposure to sex-role debates, beliefs that women can be interested in both home and a career, that fathers can be as close to their children as mothers, and that fathers are as capable in the domestic sphere as mothers. These characteristics were positively related to the assumption of a willing breadwinner role.

Haas's approach does not specifically address the question of the components of gender concepts, but it illuminates relevant factors, such as a balance of those characteristics probably necessary for success in economic and domestic realms: independence, empathy, interpersonal skills, competence, persistence, and the like. In both this study and in her work on the sharing of child care (Haas, 1982), exposure to sex-role debates in the mass media was also related to the sharing of financial and domestic roles, a result that points toward the malleability and dynamics of gender concepts.

Recent researchers (Foa et al., 1987) have shown that Americans distinguish between love and sex to a greater extent than Swedes do. This asymmetry reminds us of Baumgartner's (Tavris with Baumgartner, 1983) work with a change-sex question and it anticipates our results. The authors commented that "the Swedish culture induces a stronger positive relationship between love and sex as compared to the American culture" (p. 518). We agree. This positive relationship is also compatible with the Swedish focus on joining parental responsibilities.

The projects that include Swedish–American comparisons suggest some similarities between the countries in affective language, in gender typing of ideal persons of each sex, in work ethics, and in the linking of love and sex. Gender typing—at least of ideal persons—may be less prevalent in Sweden than in the United States, a possibility that accords with our hypotheses. Also in line with our model are Haas's findings that imply that gender concepts are susceptible to change, even though her research did not explicitly probe the components of gender concepts or their susceptibility to change.

Other Research on Gender Concepts Not Including Swedish–American Comparisons

We also examined other cross-national research that investigated gender concepts from various perspectives, even though no Swedish–American comparisons were made.

Probably the most systematic comparisons have been made by Williams and Best (1982), who studied females and males of varying ages in as many as 30 countries. The adults (university students) in 25 countries decided whether each of the 300 adjectives on the ACL were "more frequently associated with men rather than women, or more frequently associated with women than men" (p. 51). In previous research, but not in the projects described in their book, the subjects had a third response category of the trait not being differentially associated with the two sexes. Apparently, none of their work included the alternative of the trait being associated equally often with the two sexes. University students in three other countries followed the same procedure with a shorter list of 52 items.

Williams and Best also tested 5-, 6-, 8-, and 9-year-old children in 23 countries, and a group of 8- and 9-year-olds in Australia. The United States' sample also contained children of other ages. These respondents received a modification of the ACL. They were exposed to short stories that were designed to describe the essential characteristics of 32 traits taken from the ACL. The children indicated whether the traits were more often associated with females or males by pointing to a silhouette of a boy or a girl. A written version was prepared for older children.

Williams and Best found marked cross-national stability in the gender stereotypes assigned to the two sexes. Deviations occurred, of course, but the overwhelming impression created by the data was one of overlapping cross-national stereotypes, regardless of the ages of the subjects. Should their results be taken as evidence for the universality of at least cultural gender stereotypes or schemata?

At this point the answer is no, for a number of reasons, most of which are cited by the authors.

First, the sample of nations, although extensive, included no Eastern European, Middle Eastern, or Soviet-bloc countries, only three African nations, and two Oceanian nations.

Second, all of the test adjectives were drawn from previous American research. These adjectives were of undetermined relevance for the other countries. Moreover, all of the adjectives denoted personality traits, so that other potential differentiators were excluded. Furthermore, the 32-item pool of adjectives used for children may have been overly restrictive. It is impossible to assess the validity or significance of these potential problems, because no converging, possibly corroborating additional measures were included in the design.

Third, no evaluations of the adequacy of translations were given, although the authors used both a committee approach to translation and back translation, so it is reasonable to assume satisfactory translations.

Fourth, many of the derived analyses are based on scoring systems developed in the United States. Their appropriateness and equivalence as applied to other nations is not known.

Fifth, the significance of differential attribution of the traits to the two sexes was not assessed. The report contained neither statistical analyses nor converging measures at each age level that might have documented parallel patterns.

Sixth, the task itself, which required the subjects to choose one sex or the other, without the options of indicating that the adjectives apply to both or to neither sex, undoubtedly introduced a bias toward finding differences in attribution of the adjectives to the sexes. There is no reason, however, why the task's characteristics would bias the particular adjectives that were differentially associated with each sex.

Seventh, because the responses were dichotomous, the subjects had no opportunity to indicate the extent to which females and males had a particular trait. Substantial cross-national differences might have been revealed by a more finely tuned instrument.

Eighth, the task may have been interpreted differently in the various countries. This effect could arise from variations in the instructions, in the cultural perspectives the various respondents brought to the task, or both.

Clearly, it is premature to conclude that cultural gender concepts or schemata are universal, but Williams and Best (1982) have provided a very provocative and informative monograph. Additionally, they reported an intriguing developmental trend: Male stereotypes tended to be learned faster than female ones. This result was soon challenged. Carlsson, Andersson, Berg, Jaderquist, and Magnusson (1984) were not able to replicate the finding with most of their Swedish children, nor were Lee and Sugawara (1982) with Korean children, or Trautner, Sahm, and Stevermann (1983) with German children. Moreover, Tarrier and Gomes (1981) reported the opposite effect for 5-, 8-, and 11-year-old Brazilian children. They found that the Brazilian children were more knowledgeable about female than about male stereotypes.

Other research suggested that gender differences are less pronounced among Americans than among Chicanos (Gonzalez, 1982), Turks (Sunar, 1982), and Israeli men (Maloney et al., 1981), whereas the perceptions of gender differences were more pronounced among American children than among Brazilian children (Tarrier & Gomes, 1981).

SUMMARY

In this chapter, we discussed some perils of cross-cultural research, beginning with the basic questions of whether or not valid cross-cultural comparisons could be made. Such comparisons are inherently invalid, according to Malinkowski (1922), because each culture must be interpreted within its own framework of customs. The contemporary escape from this dictum is to acknowledge both the individual culture and its constituents (the emic approach) and broader cross-cultural perspectives (the etic approach), a procedure adopted in the current project.

Other hazards of cross-national research include national sensitivities, the likely constraints imposed by the experimenter's own cultural beliefs, language barriers, and difficulties with methodological design and data interpretation. Sensitivity to the differences in language pervades all of these domains.

The chapter ended with a brief summary of relevant literature. Unfortunately, only a limited number of projects were found that included comparisons of Sweden and the United States. Osgood et al. (1975) concluded that the affective aspects of language in these two (and other) countries were quite similar. In the only study that considered gender attitudes, Block (1973) reported that although marked cross-cultural similarities occurred in the traits attributed to an ideal person by respondents from six countries, Swedish respondents differentiated less between the two sexes than did American respondents. Haas (1986) did not attempt to assess gender attributes as such. Instead, she examined the extent to which Swedish and American women consider workforce participation to be obligatory or optional. Consistent with Swedish philosophy, Swedish women were more likely than American women to treat employment as obligatory and this attitude was more pronounced among full-time workers than among part-time workers. Although these results generally support the Swedish commitment to gender equality, a surprising number of Swedish women did not consider workforce participation obligatory. These results suggest that we may find diverse gender role attributes among Swedes, as well as among Americans.

Similarly, Foa et al. (1987) did not focus in gender concepts but, rather, in the differentiation of sex and love. They found greater differentiation by Americans than by Swedes, suggesting that Swedes are more likely to view the two as positively related. Such an attitude should nourish Sweden's view that both parents share domestic responsibilties.

In general, other research that considered gender stereotypes in various countries, not including Sweden, tended to find more cross-national similarities than differences in the stereotypes associated with women and men. Our question was whether the same findings would emerge in comparisons of gender concepts in the United States and Sweden.

To answer this question, we embarked on a substantial research project involving youth of varying ages in both countries. Multiple measures were used to probe different aspects of gender roles. These measures, and the overall experimental design, are described in the next chapter.

4

Method and Predictions

In this chapter, we describe our procedures for investigating the gender concepts of Swedish and American 11-, 14-, and 18-year-olds. These procedures were dictated by a number of concerns and principles. The first was that the measures should assess gender concepts from different perspectives. Such an approach increases the comprehensiveness of the evidence. The second was that the measures should be acceptable to both countries, and the third was that the design minimize the hazards of cross-cultural research described in the previous chapter.

In general, our central plan was to use measures designed to achieve both naturalness and standardization. For naturalness, we asked the subjects to list the characteristics that they most admired in people (sex unspecified), and to list the attributes that they thought characterized each of the stimulus groups (most women, most men, most boys, most girls). The purpose of asking about the attributes that they most admired in people was to obtain an estimate of culturally desirable traits. Certain characteristics may be considered particularly important in each culture/nation. These characteristics may function as cultural imperatives, as patterns for what all members of the culture should emulate if they are to be considered "good" representatives of their country. One other "natural" measure was used, the "change-sex" story. In this measure, subjects were asked to write short stories about what their lives would be like if they wakened to find that they had become the other sex. We assumed that responses to this question would reveal components of their personal gender schema, whereas responses to the other open questions would disclose components of their cultural gender schemata.

These open measures impose minimal constraints on responses and thus offer opportunities for unexpected, unusual comments. They also may yield a confusing, diverse multiplicity of data that defy systematic interpretation, but we believed that the gain in naturalness was worth the risk.

As noted in chapter 3, standardization is also important. To make valid cross-cultural comparisons, we need to be sure that all subjects respond to at least some items that are as cross-nationally similar as possible. Hence, we selected 59 adjectives that have differentiated between the sexes in past research. These adjectives referred to personality and physical traits. The traits were translated from English into Swedish by a colleague who had spent approximately half of her life in Sweden and half in England. The translations were then checked by two other Swedish colleagues who had spent between 5 and 10 years in the United States or in England. I then back translated the items. Although my back translations were the weakest link in the chain, the other translations were made by impressively fluent speakers of both languages. These 59 traits were rated for importance of defining most women, most men, most boys, most girls, self, and (for the Swedish respondents) ideal self.

The full details of the method are given in the next section.

METHOD

Subjects

The numbers of females and males tested at each age level in the two countries are listed in Table 4.1. Also given are the age ranges and the mean ages for each age level. The Swedish youth were students in school districts close to Stockholm. The districts were chosen to represent a reasonable cross section of the Swedish population, except that no data from immigrant children were included in the analyses (because immigrant children would not necessarily have the same gender concepts as Swedish natives). It is important to note that, in part because of Sweden's highly advanced welfare system, most Swedes would be considered middle class. No attempt was made to recruit subjects from a lower class group.

The American youth attended public schools in the midwestern section of the United States. These subjects also represented a middle-class group.

TABLE 4.1
Number of Subjects in each Age Group by Sex in Sweden and in the United States

	11		14		18		Totals		
	Female	Male	Female	Male	Female	Male	Female	Male	All
Sweden	118	107	119	103	97	75	334	285	619
U.S.A.	56	54	54	59	54	54	164	167	331
Totals	174	161	173	162	151	129	498	452	950

On occasion, students were unable to complete all of the booklets in the available time. The exact numbers of subjects completing each task appear in the tables of results.

Stimulus Materials

The basic tests were divided into the three booklets described here. All tests were translated into Swedish for the Swedish subjects. For expediency only the English translations are stated in the text, but examples of both forms appear in Appendix I (English version) and Appendix II (partial Swedish version).

Booklet 1. Indirect Assessments of Gender-Role Schemata: The "Change-Gender" Test

The first page contained spaces for the subject's name, age, birthdate, sex, school, and city. Then, on the second page, the students wrote their story in response to the instructions at the top of the page. The instructions for female subjects stated, "Suppose, when you awaken tomorrow, you discover that you are a boy. What will your life be like? Write a little story telling what your life would be like as a boy. Use the rest of the page and the reverse side, if necessary." The word "boy" was changed to "girl" for the male subjects. On the third page, the subjects rated aspects of their "new life" on the five statements: I would be able to do many more things than I do now; My new life would be much harder than my life is now; My new life would be much worse than my life is now; My new life would be much more satisfying than it is now; and My new life would be much happier than it is now. The subjects answered by selecting the most appropriate response on a 7-point rating continuum that ranged from 1 (Very strongly agree) to 7 (Very strongly disagree).

Booklet 2. Direct Assessments of Gender-Role Schemata: Open-Ended Descriptions of the Sexes

To determine the characteristics, the subjects voluntarily associated with young and adult individuals of both sexes, we asked for open-ended descriptions of each of the four stimulus groups (most girls, most boys, most men, and most women). One example is given in the appendices for the Swedish and the English forms of the instrument. At the bottom of each of these four pages, they were asked to give a "good first name for a person like the one you described." This latter query was used to assess their awareness of first names as gender indicators. The 14- and 18-year-old subjects described all four stimulus persons, but, to adapt the testing to the more limited attention span of the 11-year-olds, these children described only two stimulus persons, either most girls and most boys, or most men and most women. The orders of administration were counterbalanced for all subject groups.

Direct Assessments of Cultural Attributes: Descriptions of Admired Traits. On another page, the subjects were asked to write down the traits that they most admired in other people, regardless of sex. These data should identify traits generally considered desirable and important for all members of the culture.

Direct Assessments of Cultural Gender-Role Schemata: Ratings of Importance of Gender-Associated Traits for Most Girls, Most Boys, Most Men, and Most Women. Using scales that ranged from 1 (extremely important) to 7 (extremely unimportant), the subjects first rated one group of stimulus persons, such as most girls, on 59 traits. Then they rated another group of stimulus persons, such as most boys, on the same 59 traits. Half of the 11-year-old subjects rated most girls and most boys; the other half rated most women and most men. The 14- and 18-year-olds rated all four stimulus groups. The order of the groups was counterbalanced.

The 59 traits contained personality traits taken from the Bem Sex Role Inventory (BSRI; Bem, 1974), because they differentiated between the ratings of female and male college students in both the United States (e.g., Edwards & Ashworth, 1977; Myers & Gonda, 1982; Pedhazur & Tetenbaum, 1979) and Sweden (Carlsson, 1981). Other personality traits were taken from the Extended Personal Attributes Questionnaire (Spence et al., 1979). These traits, not previously tested with a Swedish sample, seemed promising on the basis of preliminary testing. In addition, some traits were included to assess possible cultural imperatives, such as being hardworking, having social adeptness, and being good looking. Another group of trait adjectives tapped physical characteristics, such as strength, having straight hair, and having blue eyes. These latter adjectives were included, because previous pilot work in both Sweden (Carlsson, personal communication) and the United States (Intons-Peterson, in press) found them to differentiate between the sexes. Finally, four pairs of similar attributes were included to assess the reliability of the instrument. These traits were: active and lively; acts as a leader and has leadership abilities; artistic and creative; and aggressive and assertive. The resulting coefficients all exceeded .90, indicating that the instrument was reliable. In some cases, the Swedish and English translations had slightly different connotations so both are listed in the tables. For example, the Swedish translation of kind also connotes niceness. The entire list of attributes appears in a number of tables (e.g., Table 6.1).

Direct Assessments of Personal Gender-Role Schemata. The subjects then rated themselves on the 59 traits. For the first self-rating, they were told to rate how they thought they really were at the time. The Swedish subjects then rated their ideal selves. These tests were assumed to assess the subjects' self- (personal) schemata.

Booklet 3. Lifestyle Expectations and Related Beliefs of 18-year-olds

Booklet 3 was designed to probe the expectations of 18-year-olds about their adult lives. The booklet began with the statement: "We are interested in what you think that you will be doing in 10 years' time—in 1994. Ten years is a long time, and you may not be sure of your plans, so we want you to answer the questions in two ways. First, answer by indicating what you would really like to be doing. Then answer by indicating what you think that you will most likely be doing." The subjects used this system to answer six multiple choice questions about the amount of time they expect to devote to paid employment outside the home, with whom they would live, how many children they would have, where they would live, the amount of education that they will have completed, and how satisfied they will be with their lives. Next, using a list of 45 occupations taken from Andersson, Magnusson, and Duner (1983) plus blanks for filling in other occupations, they rank ordered the five occupations they would most like to have, and the five jobs that they would least like to have. In the next section, the students rated 16 statements dealing with attitudes toward employment and the family (see Appendices I and II), using a scale from 1 (very important) to 7 (very unimportant). These questions were designed to investigate how important they thought friends, money, advance planning, and holidays were to a happy and contented life. In addition, four questions asked how important they thought it was for girls (boys) to decide early (say before they were 16 years old) what occupation they want as an adult and how important they thought it was for boys (girls) to take special courses in mathematics, languages, and natural science early in their academic careers. The students also were asked to list the mathematics, language, and science courses they had taken. The last section of Booklet 3 asked them to write the advice they would give to an 8-year-old boy about planning his life, and the question was repeated for giving advice to an 8-year-old girl.

Procedure

The subjects were tested in groups ranging in size from 12 to about 35. The subjects filled in the blanks on the first page of Booklet 1, except that the 18-year-olds entered a code number for their names. (Code numbers also were substituted for the names of the younger subjects to maintain strict anonymity of all data.) Then the "change-sex" story was introduced and the subjects were given about 10 minutes to think about and write their story. They then completed the questions on the third page of Booklet 1 and turned in the booklet. This procedure was used to emphasize the difference between Booklet 1, for which they were to imagine they were the other sex, and the other booklets, for which they answered as themselves. Both written statements and the experimenter's oral instructions further emphasized this difference. Booklet 2 then was distributed and, after coding the first page, they completed the rest of the booklet in about 45 minutes. When rating the 59 traits, subjects were told to omit the rating if they did not understand an adjective. Last, Booklet 3 was distributed to the 18-year-olds. At the end of the session, all subjects were thanked and their questions were answered.

All instructions were given in Swedish, by a native speaker, to the Swedish respondents and in English, by a native speaker, to the American subjects.

These procedures were designed to provide multiple approaches to assessing the contents of cultural and personal gender schemata. They drew in part on some standard techniques, such as rating scales, but enriched that tradition with some projective measures. It was our intention to avoid as many of the disadvantages of other techniques (see chapter 3), as possible.

The next five chapters describe the results. They are divided into six sections that correspond to the five basic measurements of cultural and personal gender schemata: (a) generally admired traits, regardless of sex; (b) spontaneously generated descriptions of most girls, most boys, most men, and most women in the culture; (c) ratings of the relative importance of specific traits to most girls, most boys, most men, and most women; (d) ratings of the relative importance of the same traits to themselves and to their ideal selves; (e) analyses of the "change-sex" story, and (f) lifestyle orientations of the 18-year-old subjects. Chapter 5 presents the generally admired traits and the spontaneously generated descriptions of the four stimulus groups. Chapter 6 covers ratings of the importance of certain traits to the four stimulus groups and chapter 7 treats the ratings of importance of the same set of traits to self and to ideal self. Chapter 8 describes responses to the "change-sex" story. Chapter 9 is devoted to the oldest groups' plans for their lives.

PREDICTIONS

The specific predictions that guided all of the analyses were the following:

1. Clusters or constellations of traits will emerge for each of the four groups (most girls, most boys, most women, most men). According to our model, these clusters or constellations identify contents of the concepts. It is possible, of course, that some traits will be considered uniquely characteristic of one group, whereas other traits may be shared by one or more groups.

2. The components or constellations will differ between the countries. Thus, we should find cross-national differences, such as those that might be associated with differences in commitment to gender equality of the two countries. We

should also find cross-national similarities. Some similarities are likely due to the commonalities between Sweden and the United States noted in chapter 2. Cross-national similarities provide a useful basis for inferring that the differences are not due to some extraneous factor, such as inadequate translations or procedures.

3. The components of cultural gender concepts will change with the ages of the respondent, as implied by the view that components gradually accrue to and disappear from gender concepts.

4. Any developmental trends will show parallel patterns in the two countries. The course of developmental trends may shed light on how culture contributes to gender concepts.

5. Female and male correspondents from the same culture will agree about the contents of the concepts for each of the four groups, as is assumed by the notion of *cultural* gender concepts.

6. The results of the various measures will show at least partial convergence. If they do not converge, we will ask whether the measures afford different pictures of gender concepts and whether some measures are too insensitive to be useful.

5

Cultural Gender Schemata: Generally Admired Attributes and Spontaneously Generated Descriptions

Do free listings of traits show cross-national similarities and differences in terms of the attributes generally admired in citizens of Sweden or the United States, regardless of their sex? Alternatively stated, do Swedes treasure some attributes as part of their Swedishness that may or may not differ from the attributes valued by Americans as representing Americanism, disregarding sex? We need this information to serve as a backdrop for the second type of free listings, the attributes the respondents thought were highly descriptive of each of the four stimulus groups (most girls, most boys, most women, and most men) in each country. Both types of listings are described in this chapter.

CULTURAL DIFFERENCES IN GENERALLY ADMIRED ATTRIBUTES, REGARDLESS OF SEX

The first set of the ratings of people, in general, should inform us about attributes universally or commonly admired in the two countries. Because these ratings do not take the sex of the stimulus persons into account, these ratings reflect general characteristics assigned to each nationality, but do not divulge the components of gender concepts in the two countries. Those components of gender concepts, traits generally admired for each sex, are considered as our second topic in this chapter.

One reason for studying generally admired attributes for each nationality is to assess certain expectations about each country, including those mentioned in chapter 2. For example, do Swedes manifest the commitment to the group, to patriotism so often described in writings by the Swedish Institute? Do

Americans value the competitive, self-enhancing kind of individualism suggested by the concept of Lederer and Burdick's (1958) *The Ugly American* and other self-promotional books, (e.g., Peters & Austin, 1986; Ringer, 1977). To this list, I add some hypotheses formed haphazardly as an American in Sweden. These hypotheses emerged while I spent August 1983 traveling around Sweden with the intention of simply sampling the culture (and comparing it with impressions formed during previous visits). In brief, I was curious about the Swedish view of their national image. Are Swedes as austere as Americans think (Anderson, 1986)? Are they as conscious of and committed to the group (read "Swedish society") as my readings and observations have suggested? Does this commitment to the group produce a rejection of the kind of American individualism that is so often considered integral to the American self-image (e.g., Ringer, 1977)? Do Swedes, whose country has been pacifistic throughout this century, view themselves as being more gentle than American see themselves? Collectively, these attributes paint two rather different pictures of the national personae in the two countries. Swedes should be more concerned about interpersonal relations, emphasizing the group plus individual responsibility to the group. Americans should be more concerned with individual achievement, with less regard for the group. They should be less gentle and more aggressive.

Are these expectations valid? How far from the mark were my initial impressions as a visiting American scholar—and those conveyed by the media? This is an important question to answer, for it provides a tentative, albeit tenuous measure of the extent to which my cultural heritage influenced my perceptions of another culture. More important, these questions may supply information about the views of the Swedish people that must be incorporated into any sensitive, comprehensive comparison with Americans. In other words, it is important for insightful cross-cultural research to try to ascertain the variables that are important in each of the targeted countries and to then study about the relevance of these variables in the other investigated countries.

Are there distinctive Swedish and American national characters? If so, do generally admired attributes function as "cultural imperatives," attributes that singularly define and set forth most members of a particular country or nationality? Such attributes may be the very heart of national integrity.They constitute the background fabric that contributes to gender- or other-related modifications. They may signal aspects so distinctive, so distinguishing of each national culture that they override or supercede gender-related attributes. In short, we might expect gender-related modifications to represent variations of a single underlying national motif.

How do we index this underlying motif? Our approach was to ask whether, within Sweden and the United States, certain attributes are routinely endorsed as admirable for both sexes. Unfortunately, there are no guidelines for the percentages of subjects who must agree upon attributes before they are considered cultural imperatives, but the data spoke clearly. In no case did the agreement approach unanimity: The highest percentage of agreement occurred when 74% of 11-year-old Swedish children agreed that they admired people who are kind/nice (the term "kind/nice" is used as the most satisfactory English translation of the Swedish word "snell"). Similarly, 69% of American 11-year-olds identified kind/nice as a trait they admired in people. These percentages reflect surprisingly high agreement, given that the listings were completely open-ended. Thus, for 11-year-olds in both countries, being kind/nice is the single attribute they most admire. Despite the high agreement by the 11-year-olds, the kind/nice attribute cannot be considered a cultural imperative because the highest percentages of agreement shown by each age and nationality group declined considerably for the older groups, who tended to admire somewhat different characteristics. For example, as Table 5.1 shows, "honesty" was most admired by American and Swedish 18-year-olds, but by the lower percentages of 51% and 33%, respectively. The findings strongly suggest that no single attribute functioned as a national feature. In other words, although some attributes were often admired in each country, a heterogeneous set of attributes were admired by the natives of each country. This outcome is remarkable only because it reflected so distinctly the diversity expected in each country.

More intriguing are the systematic similarities and differences, themselves. We probe these patterns by examining the five most commonly listed traits, which appear in Table 5.1, along with the percentages of subjects listing each trait.

The specific traits frequently listed for the two countries were surprisingly similar (Table 5.1). The 11- and 14-year-old respondents from both countries listed kind/nice more often than any other attribute. For the 11-year-olds, being

TABLE 5.1

Percentage of Swedish and American 11-, 14-, and 18-year-olds Listing the Five Attributes They Admired in All People, Regardless of Gender

	Age 11		Age 14		Age 18	
Sweden	n = 116		n = 222		n = 172	
	Kind/nice	74	Kind/nice	46	Honest	33
	Helpful	41	Sensitive	24	Sense of humor	30
	Generous	17	Helpful	21	Kind/nice	21
	Happy	15	Good looking	20	Sensitive	21
	Capable	15	Sincere	18	Gentle	19
			Sense of humor	18		
USA	n = 110		n = 113		n = 108	
	Kind/nice	69	Kind/nice	49	Honest	51
	Helpful	32	Helpful	33	Sense of humor	48
	Happy	19	Sensitive	22	Compassionate/ caring	46
	Generous	15	Sincere	17	Friendly	46
	Friendly	15	Friendly	15	Intelligent	46

helpful, generous, and happy also were often cited. The 14-year-olds often added being sensitive, helpful, and sincere. By age 18, the respondents from the two countries showed more divergence in the five most often noted traits, although they agreed that being honest was the most admired trait and that having a sense of humor was the second most memorable trait.

How should we interpret these results? Do they correspond to various stereotypes about the two countries? For example, do Swedes value gentleness and other expressive, communal traits to a greater extent than Americans? Do Americans value instrumental, agentic traits, such as aggression and individualism more than the Swedes? The answer is clear: In both countries, expressive traits are valued more highly than instrumental ones. Thus, when asked about what they most admire in their compatriots, our American respondents expressed as much endorsement of expressive, pacific-type traits as did our Swedish respondents. These comparisons were made by having 10 independent judges rate the traits for their instrumental and expressive implications. Of the traits with the five highest frequencies for each country and age of respondent, only three, being capable, instrumental—rather than expressive—implications. The rest were traits such as being kind/nice, helpful, generous, happy, sensitive, sincere, and honest. Why should this be?

One possibility is that our 11- to 18-year-old American respondents do not value the image of the hard-driving, tough, aggressively competitive individual as much as has been thought. In short, this perception may be a myth. Another possibility is that the respondents routinely interpreted the question as asking about interpersonal qualities. This seems unlikely, because there was no reason for such an interpretation. Moreover, the mention of expressive attributes was by no means universal. A third possibility is that the results may represent the youngsters' greater exposure to female than to male role models. This explanation assumes that American and Swedish women behave more expressively than instrumentally and that youngsters assume that the characteristics of these female role models are typical, desirable, or both. Such attitudes may change as the youngsters encounter divergent views as they mature. This explanation is not the only answer, however, for this explanation implies that knowledge about male roles would develop later than knowledge about female roles, a prediction that is negated by Thompson's (1975) finding that children as young as 3 are as cognizant of male cultural gender stereotypes as they are of female roles. In addition, the 18-year-old respondents can hardly be considered youngsters, and yet they also emphasized expressive attributes as highly desirable. Finally, another, somewhat more appealing possibility, in our view, is that as their awareness of human interaction develops, children come to realize the role of expressive—or more significantly—communal attributes to mediate, integrate, smooth, and generally facilitate the cooperative, cordinative functioning of people, just as they recognize the importance of being a capable, decisive, independent individual, particularly when that individual resides in an industrial, complex, and technical society.

Four other interesting results emerged. First, although there was substantial overlap among the attributes listed by Swedish and American respondents at each age level, the overlap was greater for the two younger groups than for the 18-year-olds. To evaluate the extent of the overlap, we computed Spearman rank order (ρ) correlations between the frequencies of listing an attribute by Swedish and American subjects at each age level. Those traits listed by one nationality group but not the other were excluded from these calculations, so all correlations exaggerate the overlap somewhat. Corroborating the view that the younger subjects of the two countries agreed more than the older subjects, the rank order correlations between the frequencies of citation of traits by 11-year-old Swedes and Americans ($\rho = .93$) and between 14-year-old Swedes and Americans ($\rho = .78$) exceeded the rank orderings of the traits rated by 18-year-old Swedes and Americans ($\rho = .57$). These results also could be interpreted as support for the view that the female role model is more pervasive at earlier ages or that, with increasing maturity, people realize that independence and other instrumental traits also may be useful in some situations.

The statistics just given and all others used the .05 level of statistical significance, although we focus mainly on the differences that achieve at least a .01 level. This latter approach seems prudent in view of the sizable numbers of statistical tests that are computed. Obviously, we want to minimize the risk of calling a difference statistically significant when it actually represents a chance perturbation.

Second, the female respondents from the two countries agreed more than the males did. The coefficients comparing the rank order correlations between the three age groups of Swedish females were .89, .87, and .89 for the 11-year-old with 14-year-old, 11-year-old with 18-year-old, and 14-year-old with 18-year-old comparisons, respectively. The counterpart coefficients for American females were .91, .92, and .89. The analogous comparisons for Swedish (.67, .59, and .63) and for American (.65, .64, .58) males were considerably lower, although all of these coefficients indicated statistically reliable associations. This finding of greater agreement about generally admired traits among women than among men was unanticipated, but the differences present an easily interpreted pattern, as the men included a greater variety of attributes they admired than women did. Specifically, men included relatively more instrumental traits than women did, thereby increasing variability for the men, because both sexes identified expressive characteristics among their most generally admired attributes.

Third, the overall rankings from the two countries were highly similar, as were the overall rankings from both sexes of respondents.

Fourth, the sexes at each age level for each country identified highly similar admired traits. These rank order correlations ranged from .74 for American 18-year-olds to .97 for Swedish 11-year-olds, suggesting substantial within-culture agreement about the most admired traits for the citizenry, although the most often endorsed attributes showed some developmental differences between the two younger and the older respondents.

Hence, when asked to list the attributes that they most admired in people, regardless of sex, 11- and 14-year-olds value being kind/nice more than other attributes, 18-year-olds value honesty and having a sense of humor more than the other traits, and these rankings are not substantially modified by either the nationality or the sex of the respondent. Obviously, our respondents in the two countries showed remarkable agreement about the traits they most admired, suggesting that, at least among these young people, similar values are held for personal characteristics when gender is not a criterion. These attributes presumably reflect generalized opinions about national characteristics. Do they correspond to cultural gender concepts? Not necessarily, as we see as we turn to our next topic.

FREE LISTINGS OF GENDER ATTRIBUTES

The free listings of gender attributes give us our first opportunity to examine the components of gender concepts that are highly salient and accessible in memory when our subjects were asked to describe the characteristics of most women, men, boys, and girls. Hence, a brief summary of our predictions is in order. First, different clusters of traits will emerge for the four groups. One likely form of these clusters is that females will be described by terms relating to interpersonal relations (expressive terms) more often than males, whereas males are more likely to be described by agentic, instrumental terms than are females. This is the prediction of distinctive cultural gender concepts, of course.

Second, the gender concepts will differ for the two countries. Specifically, Sweden's greater espousal of gender equality should produce less marked gender differences than the United States' less systematic approach. Presumably, if the efforts instituted by the Swedish government have affected the attitudes of the Swedish people, along with modifications of some behavior, the youth of the country will perceive fewer gender differences than the youth of the United States, who have not been exposed to the same systematic and coordinated system of sponsoring equality of opportunity for the two sexes. The first and second predictions should hold for both countries, thereby reflecting evidence of some cross-national similarity.

Third, these cultural gender concepts will change with age, reflecting the dynamic character of gender concepts. Such developmental trends should capture the greater awareness of older, rather than younger, respondents that people of both sexes are capable of performing diverse tasks and of assuming many different roles. These developmental trends should be roughly parallel in the two countries, the fourth prediction. Fifth, both sexes should agree about the gender concepts if these concepts accurately reflect *cultural views*, as handled by our model. The final prediction about convergence of the results cannot be assessed until later, of course.

The simplest way to investigate support for the first four predictions is to handle them together. Consequently, we now consider whether distinctive clusters of traits were found for the four stimulus groups by respondents in both countries. For the free listings of gender attributes, the subjects were asked to write down the characteristics that came to mind when they thought about most girls. They performed the same task for most boys, most women, and most men (in a randomized order across subjects). The percentages of Swedish and American 11-, 14-, and 18-year olds listing the five adjectives most often attributed to most girls, most boys, most women, and most men appear in Table 5.2.

We focus first on the five attributes most commonly identified for most girls, most boys, most women, and most men of each country. These attributes deliver the seemingly most accessible components of cultural gender concepts. We then make various comparisons to examine the support for the various predictions.

Our results do not quite fit the rhyme of what girls and boys are made of, but they come close. Most Swedish girls, we are told, are concerned about their appearance and are kind/nice. Most of the attributes used to describe them are expressive. Indeed, we were surprised by the relative absence of instrumental traits, a situation to which we return later. By way of a preview, the apparent emphasis on expressive qualities and the absence of instrumental ones suggests that Swedish girls are expected to behave in markedly traditional ways—that is, to cultivate interpersonal skills while ignoring more instrumental ones.

In contrast, most American girls are accorded more instrumental qualities, although they, too, are most often characterized by expressive ones. For example, most American girls are said to be playful and active/lively (instrumental traits), but to also be concerned about their appearance, and to laugh/giggle (expressive traits). Surprisingly, these data from the open-ended descriptions of most girls imply more latitude of expectation for American than for Swedish girls.

Most boys may not be made of snails and puppy dog tails, but they certainly are expected to exhibit instrumental traits. In both countries, boys are thought to be athletic, competitive, tough-minded, active/lively, aggressive, and (in the United States) mischievous. The expectations are clear for boys in both countries: be physically active, energetic, and driving. Contemplation, caring for others, and similar expressive attributes are not a part of the "boyness" concept, a concept that shows strong cross-national similarity.

The cross-national similarity of the male model is partially age bound. When our American respondents are describing most men, they continue along the same instrumental track that characterizes their descriptions of most boys. If anything, the descriptions become more instrumental: Most American men are said to be strong, ambitious/hard working, competitive individuals who cannot show their feelings. Most Swedish men are also instrumental, being strong, competitive, acting as leaders, and unable to show their feelings, but they are also seen as kind/nice (at least by 11-year-olds) and as watchers of television by 18-year-old males! In general, men of both countries are described instrumentally, but Swedish men, more than American men, are also accorded some expressive traits.

TABLE 5.2
Percentages of Swedish and American 11-, 14-, and 18-year-olds Listing the Five Adjectives Most Often Freely Attributed to Most Girls, Most Boys, Most Women, and Most Men

Most Girls		Most Boys		Most Women		Most Men	
Swedish 11-year-old females, n = 65							
Concerned with appearance	35%	Tough-minded	28%	Concerned with Appearance	17%	Kind/nice	22%
Calm	20	Active/lively	22	Kind/nice	14	Strong	9
Kind/nice	17	Competitive	18	Loves children	14	Tall	8
Assertive	5	Dominant	15	Helpful	9	Fun	8
Whiny	5	Athletic	14	Whiny	9	Helpful	6
Shy	5			Calm	9	Competitive	6
				Lazy	6	Ambitious/hard working	6
Swedish 11-year-old males, n = 51							
Kind/nice	33	Athletic	45	Kind/nice	25	Kind/nice	27
Whiny	27	Aggressive	27	Helpful	14	Strong	22
Concerned with appearance	22	Tough-minded	27	Whiny	12	Tough-minded	10
Calm	12	Strong	22	Devotes self completely to others	8	Ambitious/hard working	8
Helpful	10	Active/lively	20	Tidy/neat	8	Athletic	6
						Shy	6
						Lazy	6
Swedish 14-year-old females, n = 119							
Concerned with appearance	92	Tough-minded	34	Ambitious/hard working	19	Acts as a leader	12
Shy	9	Competitive	17	Devotes self completely to others	14	Strong	10
Gossipy	9	Cannot show one's feelings	8	Loves children	13	Kind/nice	8
Kind/nice	7	Aggressive	13	Concerned with appearance	13	Cannot show one's feelings	8
Emotional	7	Athletic	11	Kind/nice	8	Capable	7
Swedish 14-year-old males, n = 103							
Concerned with appearance	48	Athletic	23	Concerned with appearance	18	Strong	18
Shy	14	Aggressive	22	Devotes self completely to others	15	Acts as a leader	13
Kind/nice	12	Competitive	16	Whiny	13	Stern/strict	7
Good looking	8	Tough-minded	14	Kind/nice	11	Assertive	6
Tidy/neat	7	Dominant	12	Sensitive	10	Has leadership qualities	6

(*Continued*)

TABLE 5.2
(*Continued*)

Most Girls		Most Boys		Most Women		Most Men	
Swedish 18-year-olds females, n = 97							
Concerned with appearance	59	Competitive	25	Concerned with appearance	33	Competitive	11
Emotional	23	Tough-minded	21	Ambitious/hard working	19	Cannot show one's feelings	10
Laughs/giggles	11	Cannot show one's feelings	20	Devotes self completely to others	14	Acts as a leader	10
Good looking	10	Feels insecure	13	Whiny	9	Lazy	10
Gossipy	10	Kind/nice	11	Liberated	8	Dominant	9
				Self-sacrificing	8	Self-confident	9
Swedish 18-year-old males, n = 75							
Concerned with appearance	40	Tough-minded	23	Devotes self completely to others	13	Competitive	15
Emotional	9	Athletic	15	Concerned with appearance	12	Cannot show one's feelings	11
Feels insecure	8	Competitive	12	Emotional	11	Watches TV	11
Kind/nice	7	Self-confident	9	Ambitious/hard working	9	Dominant	9
Sensitive	7	Cannot show one's feelings	9	Liberated	8	Strong	9
				Self-sacrificing	8		
				Tender	8		
American 11-year-old females, n = 56							
Playful	43	Athletic	41	Kind/nice	45	Strong	38
Silly	36	Active/lively	38	Loves children	39	Competitive	30
Concerned with appearance	30	Mischievous	38	Helpful	32	Stern/strict	29
Shy	18	Loud	38	Compassionate/caring	27	Ambitious/hard working	27
Athletic	16	Silly	25	Whiny	21	Loud	14
American 11-year-old males, n = 54							
Playful	28	Athletic	24	Kind/nice	26	Strong	33
Whiny	22	Playful	20	Devotes self completely to others	22	Ambitious/hard working	22
Concerned with appearance	15	Tough-minded	19	Helpful	19	Loud	19
Kind/nice	15	Aggressive	17	Loves children	15	Athletic	12

(*Continued*)

TABLE 5.2
(*Continued*)

Most Girls		Most Boys		Most Women		Most Men	
American 11-year-old males, n = 54							
Helpful	12	Active/lively	12	Compassionate/ caring	11	Tough	11
		Competitive	12			Lazy	11
American 14-year-old females, n = 54							
Concerned with appearance	26	Athletic	22	Devotes self completely to others	35	Strong	33
Playful	24	Aggressive	20	Loves children	31	Acts as a leader	28
Laughs/giggles	19	Mischievous	15	Compassionate/ caring	24	Cannot show one's feelings	22
Active/lively	13	Cannot show one's feelings	11	Sensitive	19	Aggressive	17
Shy	7	Competitive	7	Concerned with appearance	9	Competitive	9
		Shy	7				
American 14-year-old males, n = 59							
Concerned with appearance	27	Athletic	20	Good looking	29	Strong	25
Active/lively	22	Active/lively	17	Sensitive	20	Cannot show one's feelings	25
Emotional	17	Aggressive	12	Affectionate/ loving	17	Aggressive	19
Tidy/neat	12	Competitive	10	Compassionate/ caring	15	Competitive	10
Laughs/giggles	10	Mischievous	10	Whiny	15	Stern/strict	8
American 18-year-old females, n = 54							
Good looking	44	Active/lively	56	Compassionate/ caring	39	Athletic	46
Playful	35	Athletic	43	Concerned with appearance	35	Self-centered/ egocentric	35
Laughs/giggles	24	Curious	33	Sensitive	28	Sense of humor	28
Active/lively	22	Mischievous	33	Loves children	28	Strong	26
Concerned with appearance	20	Playful	31	Good looking	22	Cannot show one's feelings	26
American 18-year-old males, n = 54							
Good looking	41	Playful	41	Good looking	48	Athletic	39
Playful	33	Athletic	39	Sensitive	26	Self-centered/ egotistical	35
Emotional	22	Active/lively	37	Kind/nice	26	Intelligent	31
Shy	20	Mischievous	37	Compassionate/ caring	26	Ambitious/hard working	31
Laughs/giggles	19	Curious	28	Affectionate/ loving	22	Cannot show one's feelings	26

The cross-national similarity of the model for females is also partially age bound, except in this case, Swedish women are assigned somewhat more instrumental qualities than American women, who rated almost none. In both countries, however, most women are described with primarily expressive traits, although the particular traits vary somewhat for the two countries. For example, most Swedish women are described as concerned with their appearance, as kind/nice, as devoting themselves completely to others, and as being whiny. American women are compassionate/caring, kind/nice, sensitive, and they love children. They are sometimes seen as whiny. They are never described as *liberated*, a term used by 18-year-old Swedish correspondents to describe Swedish women. Briefly, although women from both countries are described with expressive terms, Swedish women are more likely than American women to be assigned some instrumental traits.

What support do these results bring to the predictions? A substantial amount, as we see here. In the first place, the distinctive clusters of traits ascribed to each of the four stimulus groups in each country signaled some clear differences in the conceptions our respondents had for females and males in their societies. Further, these cultural gender concepts were quite consistent with predictions that females would be accorded more expressive than instrumental attributes, whereas males would be accorded more instrumental than expressive ones. These general notions must be modified somewhat, however, because the results also indicated that both sexes are frequently assigned both instrumental and expressive attributes. The particular attributes assigned to the four stimulus groups differed somewhat for the two countries, with Swedish women generally being described as more instrumental (particularly, more liberated) than American women and Swedish men being described as more expressive than American men. Expectations for most girls were about the same in both countries, showing some cross-national similarity. In brief, in their free listings, Swedes showed fewer gender differences in their ascriptions than Americans did. Obviously, these results support the predictions that cultural gender concepts will emerge for the stimulus groups and that the contents of these concepts are culture-sensitive. The cultural gender concepts also change somewhat with age of the respondents, as predicted by our contention that cultural gender concepts are dynamic, and the exact changes, such as the change from the 11-year-old Swedish respondents who think that Swedish men are kind/nice, whereas 18-year-olds substitute watching television, differ somewhat for the two countries.

The fifth prediction targets the very heart of the notion of *cultural* gender concepts. If gender concepts are to be considered representative of a culture, they should be commonly endorsed by both sexes. Again, we found support. Table 5.2 shows that the female and male respondents showed substantial agreement in their free listings of attributes assigned to each of the stimulus groups. Thus, female and male respondents alike share similar views about attributes characteristic of females, just as they share similar views about attributes characteristic of males. These results suggest that the components of gender concepts identified by the free listings did indeed function as cultural gender concepts.

Although the brief summary given here focused more on cross-national differences than on cross-cultural similarities, one of the striking aspects of the data was the appearance of the same components in various gender concepts. Being kind/nice, for example, is manifestly salient in both countries for both sexes. Does this mean that the free listings are tapping more than gender-related attributes? Why would they use identical terms to describe different sexes? Perhaps our respondents misinterpreted the instructions. Perhaps certain components really are part of more than one cultural gender concept. Perhaps these components insinuate themselves in more than one gender concept because they are integral to each. We cannot decide between these alternatives on the basis of a single measure, and so we delay resolution of the issue until we have examined other results.

Another message may be gleaned from the results of the free descriptions: Gender-role expectations appear to be quite rigid for Swedish youngsters. Girls are expected to be oriented toward interpersonal matters, and boys toward more agentic ones. When they grow up, they are expected to leaven these approaches with characteristics often associated with the gender roles of the other sex. Note that these expectations, if they exist as suggested by the free listings, provide a difficult developmental sequence for Swedish youngsters. After childhood training in one gender role, their nation expects a broadened horizon that incorporates at least some elements of the other gender role. Such a transition would be an arduous challenge.

Lifetime expectations seem a little easier in the United States. American boys are expected to learn instrumental roles at early ages and to continue to express these characteristics as men. American girls are given some latitude as youngsters, and are then expected to relinquish some instrumental traits as they mature. This should be an easier task than trying to acquire new skills as an adult, the approach that the free listings imply is part of the Swedish model.

If these patterns emerge for other estimates of the components of gender concepts, they might offer some insight into the current discrepancies between the theory and practice of gender equality in Sweden. Specifically, if pronouncedly stereotypic gender roles are expected for youngsters in Sweden, it is not reasonable to assume that these influences will be easily outgrown, unlearned, or overthrown as adults. Although speculative, it is tempting to conclude that the efforts of the Swedish government on behalf of gender equality have not yet modified descriptions of and expectations for characteristics of the Swedish people. The same is true for the United States, of course, except that the seemingly greater tolerance of a variety of attributes for girls offers greater flexibility for subsequent development than more restricted expectations.

The data from the open-ended questions thus supported the predictions that, for both countries, females would be more likely than males to be described by expressive traits, whereas males would be more likely than females to be described by instrumental traits. These trends index some cross-national similarities. Implying cross-national differences were the trends for Swedish adults of both sexes to be assigned more traits often associated with the other sex than was true for American adults, and this was increasingly true as the age of the respondent increased.

SUMMARY

This chapter has considered the attributes that are generally admired in each country without regard to sex and the attributes that are freely listed for children and adults of each sex. The generally admired attributes should index those characteristics that distinguish members of one nationality from those of another. Presumably, these characteristics form a national ethos within which gender- and other individualistically related distinctions develop.

To our surprise, relatively few national differences appeared. Apparently, Swedes and Americans share similar values about the traits that are considered generally important for all members of the country. These pannational traits for Sweden and the United States varied as a function of age: 11-year-olds admired being kind/nice, helpful, generous, and happy more than other characteristics for all of their compatriots whereas the 18-year-olds admired honesty and having a good sense of humor more than other traits. This pronounced similarity in the generally admired traits shown by respondents from the two countries is most sensibly interpreted as an indication that the personal values of the two countries are similar. These fortuituous and unexpected similarities establish a reasonably firm foundation for evaluating gender-related differences, for they define the values common to both countries. The existence of some cross-national agreement makes more plausible the argument that gender-related differences result from societal foci on equality of opportunity for the two sexes than if national characteristics had differed.

The second topic of the chapter, the free listings of attributes that the subjects thought characterized most girls, most boys, most women, and most men, offer our first estimates of cultural gender concepts. These attributes do not necessarily tell us how important the attributes are for distinguishing between the sexes, but, rather, signal traits so salient that they are accessed immediately as typical of each of the four groups. These adjectives constitute indications of the components of cultural gender concepts.

What are the descriptions that we assume represent components of the cultural gender concepts? According to our Swedish respondents, most girls are concerned with their appearance and are kind/nice. American respondents think that most girls are good looking and playful. Swedish women also are seen as concerned about their appearance. Moreover, they are viewed as devoting themselves to others, as being ambitious/hardworking, and as being liberated. American women are described as sensitive, compassionate, and caring. In brief, most girls and most women are accorded expressive/communal traits, but Swedish women have additional instrumental attributes. No other stimulus group was described as liberated.

Most boys are described as athletic and competitive in both countries. The other most commonly mentioned adjectives are variations on the same theme, with Swedish boys being called tough-minded, and American boys labeled playful and mischievous. Some similarities appear for most men, as well. In both countries, the 18-year-old respondents think that most men do not show their feelings. Other attributes are largely instrumental. When the respondents are younger, only the Swedes attribute expressive traits (e.g., kind/nice) to most men.

Overall, the free listings of traits suggest that the cultural gender concepts for females in the two countries differ for women (by including some instrumental traits along with the expressive ones) but not for girls. The components of cultural gender concepts for most men share some attributes, although the 11-year-old Swedish respondents see most men as kind/nice. Thus, the Swedish cultural gender concepts are more likely than American cultural gender concepts to include both expressive and instrumental attributes for women and for men. These results suggest that the differences in cultural gender concepts are less pronounced in Sweden than in the United States, as we predicted.

The data carry another intriguing message. Some attributes are assigned to more than one stimulus group, suggesting that cultural gender concepts overlap to some extent. It is difficult to know how seriously to take this result, because it is based on a single response measure. Hence, we reserve judgment about its significance until other data have been evaluated.

The free listings of attributes accorded the four stimulus groups do not tell us how important each attribute is to girlness, boyness, womanness, or manness. They do not necessarily elicit the same information from each participant, because each person was free to record whichever attributes came to mind as characteristic of the stimulus group. For uniform ratings of importance of attributes to defining the gender concepts, we turn next to the importance ratings.

6

Cultural Gender Concepts: Importance Ratings

In this chapter, we consider a second way to try to identify the components of cultural gender concepts, ratings of how important specific attributes are to definitions of most girls, most boys, most women, most men. This approach has the obvious advantage of obtaining ratings for all stimulus groups, from all respondents for each of the attributes. It also has its own set of problems, the most important being that its utility depends on a judicious, comprehensive selection of attributes. If only a small set of attributes is rated, some salient discriminators may be overlooked. If a large number is rated, respondents may become weary and uncooperative, and the voluminous data are likely to become unwieldy. Even our compromise number of 59 items produced data rich to the point of almost swamping us with numbers.

Grapple with the numbers we did, first by conducting an omnibus analysis of variance to identify the significant effects. We then explored support for each of the predictions stated in chapter 4.

The analysis of variance treated the three characteristics of our respondents (nationality, sex, and age) as between-subjects variables and stimulus groups and traits as within-subject variables. The results were intriguing. Nationality was the first reliable main effect, $F(1, 1572) = 8.75$. Americans apparently think that the adjectives are more important descriptors of cultural gender concepts than Swedes do. The mean ratings for Americans and Swedes were 3.12 and 3.39, respectively, on a scale that ranged from 1 (extremely important) to 7 (not at all important). Does this peculiar result reflect a general tendency of Americans to rate all items as more important than Swedes do, a sort of "enthusiasm" or "endorsement" difference? Does it show a bias produced by the fact that many of the adjectives were taken from American sources? The latter seems more likely because an examination of the range of responses showed no overall differences between the two countries. Moreover, similar patterns surfaced for both countries. Most men had higher mean importance ratings (3.20) than most boys (3.22), most women (3.26), or most girls (3.33), $F(3, 4716) = 2.78$. Apparently our adjectives were judged as more important for males than for females, despite our original efforts to find attributes characteristic of each sex. How should we interpret this result? At least two possibilities exist. The first is that males, more than females, are assigned distinctive traits. The second is that both sexes are seen as possessing the attributes, but men possess them to a greater extent. As we see here, the detailed data support the latter interpretation.

The third main effect to be significant, Traits, showed a tremendous range, from 1.40 to 6.35, $F(58, 91176) = 12.25$, giving us license to examine the individual traits. Obviously, some adjectives define the stimulus groups better than others do.

A number of interactions were significant. Most striking are those involving Nationality, Stimulus Groups, and Traits. The triple interaction of these variables was highly reliable, $F(174, 273528) = 9.15$, as were the double interactions contributing the triple interaction. These interactions are analyzed in detail in the following sections. One other interaction was noteworthy: 18-year-old Swedes rated the traits as generally less important (3.49) than did their 11- and 14-year-old compatriots (3.35 and 3.34 respectively), consistent with the view that the concepts of gender equality require years to develop. Americans showed no reliable differences as a function of the age of the respondent, although notable trends appeared.

This quick sketch of the results says little about either the components of gender concepts or the importance of the components to the cultural gender concepts, largely because we have not yet tackled the ratings of the individual traits for the four stimulus groups, our central interest. We move now to such a consideration, but the data management problem is still acute. We decided to use two techniques, two prisms to look at the data on the assumptions that the two views would yield complementary information. In one approach, we explore the five top-rated attributes. Presumably, these attributes are the most important markers of each group. In the second approach, we examine ratings on all of the items, a plan that takes into account the rating assigned to every item. These two approaches are supplemented by complete listings of the ratings in Tables 6.1–6.4 to give interested parties full access to our data.

CONTENTS OF CULTURAL GENDER CONCEPTS

Do the importance ratings offer different clusters of attributes rated most characteristic of each group by each nationality of raters, as the freely listed attributes did? Alternatively, do the importance ratings yield answers to the predictions that distinctive gender concepts will emerge for each of the stimulus groups and that these concepts will differ for the two countries? Responses to these queries are contained in Tables 6.1–6.4. These tables list mean importance ratings given by respondents to each attribute for each stimulus group. Each table lists the traits from highest to lowest in terms of the overall mean rating assigned by Swedish correspondents.

Most Girls: Cross-National Comparisons. What are the five most important attributes for defining most Swedish girls? Being kind/nice, trying to do one's best, never giving up, being gentle, and being friendly (Table 6.1). Thus, of the five most highly ranked attributes for Swedish girls, two are generally considered instrumental, whereas three are more expressive in nature, a combination that nicely accords with the view that the Swedish emphasis on equality is instantiated in their cultural gender concepts. But is this true across all of the rated traits? To answer this question, we subtracted an "instrumental index" (the mean of the 29 instrumental traits designated by "I" in Table 6.1) from an "expressive index" (the mean of the 29 expressive traits designated by "E" in Table 6.1). (One trait, patriotic, was not reliably classifed as either expressive or instrumental. Its ratings were ignored in the calculation of expressive and instrumental indices.) For most girls, Swedish respondents assigned reliably higher ratings to expressive than to instrumental traits, $t(332) = 3.76$.

Overall, the cultural gender concept for most Swedish girls contains somewhat more expressive than instrumental traits, with being kind/nice, trying to do one's best, never giving up, being gentle, and being friendly as the top-ranked attributes. Note that of these esteemed attributes, two (trying to do one's best and never giving up) are instrumental and were suggested by Swedish informants. Evidently, the suggestion from free listings that Swedish girls are expected to be primarily oriented toward interpersonal, communal, and noninstrumental concerns is misleading or incomplete. Although expressive traits may be the most salient descriptors of Swedish girls, the instrumental qualities of trying to do their best and of persisting (never giving up) also are judged important. These results nicely document the desirability of using multiple measures.

What about American girls? They were assigned both expressive and instrumental traits in the free listings. Their importance ratings yielded a similar pattern. Most American girls are rated as kind/nice and friendly, but their other top-rated attributes are being warm, feeling good about themselves, and being affectionate. These results also suggest that raters from the two countries agreed that friendliness and kindness were particularly salient characteristics of most girls, but Americans placed a stronger premium on expressive-communal traits by including affectionateness and warmth and by not including the top instrumental Swedish attributes of trying to do one's best and never giving up. Further bolstering this conclusion was the expressiveness/instrumental index: Americans attributed reliably higher ratings of expressive than instrumental traits to most girls, $t(299) = 4.98$.

TABLE 6.1
Mean Importance Ratings for Most Girls

Country	Sweden						U.S.A.					
Sex of respondent	Female			Male			Female			Male		
Age Group	11	14	18	11	14	18	11	14	18	11	14	18
Attributes (type)[f]												
Kind/nice (E)	1.85	1.83	2.09	1.80	1.86	2.09	1.97	1.93	2.09	2.25	2.41	2.55[b]
Tries to do one's best (I)	1.84	1.84	2.10	1.70	2.17	2.19[b]	2.19	2.11	2.73	2.21	1.93	2.09
Gentle (E)	2.04	1.95	2.15	1.95	2.01	2.27[b]	2.15	2.03	2.36	2.47	2.15	2.73
Never gives up (I)	1.89	1.92	2.13	1.80	2.27	2.41[a,b]	1.85	2.06	2.73	1.81	2.22	2.91[a,b,d]
Friendly (E)	2.02	1.94	2.26	1.96	2.21	2.35	2.15	1.93	1.91	2.01	2.12	2.09
Sincere (E)	2.24	2.06	2.13	2.25	2.24	2.36	2.28	2.23	2.27	2.56	2.61	2.64
Willing to take a stand (I)	2.35	2.20	1.93	2.11	2.41	2.51[a,c]	2.36	2.35	3.64	2.10	2.38	3.27[a,d]
Helpful (E)	1.84	2.14	2.47	2.00	2.36	2.49[b]	1.92	2.18	2.64	2.05	2.41	2.73[b]
Cooperative (E)	2.54	2.36	2.35	2.30	2.49	2.63[a]	2.35	2.41	2.73	2.45	2.30	2.36
Thinks one is a good person (I)	2.78	2.40	2.62	2.63	2.35	2.61	2.64	2.39	2.45	2.51	2.42	2.91
Aware of feelings of others (E)	2.70	2.25	2.48	2.89	2.72	2.64[a]	2.40	2.57	2.55	2.38	2.41	2.27
Strong personality (I)	2.29	2.60	2.54	2.42	2.66	2.77	2.31	2.58	2.64	2.61	2.35	2.55
Loves children (E)	2.60	2.33	2.68	2.48	2.81	2.69[a]	2.25	2.32	2.27	2.78	2.83	3.18
Warm (I)	3.09	2.37	2.57	3.11	2.35	2.51[b]	1.87	1.99	2.00	2.12	2.20	2.18[b]
Emotional (E)	2.84	2.40	2.40	2.83	2.74	2.68	3.01	2.98	2.64	3.40	3.48	3.36[d]
Eager to soothe hurt feelings (E)	2.48	2.23	2.97	2.52	2.57	3.05[b]	2.03	2.15	2.27	2.05	2.28	3.00[b]
Stands up under pressure (I)	2.76	2.58	2.66	2.50	2.61	2.89	3.45	3.61	3.73	2.40	2.52	2.64[e]
Fun (I)	2.58	2.55	2.71	2.54	2.63	3.04	2.48	2.42	2.45	2.41	2.49	2.45
Humorous (I)	2.73	2.61	2.63	2.88	2.64	2.78	2.89	2.87	3.10	2.78	2.84	2.64
Tender (E)	3.68	2.39	2.60	2.93	2.61	2.53[b]	3.49	2.41	2.36	3.01	2.98	2.82[b]
Affectionate (E)	3.16	2.52	3.00	2.95	2.57	2.68[b]	2.04	2.05	2.00	2.37	2.31	2.36[d]
Active (I)	2.91	2.73	2.67	2.78	2.76	3.01	2.91	2.80	2.82	2.80	2.58	2.64

(Continued)

TABLE 6.1
(Continued)

Country	Sweden						U.S.A.					
Sex of respondent	Female			Male			Female			Male		
Age Group	11	14	18	11	14	18	11	14	18	11	14	18
Likable (E)	3.29	2.90	2.85	2.76	2.61	2.57[a]	2.47	2.49	2.45	2.25	2.31	2.27
Loyal (E)	3.46	2.88	2.69	3.12	2.87	2.69	2.65	2.41	2.45	2.77	2.93	2.82
Patriotic	2.43	2.86	2.94	3.15	2.85	2.69	3.38	3.39	3.64	3.91	3.78	3.82[d]
Self-confident (I)	2.53	2.98	3.03	2.18	2.77	3.24[b]	2.44	2.38	2.45	2.09	2.24	2.18[a,d]
Generous (E)	2.66	2.80	3.01	3.08	2.70	2.95	2.81	2.65	2.73	2.66	2.78	2.64
Hardworking (I)	2.61	2.82	2.99	2.38	2.83	3.44[b]	2.78	2.75	3.18	2.53	2.49	2.45[b]
Has self-esteem (I)	2.77	2.95	2.77	2.82	2.98	3.18[a]	2.38	2.95	2.91	2.69	2.42	2.36
Feels good about oneself (I)	2.49	3.00	2.89	2.93	3.12	3.07[b]	2.07	2.18	2.45	2.23	2.15	1.82[d]
Compassionate/caring (E)	2.98	2.68	3.02	2.08	2.93	3.19[b]	2.29	2.19	2.27	2.53	2.55	2.55[d]
Makes decisions easily (I)	3.04	2.83	3.05	2.78	2.88	3.25[b]	2.89	3.03	3.27	2.41	2.68	3.73[b]
Liberated (E)	3.25	3.15	3.30	2.82	3.20	3.42[b]	4.03	4.25	4.18	3.93	3.97	3.80[d]
Capable (I)	3.54	3.29	3.24	2.83	2.92	3.65[c]	3.01	3.11	2.73	2.58	2.60	2.64[a,d]
Creative (E)	3.36	3.65	3.35	3.62	3.30	3.11	3.25	3.25	2.37	2.98	3.13	2.82
Has social adeptness (E)	3.03	3.22	3.72	3.05	3.19	3.68	3.13	3.15	3.10	3.08	2.87	2.82
Good looking (E)	4.33	3.73	3.84	3.80	2.77	2.88[a,b]	3.68	4.10	2.64	3.28	3.37	4.64[a,e]
Assertive (I)	4.23	4.02	3.91	3.60	3.64	4.06	3.63	3.61	3.70	3.12	3.15	3.09
Lively (I)	4.05	3.82	3.74	4.07	4.11	4.08[a]	3.35	3.19	3.27	2.60	2.62	2.55[a,d]
Artistic (E)	4.24	4.25	3.97	3.66	3.82	4.18[c]	3.10	4.11	3.09	4.12	3.32	3.64[c]
Popular (I)	4.67	4.08	4.02	4.21	3.84	3.87[a,b]	3.15	3.10	3.09	4.23	4.21	4.27[e]
Tough-minded (I)	4.09	4.24	3.96	4.02	3.81	4.34[c]	4.21	4.32	4.45	4.11	4.03	4.09
Strong (I)	4.41	4.18	3.67	4.32	4.15	4.24[a]	4.09	4.24	4.36	4.21	3.84	4.09
Athletic (I)	3.00	4.25	4.24	3.79	4.25	4.91[b]	4.68	4.97	4.73	4.18	3.94	4.00[a]

78

TABLE 6.1
(Continued)

Country	Sweden						U.S.A.					
Sex of respondent	Female			Male			Female			Male		
Age Group	11	14	18	11	14	18	11	14	18	11	14	18
Devotes self completely to others (E)	4.23	4.35	4.46	4.34	4.47	4.69	3.98	3.67	3.82	3.35	4.31	4.27
Competitive (I)	4.68	4.98	4.78	4.15	4.38	4.45[a]	3.58	3.81	3.73	3.35	3.21	3.00[a,d]
Has leadership abilities (I)	5.43	5.06	4.91	4.73	4.34	4.72	3.38	3.31	3.36	3.36	3.22	3.18[d]
Shy (E)	4.95	4.78	4.56	5.32	4.81	4.79	4.58	4.57	4.36	4.63	4.39	4.55
Dominant (I)	4.84	5.20	4.97	4.64	4.31	4.92[a,c]	4.22	4.93	4.82	4.88	4.06	4.18
Acts as a leader (I)	5.28	5.00	4.91	4.87	4.55	4.73[a]	4.38	4.10	4.00	3.09	3.25	3.18[a,d]
Cannot show one's feelings (I)	5.27	5.09	4.57	4.65	4.84	5.25	5.21	5.35	5.18	5.01	5.31	5.00
Quiet (E)	5.13	5.16	4.92	4.72	4.73	4.97	5.55	5.53	4.55	5.78	5.03	4.63
Subordinates self to others (E)	5.14	5.18	5.18	4.23	4.70	4.99[a]	5.68	5.13	4.00	5.03	4.61	4.78[a]
Feels insecure (E)	5.24	5.38	4.89	5.22	4.91	5.23	4.54	5.55	4.45	4.36	4.89	5.27
Tall (I)	5.15	5.33	5.14	5.27	4.81	5.20	5.14	5.16	5.09	5.27	5.09	5.36
Aggressive (I)	5.66	5.44	5.03	5.02	4.99	5.23	5.24	5.38	4.18	5.22	4.91	3.91
Has Blue Eyes (E)	5.94	5.93	5.97	5.27	5.16	5.77[a,b]	5.53	5.32	4.55	6.10	5.96	5.91[a,e]
Whiny (E)	5.81	5.59	5.60	6.05	5.52	5.90	5.18	5.88	5.36	5.46	5.11	5.82
Has straight hair (I)	5.82	5.94	5.87	5.39	5.54	6.07[c]	5.96	5.83	5.18	4.88	5.01	5.82[a]

[a]Reliable differences between the two sexes of respondents
[b]Reliable differences between age groups
[c]Reliable interaction between sex and age
[d]Reliable differences between countries
[e]Reliable interaction between sex and country
[f]Type of attribute, E = expressive; I = instrumental

79

Obviously, there are both similarities and differences in the ratings of importance for most Swedish and American girls, although, in general, the traits considered most important are primarily expressive. These are fairly global comparisons of cross-national differences. For more precision, we ask which of the 59 traits yielded reliable differences between the two countries? Across all 59 traits, statistically significant nationality differences emerged on only 14. In other words, for most girls cross-national differences were far less common than cross-national similarities. Despite their relative scarcity, however, many of the differences corresponded to differences predicted in chapters 2 and 3. For example, Swedish girls were rated as being more patriotic and liberated than American girls. Swedish patriotism presumably is fostered by a strong cultural belief in the common good, in working for and with society, and in democratic participation. Swedish liberation should follow from the commitment to gender equality. In contrast, most American girls were rated as more capable, more competitive, more likely to have leadership qualities, and more likely to act as a leader than Swedish girls, all traits that contribute to an American theme of "competitive individualism." Of the other attributes that showed cross-national differences, the following traits were rated as reliably more important for Swedish than for American girls: never gives up, willing to take a stand, and emotional. The traits of being affectionate, self-confident, feeling good about self, being compassionate, and being lively were rated as more important for American girls than for Swedish girls.

In summary, these data tell us that the cultural gender concepts for most girls in both Sweden and the United States contain both expressive and instrumental components. In both countries, young girls clearly are expected to be concerned about interpersonal matters and to develop the requisite coping skills. In Sweden, more than in the United States, most girls also are expected to try to do their best and to never give up, traits that should stand them in good stead in most adult endeavors, including the work force.

Most Boys: Cross-National Comparisons. The most important characteristics of most Swedish boys are trying to do one's best, never giving up, and being kind/nice, sincere, and gentle (Table 6.2). Note that these top-rated adjectives contain both instrumental and expressive traits, as did the top-rated traits assigned to most Swedish girls. In fact, three of the top-rated traits were the same for both Swedish girls and boys: trying to do one's best, never giving up, and being kind/nice. These results add to the evidence that Sweden's emphasis on equality of the sexes has influenced cultural gender concepts in the country.

Also interesting is the observation that three of the five top-rated attributes for most Swedish boys were expressive and two were instrumental. But is this true across all traits? Again, we computed the expressiveness/instrumental index by comparing the mean ratings given to the 29 expressive traits to those assigned for the 29 instrumental ones. The means did not differ significantly,

TABLE 6.2
Mean Importance Ratings for Most Boys

Country	Sweden						U.S.A.					
Sex of respondent	Female			Male			Female			Male		
Age Group	11	14	18	11	14	18	11	14	18	11	14	18
Attributes												
Tries to do one's best	1.71	1.90	2.05	1.62	2.00	2.20^b	2.19	2.21	2.38	1.71	2.10	2.15
Never gives up	1.89	1.96	2.01	1.70	2.10	2.42^{a,b}	1.73	2.09	2.42	1.74	2.12	2.92^{a,b}
Kind/nice	2.02	1.79	2.08	1.77	2.16	2.62^{a,c}	1.43	1.55	1.69	2.47	2.30	1.85^{a,b}
Sincere	2.02	2.13	2.11	1.97	2.08	2.49	3.34	2.60	3.31	2.79	2.90	2.89
Gentle	2.35	2.03	2.17	1.75	2.27	2.48^c	3.05	2.42	2.65	2.27	2.65	3.04^d
Friendly	1.45	1.54	1.41	1.37	1.55	1.35^{a,b}	2.23	2.30	2.31	1.93	2.39	2.54^{a,b}
Willing to take a stand	2.48	2.29	1.88	2.05	2.49	2.46^{a,c}	3.56	3.10	3.28	3.39	2.96	2.85^a
Helpful	2.09	2.21	2.46	1.95	2.39	2.58^b	2.18	2.22	1.85	2.12	2.00	2.30^d
Cooperative	2.27	2.37	2.35	2.20	2.37	2.56	3.58	3.41	3.50	3.38	2.71	2.74
Emotional	2.76	2.25	2.25	2.63	2.65	2.91^a	4.20	4.18	4.08	3.84	3.76	3.30^d
Stands up under pressure	2.71	2.52	2.54	2.32	2.57	2.68^c	3.00	2.73	2.96	2.95	3.11	3.33
Humorous	2.38	2.40	2.64	2.60	2.68	2.68	2.65	2.87	2.81	2.75	3.21	3.69
Strong personality	2.55	2.66	2.35	2.43	2.61	2.79^a	4.00	3.67	3.28	3.41	2.74	2.93
Thinks one is a good person	2.80	2.39	2.54	2.31	2.78	2.90^c	2.35	2.35	2.69	2.88	2.76	2.33
Aware of feelings of others	2.92	2.22	2.61	2.84	2.71	2.86^{a,b}	1.90	1.95	1.81	1.80	2.29	2.04
Fun	2.56	2.36	2.77	2.64	2.66	2.96^{a,b}	2.65	2.47	2.35	1.81	2.08	2.42^b
Active	2.46	2.77	2.63	2.55	2.75	2.80	2.25	2.39	2.31	2.34	2.80	2.96^d
Hardworking	2.63	2.81	2.87	2.23	2.58	3.09^b	2.32	2.25	2.00	2.41	2.07	2.46
Tender	3.02	2.35	2.42	3.11	2.80	3.28^a	4.42	4.10	4.27	2.95	3.02	3.59^a
Affectionate	3.05	2.42	2.67	2.76	2.81	3.17^a	2.59	2.83	3.00	2.80	2.85	2.93^a
Loyal	3.17	2.81	2.48	3.39	2.69	2.87^b	2.33	2.13	2.19	2.91	2.93	2.50^{a,b}

(Continued)

81

TABLE 6.2
(Continued)

Country	Sweden						U.S.A.					
Sex of respondent	Female			Male			Female			Male		
Age Group	11	14	18	11	14	18	11	14	18	11	14	18
Self-confident	2.58	2.86	3.02	2.27	2.65	3.07[b]	2.73	2.35	2.27	1.81	2.00	2.41[d]
Patriotic	2.84	2.79	2.77	2.90	2.97	2.55	2.83	2.99	2.96	3.89	3.81	4.07
Loves children	2.49	2.59	2.77	2.40	3.10	3.45[a,b]	2.97	2.83	3.19	5.01	3.76	4.38[a]
Warm	3.32	2.32	2.49	3.29	2.88	3.17[a,b]	2.53	2.87	2.96	3.95	3.81	3.78[a]
Has self-esteem	2.67	2.84	2.82	2.76	2.88	2.94	2.31	2.42	2.31	2.41	2.67	2.74
Eager to soothe hurt feelings	2.31	2.44	3.18	2.67	2.96	3.47[a,b]	4.01	3.53	3.46	2.79	2.89	2.76
Generous	2.80	2.98	2.85	2.82	2.88	2.96	2.41	2.75	2.65	1.85	2.18	2.22
Likable	3.00	2.73	2.85	3.12	2.96	3.13	3.17	2.85	2.58	2.25	2.59	3.07[d]
Feels good about oneself	2.67	2.84	2.85	3.02	3.01	3.29[a]	3.05	2.96	3.04	2.51	3.12	3.00[d]
Makes decisions easily	3.07	2.90	3.06	2.79	2.90	2.99	3.41	3.57	3.50	2.73	3.28	3.63
Compassionate/caring	2.94	2.92	3.16	2.94	3.00	3.32	2.83	2.93	2.92	3.09	2.83	3.26
Creative	3.58	3.41	3.50	2.50	3.12	3.04[a]	4.15	4.00	2.81	1.85	2.11	2.22[a]
Capable	3.62	3.40	3.01	2.95	3.02	3.56[c]	3.02	2.77	2.85	3.30	2.85	3.15[a]
Has social adeptness	3.34	2.60	3.32	2.73	3.36	3.57[b]	2.27	2.37	2.24	2.35	2.03	2.22
Liberated	3.56	3.35	3.34	3.10	3.18	3.37	5.20	4.85	4.69	3.89	3.75	4.15
Strong	4.06	3.50	3.24	3.92	3.72	3.76[a]	2.63	2.71	3.88	2.95	2.78	2.93
Good looking	4.27	3.42	3.33	3.88	3.63	4.01[b,c]	3.51	4.17	4.36	4.61	4.39	4.40[a]
Assertive	4.16	3.99	3.81	3.63	3.50	3.97[a]	3.13	2.96	3.12	3.13	2.85	3.30[d]
Lively	4.15	3.68	3.63	3.76	4.00	4.07[a]	3.27	2.89	3.12	2.65	2.83	2.81[d,e]
Athletic	3.20	3.88	3.80	3.88	3.75	4.15	2.45	2.63	2.81	2.10	2.39	2.59[d]
Tough-minded	4.55	4.15	3.90	3.94	3.53	4.07	2.54	2.38	2.77	4.06	3.50	3.26
Popular	4.60	4.25	3.89	4.45	3.73	3.79[a,b]	2.65	2.89	3.42	3.88	3.90	3.93[a,b]

TABLE 6.2
(Continued)

Country	Sweden						U.S.A.					
Sex of respondent	Female			Male			Female			Male		
Age Group	11	14	18	11	14	18	11	14	18	11	14	18
Artistic	4.44	4.19	4.15	3.97	3.92	4.12	3.91	3.52	3.92	3.58	3.43	3.50
Competitive	4.65	4.76	4.48	3.93	3.80	3.97[a]	2.43	2.78	2.65	2.45	2.88	3.11[a,d]
Has leadership abilities	5.21	4.81	4.68	4.51	3.99	3.93[a]	2.41	2.63	2.77	2.75	2.89	3.19[a,d]
Devotes self completely to others	4.09	4.28	4.80	4.53	4.23	4.99[b]	3.02	3.10	3.31	3.08	3.42	3.58[b]
Acts as a leader	5.05	4.90	4.43	4.45	4.22	3.94[a,b]	2.97	3.20	2.45	2.48	3.65	3.40[d]
Dominant	4.54	4.62	4.91	4.53	4.14	4.34[a]	2.38	2.41	2.19	2.10	2.00	2.19[a]
Shy	4.96	4.67	4.64	5.37	4.52	4.83[b]	4.68	5.01	3.54	4.32	5.03	3.31[b]
Subordinates self to others	4.96	5.00	4.98	4.68	4.36	4.72[a]	4.53	4.10	3.92	3.70	3.84	3.64[a]
Tall	5.49	4.78	4.33	5.23	4.60	4.78[b]	4.10	4.53	4.23	4.61	4.32	4.89
Quiet	5.00	4.92	4.87	5.33	4.62	4.84	4.13	3.65	3.50	3.19	3.90	3.77
Cannot show one's feelings	5.38	5.08	4.57	5.12	4.70	5.10	3.20	4.27	3.69	4.10	3.36	4.04
Aggressive	5.37	5.39	5.10	5.09	4.43	4.90[a,c]	1.87	1.74	1.75	2.60	2.83	2.50[a,d]
Feels insecure	5.48	5.26	4.95	5.44	5.01	5.35	4.89	5.41	3.35	5.38	5.01	3.64
Has blue eyes	5.70	5.74	5.69	5.36	5.44	5.83	4.15	4.16	4.12	4.15	4.28	4.33
Whiny	5.75	5.57	5.54	6.09	5.42	5.90	4.08	4.17	4.04	3.85	4.35	3.96
Has straight hair	5.70	5.94	5.62	5.53	5.28	5.97[c]	3.76	3.76	3.58	3.53	3.67	3.96

[a]Reliable differences between the two sexes of respondents
[b]Reliable differences between age groups
[c]Reliable interaction between sex and age
[d]Reliable differences between countries
[e]interaction between sex and country

83

$t(332) = 1.13$, indicating that, on the average, the two types of traits were deemed about equally important for most Swedish boys. This contrasts with assignments to most Swedish girls, for whom expressive traits were rated as reliably more important, on the average, than instrumental traits.

What about most American boys? Were both instrumental and expressive attributes considered to be highly important characteristics? The answer is clearly yes: Most American boys were considered as kind/nice, aware of the feelings of others, helpful, trying to do one's best, and never giving up (Table 6.2). Thus, the respondents from the two countries agreed that being kind/nice, trying to do one's best, and never giving up are highly salient attributes of most boys, but the other top-rated components differed for the two countries. Moreover, echoing the data for most Swedish boys, American boys were assigned approximately equal ratings on instrumental and expressive traits, $t(332) < 1$. The cultural gender concepts for most boys in the two countries seem quite similar, with both instrumental and expressive traits being important components. Topping the list for both countries are the three attributes of trying to do one's best, never giving up, and being kind/nice.

To be more precise about the cross-national comparisons, we compared the mean ratings assigned most boys of each country on each of the 59 attributes. About one quarter (15 traits) showed reliable nationality differences. Most striking among these differences were the reliably higher ratings accorded by Americans to being self-confident, assertive, athletic, aggressive, competitive, having leadership qualities, and acting as a leader—all traits often associated with an American macho image.

Briefly summarizing the message from the importance ratings for most girls and most boys, the data describe both cross-national similarities and differences. In both countries, expressive, communal, interpersonally related attributes are rated as important as more instrumental, agentic ones, a surprising but robust result. Girls rate expressive attributes reliably higher than instrumental ones, on the average.

The importance ratings for most girls and boys yielded another noteworthy result: Some attributes appeared in all of the gender concepts. Specifically, being kind/nice, trying to do one's best, and never giving up were among the five top-ranked traits for most Swedish girls and boys and for most American boys. Most American girls were also thought to be kind/nice, but the other attributes of trying to do one's best and never giving up were given lower ratings of importance. The appearance of attributes in more than one gender concept supports the data from the free listings of traits.

Before moving on to the ratings for most women and most men, we comment on two more aspects of the data: Trying to do one's best and never giving up, despite their high ratings of importance, were never mentioned in the free listings. These two traits were recommended to us by Swedish informants, and they were rated as highly important by not only Swedish respondents but also by American respondents. This result is particularly interesting because, to my knowledge, neither attribute appears in any American inventory of gender roles. The second aspect is that the top-rated attributes are all personality characteristics. Physical characteristics, such as being tall, having blue eyes, or having straight hair were rated as among the least important attributes for most girls and boys in both countries. We return to these curious findings later.

These results certainly suggest that there is substantial agreement on the components of cultural gender concepts, at least for most girls and most boys. We now ask if this is true for most women and most men, as well.

Most Women: Cross-National Comparisons. The top-rated attributes for most Swedish women are trying to do one's best, being kind/nice, gentle, and never giving up. Being friendly and sincere tied for fifth place (see Table 6.3). Except for the last two, these attributes are beginning to look like the Swedish national image. These attributes appear to be highly salient to our large sample of Swedish respondents, regardless of the age or sex of the group being rated. Of course, we need to be cautious, because we have not yet considered rating of most Swedish men.

These attributes combine both expressive and instrumental ones. Nevertheless, when the mean ratings were compared for the 29 expressive and the 29 instrumental attributes, the expressive traits were given a higher importance ratings than the instrumental traits, $t(332) = 5.05$.

Most American women elicited a different set of top-rated attributes. They were considered as affectionate, warm, friendly, self-confident, and as feeling good about themselves. Thus, American women are thought to be confidently warm and outgoing, whereas Swedish women are viewed as combining their persistence at doing their best with kindness, gentleness, and sincerity. The components of the cultural gender concept for most Swedish women appears to be somewhat more assertive and instrumental than that for most American women. The women of both countries typically are considered friendly.

These summary statements need statistical backup. In general, the expressive traits were rated as reliably more important (3.00) for most American women than instrumental traits (3.19), $t(330) = 4.89$. Moreover, 21 traits showed cross-national differences, as shown in Table 6.3. Of these differentiating attributes, being willing to take a stand and being patriotic were rated as more important for Swedish than for American women, whereas loving children, being warm, eager to soothe hurt feelings, tender, fun, hardworking, affectionate, self-confident, compassionate, and the like were rated as more important for American than for Swedish women. These constellations pick up our contentions that the Swedish ethos promotes group solidarity and patriotism and that the American perspective assigns women to a nurturing role. The only discordant note rises from the attribute "aggressive." It was rated as considerably more important for American (3.77) than for Swedish (5.21) women. Although being aggressive is

TABLE 6.3
Mean Importance Ratings for Most Women

Country	Sweden						U.S.A.					
Sex of respondent	Female			Male			Female			Male		
Age Group	11	14	18	11	14	18	11	14	18	11	14	18
Attributes												
Tries to do one's best	1.86	1.95	2.06	1.60	2.05	2.26[b]	2.63	2.49	2.36	1.99	1.83	1.91[a]
Kind/nice	1.86	1.98	2.05	1.81	2.04	2.20	1.88	1.97	2.09	1.81	2.10	2.27
Gentle	1.87	1.93	1.99	1.83	2.12	2.28[a]	2.56	2.50	2.55	2.21	2.42	2.45
Never gives up	1.87	2.03	1.89	1.81	2.18	2.44[a,b]	1.86	1.94	1.98	1.85	2.20	2.46[a,d]
Friendly	1.90	1.98	2.12	1.95	2.25	2.34[a,b]	1.85	1.93	2.22	1.87	1.88	1.95[b]
Sincere	1.98	2.25	1.87	1.89	2.26	2.26[b]	1.85	1.97	1.91	2.03	1.97	2.00
Helpful	2.06	2.02	2.24	1.98	2.05	2.45[b]	2.20	2.12	2.27	2.51	2.62	2.55[a]
Willing to take a stand	2.05	2.34	1.84	2.33	2.47	2.40[a,b]	2.82	3.08	3.64	2.56	2.68	2.82[a,b,d,e]
Loves children	1.98	2.08	2.39	1.80	2.54	2.68[a,b]	1.94	2.06	2.00	2.06	2.12	2.27[a,d]
Cooperative	2.49	2.35	2.17	2.23	2.40	2.47	2.65	2.48	2.36	3.16	2.48	2.64
Thinks one is a good person	2.57	2.49	2.56	2.22	2.65	2.56	2.49	2.56	2.64	1.80	2.35	2.27
Emotional	2.65	2.48	2.37	2.72	2.60	2.57	2.87	2.53	2.45	2.87	2.83	3.18
Strong personality	2.57	2.41	2.52	2.51	2.74	2.90[a,c]	2.08	1.97	2.36	3.15	2.50	2.55[a]
Warm	3.00	2.38	2.50	3.16	2.48	2.51[b]	1.60	1.68	1.64	2.20	2.15	2.18[a,d]
Eager to soothe hurt feelings	2.27	2.33	2.92	2.51	2.69	3.13[b]	2.55	2.48	2.36	2.61	2.72	2.55[b,d]
Aware of feelings of others	2.89	2.48	2.44	3.18	2.74	2.57[b]	1.87	1.88	2.09	1.93	1.91	2.09
Humorous	2.71	2.57	2.59	2.68	2.70	2.90	2.67	2.71	2.91	2.67	2.61	2.73
Tender	2.98	2.50	2.45	3.05	2.80	2.65	2.07	1.93	2.00	2.55	2.43	2.27[d]
Stands up under pressure	2.63	2.78	2.65	3.05	2.49	2.85	2.72	3.01	3.09	2.49	2.35	2.18[a,e]
Patriotic	2.61	2.68	2.69	2.71	2.99	2.61	2.92	3.26	3.27	2.81	2.84	3.18[d]
Fun	2.68	2.60	2.71	2.77	2.72	3.07	2.08	2.09	2.27	2.25	2.41	2.45[d]

TABLE 6.3
(Continued)

| Country | Sweden | | | | | | U.S.A. | | | | | |
| Sex of respondent | Female | | | Male | | | Female | | | Male | | |
Age Group	11	14	18	11	14	18	11	14	18	11	14	18
Hardworking	2.56	2.68	2.82	2.24	2.62	3.37[b,c]	2.33	2.61	2.73	2.01	2.07	2.09[b,d,e]
Affectionate	2.95	2.64	2.95	2.62	2.81	2.66	1.53	1.57	1.55	2.12	2.24	2.18[d]
Has self-esteem	2.64	2.72	2.80	2.54	2.82	2.17	2.56	2.68	2.82	2.05	1.95	2.00
Likable	2.85	2.84	2.85	3.05	2.61	2.78	1.99	2.01	2.00	2.03	2.38	2.36[d]
Active	2.76	2.74	2.69	2.72	2.95	3.03[a]	2.80	3.05	2.64	2.78	2.63	2.64
Feels good about oneself	2.64	2.62	2.95	2.83	2.87	3.15	2.26	1.89	2.27	1.71	1.75	1.73[a,d]
Self-confident	2.35	2.94	2.89	2.45	3.00	3.10	1.83	2.12	2.27	2.02	1.63	1.82[d]
Generous	3.15	2.73	2.91	2.60	2.88	2.93[c]	2.48	2.65	2.36	2.05	1.98	2.45
Loyal	4.00	3.05	2.85	3.44	2.74	2.79[b]	1.89	1.93	1.91	2.85	2.71	2.18[b,d]
Makes decisions easily	3.00	2.72	3.07	2.83	3.00	3.36[b]	2.85	3.23	3.73	2.72	2.95	3.00
Compassionate/caring	3.02	2.86	3.10	3.26	2.90	3.24[b]	1.91	2.05	2.09	1.98	2.42	2.36[b,d]
Has social adeptness	2.94	3.24	3.29	2.82	3.08	3.67[b]	2.56	2.49	2.60	2.51	2.74	2.73
Capable	3.52	3.28	3.16	2.73	3.05	3.76[c]	2.68	2.56	2.82	2.65	2.41	2.09[d]
Liberated	3.33	3.07	3.12	3.08	3.39	3.74[b]	3.08	3.49	3.91	2.64	2.71	2.80
Creative	3.60	3.53	3.19	4.08	3.18	3.36	3.52	3.27	3.18	4.05	3.39	2.64
Good looking	4.23	3.62	3.98	3.79	3.05	3.23[a,b]	2.80	3.02	2.82	4.13	4.23	4.18[a,e]
Assertive	4.03	3.61	3.96	3.80	3.38	4.01[b]	3.80	3.56	3.00	3.10	3.23	2.91[d]
Artistic	3.86	4.01	4.17	3.58	3.59	4.39[b]	5.26	4.70	4.73	4.21	3.63	3.91[b]
Lively	3.95	4.00	4.01	3.61	4.04	4.23	3.73	3.51	3.64	3.98	4.01	2.82
Strong	4.48	3.93	3.54	4.32	4.13	4.46[a,c]	4.03	3.63	3.91	4.54	4.73	3.82[a]
Tough-minded	4.23	4.10	4.14	3.95	3.86	4.39	3.73	3.54	3.55	3.61	3.70	3.55
Popular	4.87	4.17	4.15	4.19	3.83	4.23[a,b,c]	4.10	3.86	3.64	4.03	3.81	4.09

(Continued)

87

TABLE 6.3
(Continued)

Country	Sweden						U.S.A.					
Sex of respondent	Female			Male			Female			Male		
Age Group	11	14	18	11	14	18	11	14	18	11	14	18
Athletic	3.79	3.88	4.44	3.53	4.12	5.14[b]	3.84	3.96	4.36	3.52	3.71	3.64
Devotes self completely to others	4.39	4.42	4.51	4.22	4.28	4.56	4.02	4.03	3.91	3.81	3.42	4.00
Dominant	5.00	4.50	4.86	4.33	4.26	5.08[b]	3.95	3.85	4.36	3.82	3.41	4.09
Has leadership qualities	5.26	4.70	4.79	4.26	4.18	4.76	3.67	3.69	3.55	3.98	3.48	2.73[d]
Competitive	4.74	4.88	4.98	4.13	4.22	4.84[a,b]	3.43	3.83	3.36	3.10	3.01	3.27[a,d]
Subordinates self to others	4.22	4.74	5.14	4.35	4.53	4.76	4.56	4.23	4.33	4.06	3.95	4.11[a]
Acts as a leader	5.02	4.92	4.89	4.65	4.26	4.75[a]	3.96	4.02	4.00	3.38	3.25	3.18[a,d]
Shy	4.98	4.73	4.80	5.51	4.68	4.59	4.56	4.32	4.27	3.80	3.86	4.45
Quiet	4.71	4.87	4.99	4.76	4.86	5.10	5.03	4.95	4.91	4.63	4.32	4.73
Cannot show one's feelings	5.04	5.13	4.74	4.93	4.90	5.18	5.06	4.98	5.00	4.86	4.93	4.80
Feels insecure	5.06	4.97	5.03	5.18	5.08	5.27	3.95	4.03	4.00	5.08	4.93	5.09
Tall	5.32	5.41	5.24	4.93	4.84	5.38[a]	4.83	4.92	5.45	4.75	4.87	5.09
Aggressive	5.54	5.38	5.15	4.69	5.06	5.33	4.43	3.95	3.55	3.96	3.54	3.18[d]
Whiny	5.56	5.59	5.64	5.91	5.63	5.93	5.55	5.53	5.36	5.19	5.51	6.00
Has blue eyes	5.75	5.84	6.05	5.57	5.22	6.13[b]	4.22	4.75	5.18	5.81	5.92	5.91
Has straight hair	5.68	6.08	6.11	5.17	5.52	6.23[a,b,c]	4.73	4.89	5.09	5.69	6.07	6.18

[a]Reliable differences between the two sexes of respondents
[b]Reliable differences between age groups
[c]Reliable interaction between sex and age
[d]Reliable differences between countries
[e]Reliable interaction between sex and country

88

not usually construed as a nurturing quality, it is consistent with another American theme, that of egotistic individualism. On balance, most Swedish women were rated as being somewhat more instrumental than most American women, consonant with expectations based on Sweden's policies of gender equality of opportunity.

Most Men: Cross-National Comparisons. One of the biggest surprises was the substantial importance ratings given to expressive characteristics for Swedish men. Being kind/nice, gentle, and helpful were among the top-rated traits for most Swedish men, as were the instrumental characteristics, trying to do one's best and never giving up (Table 6.4). Thus, being kind/nice, trying to do one's best, and never giving up appear to be hallmarks of the Swedish national character. These attributes emerged at or near the top of the importance ratings for each of the stimulus groups, signaling the salience this combination of concern and individual dedication appears to have for all age groups and both sexes in Sweden.

Over the 58 traits, expressive traits were rated slightly more important on the average (3.33) than instrumental traits (3.47) for Swedish men, a result that parallels the finding for most Swedish boys. The difference was not statistically significant, however. In other words, these two types of traits are both deemed to contribute in nearly equal measure to those characteristics that define maleness in the Swedish nation.

The American male persona is different. Here we find much more dedication to the hard-driving, macho image of lore, except for one trait, loyal, which had the highest rating, 1.78. American men try to do their best, feel good about themselves, are self-confident, and hardworking. Interestingly, however, even for American men, such traits as aggression and competition are not rated as very important, raising the possibility that some previous work may, perhaps by virtue of some subtle demands, have misrepresented American views. It is still the case, however, that, overall, instrumental traits are rated as more important for most American men (2.80) than are expressive traits (3.21), as shown in Table 6.4. This difference was reliable, $t(332) = 4.61$.

The top-rated components of the cultural gender concepts for most men show distinct national differences. Is this true for all 59 attributes? No, but 22 of the attributes did show reliable differences. This is the highest number of cross-national differences found so far, but we must remember that cross-national similarities are at least intimated by the 37 characteristics that did not yield reliable differences. The absence of reliable differences must be treated with caution, of course, and we would be treading on dangerous ground to assume that cross-national similarities are indisputably documented by the findings. Nevertheless, it is important to note that even for the most discrepant stimulus group, apparent similarities outnumbered the differences.

With adult gender concepts, as with those for children, the top-rated attributes

TABLE 6.4
Mean Importance Ratings for Most Men

Country	Sweden						U.S.A.					
Sex of respondent	Female			Male			Female			Male		
Age Group	11	14	18	11	14	18	11	14	18	11	14	18
Attributes												
Tries to do one's best	1.88	1.74	1.94	1.57	2.08	2.25[a,b]	1.86	1.78	1.82	1.83	1.81	1.82[a,b,d]
Never gives up	1.92	1.80	2.06	1.87	2.14	2.38[a,b]	1.83	1.81	1.82	1.92	2.63	2.91[a,b]
Kind/nice	2.03	1.83	2.01	1.77	2.18	2.49[a]	2.35	2.08	2.36	2.26	2.31	2.09
Gentle	2.21	1.89	2.16	1.98	2.31	2.33	2.65	2.66	2.82	2.19	2.33	2.36
Helpful	2.00	1.97	2.30	1.94	2.30	2.42[b]	2.55	2.31	2.45	2.33	2.41	2.55
Willing to take a stand	2.42	1.99	1.89	2.19	2.33	2.37[a]	2.15	2.22	2.09	2.83	2.33	2.64[a]
Friendly	2.04	1.96	2.26	1.91	2.29	2.54[a,b]	2.13	2.07	2.18	2.09	2.14	2.00
Sincere	2.26	2.02	2.01	1.79	2.35	2.58	2.22	2.16	2.18	1.87	1.95	1.91[a]
Cooperative	2.54	2.22	2.22	2.17	2.45	2.55	2.67	2.35	2.73	2.69	2.71	2.36
Loves children	2.12	2.15	2.51	2.11	2.77	3.06	2.16	2.21	2.18	2.42	2.25	2.27[a,d]
Stands up under pressure	2.83	2.38	2.55	2.60	2.51	2.69	2.23	2.14	2.45	2.15	2.39	2.18[d]
Emotional	2.68	2.36	2.21	2.79	2.88	2.93[a]	3.10	3.22	3.27	3.40	3.31	3.09[a,d]
Strong personality	2.64	2.61	2.45	2.51	2.63	2.81	2.24	2.31	2.27	2.05	2.08	2.09[a]
Hardworking	2.57	2.64	2.70	2.28	2.36	2.99[b]	1.97	2.03	2.00	2.07	2.11	2.09[d]
Aware of feelings of others	2.85	2.44	2.49	3.07	2.60	2.79[b]	2.23	2.47	2.55	2.65	2.43	2.18
Patriotic	2.42	2.70	2.68	2.35	2.81	2.70	2.68	2.67	2.82	2.68	2.63	3.00
Active	3.04	2.61	2.53	2.66	2.76	2.77	2.40	2.31	2.36	2.30	2.45	2.73
Humorous	2.69	2.60	2.64	2.85	2.75	2.81	2.67	2.68	2.82	2.36	2.78	2.64
Thinks one is a good person	2.87	2.52	2.49	2.93	2.87	2.90[a]	2.35	2.81	2.73	3.04	2.63	2.55
Fun	2.70	2.57	2.87	2.68	2.63	3.10[b]	2.79	2.76	2.55	2.98	2.85	2.45
Self-confident	2.67	2.68	2.83	2.41	2.87	2.88	1.98	2.02	2.00	1.92	1.72	1.82[d]

TABLE 6.4
(Continued)

Country	Sweden						U.S.A.					
Sex of respondent	Female			Male			Female			Male		
Age Group	11	14	18	11	14	18	11	14	18	11	14	18
Loyal	3.23	2.84	2.42	3.41	2.80	2.88	2.32	2.27	1.64	2.41	2.32	1.91[a,d]
Tender	2.86	2.45	2.49	3.10	2.90	3.35[a,b]	2.98	2.99	3.00	2.78	3.02	2.45
Affectionate	3.14	2.48	2.71	2.83	2.94	3.09[a]	2.36	2.42	2.27	2.51	2.42	2.18[d]
Warm	3.11	2.48	2.37	3.14	3.03	3.19[a]	2.25	2.27	2.27	2.41	2.38	2.36[a]
Eager to soothe hurt feelings	2.44	2.57	3.00	2.36	2.96	3.48[a,b]	2.41	2.46	2.45	2.67	2.67	2.64[a,d]
Has self-esteem	2.84	3.00	2.81	2.71	2.81	2.77	2.28	2.56	2.55	1.80	1.84	1.82
Generous	3.02	2.82	2.95	2.52	2.91	2.99	2.51	2.43	2.64	2.66	2.53	2.45
Makes decisions easily	3.31	2.84	3.12	3.38	2.65	2.86[b]	2.80	2.72	3.36	2.73	3.31	2.82
Feels good about oneself	2.96	2.88	2.78	3.00	3.14	3.29	1.80	2.20	2.00	1.79	1.85	1.82[a,d]
Likable	3.00	2.78	2.85	2.80	3.11	3.37[a]	2.20	2.34	2.36	2.50	2.41	2.45[a,d]
Compassionate/caring	3.21	2.90	3.31	2.90	2.94	3.22[b]	2.41	2.57	2.64	2.21	2.24	2.27[b,d]
Creative	3.73	2.94	3.37	4.06	2.93	3.00	2.81	2.90	3.27	3.25	2.78	2.91
Capable	3.77	3.19	3.23	2.98	2.96	3.51[c]	2.43	2.34	2.55	2.53	2.48	2.36[d]
Has social adeptness	3.62	3.40	3.41	3.00	3.11	3.26	2.89	2.45	2.60	2.58	2.43	2.91
Liberated	3.28	3.27	3.29	3.44	3.38	3.68	3.39	3.43	3.55	3.41	3.57	3.40
Good looking	4.16	3.71	3.48	3.69	3.43	3.90[c]	3.31	3.24	3.27	4.10	4.13	4.18[a]
Strong	4.58	3.70	3.29	3.77	3.42	3.89[b,c]	2.50	2.53	2.64	2.34	2.54	2.91[b]
Assertive	4.09	3.81	3.89	3.30	3.60	3.90	2.98	2.88	2.82	2.87	3.01	3.00[d]
Athletic	3.00	3.85	3.83	2.50	3.71	4.45[b]	2.89	2.58	3.82	2.67	3.80	2.91[e]
Lively	3.96	3.87	3.80	3.75	3.95	4.24	2.98	3.05	3.27	3.03	3.25	3.00[d]
Artistic	3.59	4.02	4.09	3.26	3.84	4.25	4.50	4.63	4.82	4.61	4.70	4.45[d]
Tough-minded	4.36	4.17	3.96	3.71	3.73	4.24	2.78	2.98	2.82	2.77	2.75	3.36[d]

(Continued)

91

TABLE 6.4
(Continued)

Country	Sweden						U.S.A.					
Sex of respondent	Female			Male			Female			Male		
Age Group	11	14	18	11	14	18	11	14	18	11	14	18
Popular	4.90	4.23	4.00	4.19	3.93	3.87[a,b]	4.66	4.41	3.91	4.31	4.22	4.18[a,b]
Competitive	4.38	4.68	4.41	3.71	4.00	4.20[a,b]	2.07	2.11	2.09	2.31	2.11	2.82[d]
Acts as a leader	4.84	4.75	4.55	4.56	3.82	3.65[a,b]	2.78	2.68	2.45	2.34	2.27	2.64[a,d]
Has leadership abilities	5.26	4.68	4.57	4.43	4.03	3.63[a,b]	2.35	2.38	2.36	2.58	2.60	2.64[a,d]
Devotes self completely to others	4.12	4.30	4.78	4.52	4.26	4.80[b]	3.87	3.90	3.91	4.02	4.37	4.36
Dominant	4.68	4.99	4.89	3.76	4.09	4.36[a]	3.10	3.05	3.00	3.35	3.47	3.45[a,d]
Subordinates self to others	4.22	4.70	4.62	4.08	4.29	4.99[b]	4.23	4.12	4.44	4.10	4.23	4.44
Tall	5.13	4.76	4.44	4.89	4.51	4.58[b]	4.20	4.38	4.45	4.40	4.41	4.18
Cannot show one's feelings	4.89	4.88	4.68	4.38	4.73	5.13	4.32	4.33	4.09	4.00	4.45	4.80
Quiet	4.77	5.05	4.89	4.51	4.59	5.18	4.53	4.55	4.55	4.32	4.34	4.82
Shy	5.07	4.84	4.59	5.28	4.73	4.97[b]	5.06	5.08	5.00	5.20	4.98	4.82
Aggressive	5.31	5.31	4.94	4.92	4.54	5.00	2.89	2.90	2.91	3.02	2.88	3.00[d]
Feels insecure	4.84	5.17	4.93	4.86	5.08	5.24	5.20	5.16	5.18	5.11	5.23	5.27
Whiny	5.71	5.67	5.59	5.68	5.22	5.84	6.02	5.91	5.91	5.87	5.92	6.00
Has blue eyes	5.84	6.02	5.68	5.52	5.14	5.77	5.62	5.55	5.27	5.25	5.51	5.64
Has straight hair	5.56	6.03	5.66	5.47	5.24	6.06[a]	5.07	5.10	5.09	5.98	5.93	6.18[a]

[a]Reliable differences between the two sexes of respondents
[b]Reliable differences between age groups
[c]Reliable interaction between sex and age
[d]Reliable differences between countries
[e]Reliable interaction between sex and country

were always personality characteristics; physical traits typically were among the lowest rated items.

These results seem to provide impressive support for the first two predictions, but we have not yet systematically compared ratings of most girls with those of most boys, with ratings of most women with those of most men, and so forth. This information should also afford more insight into an intriguing aspect of gender-differentiating attributes: the tendency for relatively few of them to be rated as highly important. The attributes typically rated as differing among the stimulus groups were usually rated as less important than attributes that did not differ among the stimulus groups.

Most Girls versus Most Boys. As shown in Table 6.5, Swedish females and males agree that most boys are reliably taller, stronger, more dominant, more athletic, more likely to act as a leader, and more likely to have leadership qualities, more likely to have blue eyes, and so on, than most girls. To repeat, the most important components in the cultural gender concepts for these two groups (being kind, trying to do one's best, never giving up, being gentle, and being friendly) do not differ for most girls and most boys, although they are highly salient as attributes when people are asked to rate most girls and most boys.

American female and male respondents maintained that most boys are stronger, more aggressive, more dominant, kinder, and as more aware of the feelings of others than most girls. As with the Swedish ratings, the traits showing gender differences, except *kind*, are not among the five top-rated attributes characterizing most girls and most boys. Apparently, the gender-differentiating traits are considered to be less important components of the gender concepts than some more general and nongender-differentiating attributes, a theoretically powerful result that poses a major challenge to most models of gender concepts.

Most Women versus Most Men. We turn next to the attributes showing reliable gender differences between most women and most men. According to Swedish respondents, most men are taller, more competitive, and more athletic than most women, whereas most women are more eager to soothe hurt feelings than most men. Among the attributes rated differentially for most women and most men, American respondents judge most men to be stronger, more athletic, and less likely to give up than most women. Most women are rated as warmer than most men. For both nationalities, the traits that show gender differences conform to now-familiar stereotypic assignments (see Table 6.6), and most of these gender-differentiating traits are not among the top-rated attributes.

Overall, where attributes showed reliable gender differences, the direction of the differences was usually stereotypic: Most boys and most men, regardless of their nationality, are likely to be rated as having more instrumental-agentic traits than most girls or most women. Most girls and most women are more likely than most males to be rated as having expressive-communal traits. Finally, the

TABLE 6.5
Mean Importance Ratings Showing Significant Differences Between Most Girls and Most Boys

	Swedish female raters					Swedish male raters			
		Higher ratings for most boys than most girls							
Attributes	Most boys	Most girls	(df)	t	Attributes	Most boys	Most girls	(df)	t
Tender	2.52	2.72	(236)	2.43*	Hardworking	2.63	2.89	(207)	3.12*
Affectionate	2.61	2.79	(211)	2.38*	Strong	3.79	4.26	(207)	4.49***
Likable	2.84	2.98	(229)	2.00*	Competitive	3.89	4.34	(203)	4.24***
Strong	3.55	4.04	(240)	4.17***	Athletic	4.00	4.46	(134)	3.14**
Good Looking	3.60	3.88	(246)	3.06**	Has leadership abilities	4.13	4.58	(194)	4.18***
Athletic	3.85	4.22	(214)	2.71**	Acts as a leader	4.16	4.71	(201)	4.85***
					Dominant	4.33	4.65	(177)	3.00**
					Aggressive	4.84	5.08	(206)	2.37*
					Tall	4.84	5.08	(206)	2.37*
		Higher ratings for most girls than most boys							
					Attributes	Most boys	Most girls	(df)	t
					Kind/nice	1.93	2.20	(213)	3.01**
					Warm	2.62	3.08	(200)	4.66***
					Tender	2.65	3.05	(204)	3.91***
					Likable	2.65	3.06	(194)	4.32***
					Affectionate	2.68	2.92	(182)	2.45*
					Loves children	2.68	3.02	(209)	3.37***
					Eager to soothe hurt feelings	2.72	3.04	(206)	3.48***
					Good looking	3.11	3.84	(208)	5.62***

TABLE 6.5
(Continued)

Higher ratings for most boys than most girls

American female raters

Attributes	Most boys	Most girls	(df)	t
Kind/nice	1.69	2.77	(162)	2.17*
Aggressive	1.75	3.45	(155)	4.59***
Aware of feelings of others	1.81	3.96	(162)	4.38***
Dominant	2.19	3.85	(162)	5.85***
Loyal	2.19	3.96	(162)	4.33***
Has self-esteem	2.31	3.54	(161)	2.40*
Strong	2.88	4.23	(162)	3.01**

American male raters

Attributes	Most boys	Most girls	(df)	t
Kind/nice	1.85	3.15	(163)	2.62**
Aware of feelings of others	2.04	3.26	(163)	3.33***
Dominant	2.19	3.22	(163)	4.40***
Fun	2.42	3.04	(162)	2.26*
Thinks one is a good person	2.33	3.15	(163)	2.23*
Aggressive	2.50	3.20	(155)	3.04**
Loyal	2.50	3.92	(162)	3.86***
Willing to take a stand	2.92	3.62	(160)	2.21*
Strong	3.00	3.85	(162)	2.19*

Higher ratings for most girls than most boys

American female raters

Attributes	Most boys	Most girls	(df)	t
Friendly	1.62	2.31	(162)	2.81**
Loves children	1.73	3.19	(162)	4.96***
Affectionate	1.88	3.00	(162)	2.89**
Eager to soothe hurt feelings	1.88	3.46	(162)	4.60***
Strong personality	2.00	3.28	(161)	2.92**
Tender	2.12	4.27	(162)	4.94***
Cooperative	2.31	3.50	(162)	3.13**
Emotional	2.32	4.20	(161)	4.84***

American male raters

Attributes	Most boys	Most girls	(df)	t
Likable	1.96	3.07	(163)	2.96**
Eager to soothe hurt feelings	2.28	2.76	(162)	2.49*
Loves children	2.42	4.38	(162)	5.03***
Warm	2.44	3.78	(162)	3.85***
Humorous	2.46	3.69	(162)	3.37**
Shy	2.62	3.31	(162)	2.62*
Tender	2.65	3.65	(162)	3.76***
Patriotic	2.74	4.07	(163)	3.95***

(Continued)

95

TABLE 6.5
(Continued)

	Swedish female raters				Swedish male raters
	Higher ratings for most boys than most girls				
Shy	2.50	3.54	(162)	2.61*	
Feels insecure	2.65	3.35	(162)	2.56*	
Artistic	2.96	3.92	(162)	3.58***	
Has blue eyes	3.12	4.12	(162)	3.29**	
Good looking	3.28	4.36	(161)	2.70**	

*p < .05
**p < .01
***p < .001

96

TABLE 6.6

Mean Importance Ratings Showing Significant Differences Between
Most Women and Most Men

Swedish female raters

Higher ratings for most men than most women

Attributes	Most men	Most women	(df)	t
Tries to do one's best	1.85	1.98	(243)	2.48*
Athletic	3.96	4.24	(112)	2.27*
Competitive	4.53	4.82	(233)	2.86**
Subordinates self to others	4.61	4.87	(172)	2.15*
Tall	4.76	5.35	(246)	6.27***

Higher ratings for most women than most men

Attributes	Most women	Most men	(df)	t
Eager to soothe hurt feelings	2.50	2.67	(241)	2.49*
Has self-esteem	2.73	2.88	(224)	2.00*
Has social adeptness	3.19	3.43	(177)	2.24*

Swedish male raters

Higher ratings for most men than most women

Attributes	Most men	Most women	(df)	t
Hardworking	2.56	2.77	(192)	2.83**
Active	2.70	2.93	(178)	3.12***
Makes decisions early	2.87	3.09	(189)	2.29*
Creative	3.06	3.27	(138)	2.22*
Strong	3.68	4.32	(191)	5.38***
Has leadership abilities	3.85	4.43	(148)	4.06***
Acts as a leader	3.89	4.54	(189)	5.76***
Competitive	4.01	4.45	(191)	4.47***
Athletic	4.02	4.58	(132)	4.03***
Dominant	4.18	4.64	(156)	3.32***
Tall	4.66	5.05	(193)	3.75***
Aggressive	4.86	5.12	(178)	2.73**

Higher ratings for most women than most men

Attributes	Most women	Most men	(df)	t
Loves children	2.44	2.70	(191)	2.60**
Thinks one is a good person	2.54	2.88	(188)	3.39***
Emotional	2.62	2.89	(184)	2.91**
Warm	2.66	3.09	(183)	5.12***
Affectionate	2.72	2.98	(166)	2.79**
Tender	2.75	3.12	(181)	3.32***

(Continued)

TABLE 6.6

Mean Importance Ratings Showing Significant Differences Between
Most Women and Most Men

Swedish female raters

Higher ratings for most men than most women

Attributes	Most men	Most women	(df)	t

American female raters

Higher ratings for most men than most women

Attributes	Most men	Most women	(df)	t
Never gives up	2.12	2.58	(162)	2.48*
Loyal	2.12	3.38	(162)	3.22**
Self-confident	2.35	3.46	(162)	2.55*
Friendly	2.50	3.31	(162)	2.43*
Strong	2.54	3.42	(162)	2.58*
Athletic	2.85	4.19	(162)	4.05***
Eager to soothe hurt feelings	2.88	3.80	(161)	2.78**
Willing to take a stand	2.92	5.08	(162)	3.78***
Quiet	3.27	4.19	(162)	3.40**

Higher ratings for most women than most men

Attributes	Most women	Most men	(df)	t
Affectionate	1.54	2.85	(162)	4.56***

Swedish male raters

Higher ratings for most men than most women

Attributes	Most men	Most women	(df)	t
Likable	2.77	3.12	(179)	3.71**
Eager to soothe hurt feelings	2.82	2.99	(189)	2.20*
Good looking	3.26	3.68	(190)	3.65***

American male raters

Higher ratings for most men than most women

Attributes	Most men	Most women	(df)	t
Never gives up	2.26	2.89	(163)	4.13***
Strong	2.59	3.04	(163)	2.06*
Athletic	2.75	3.41	(163)	3.34**
Shy	2.96	3.52	(163)	2.20*

Higher ratings for most women than most men

Attributes	Most women	Most men	(df)	t
Capable	1.81	2.22	(163)	3.05**

TABLE 6.6
Mean Importance Ratings Showing Significant Differences Between
Most Women and Most Men

Swedish female raters

Higher ratings for most men than most women

Attributes	Most men	Most women	(df)	t
Likable	1.77	2.69	(162)	3.09**
Kind	2.12	3.04	(161)	3.40**
Stands up under pressure	2.15	3.58	(162)	2.20*
Helpful	2.27	3.19	(162)	3.04**
Warm	2.54	3.19	(162)	2.71**
Active	2.69	3.65	(162)	2.31*
Has straight hair	3.35	4.38	(162)	3.28**
Whiny	3.73	4.69	(162)	3.40**
Tender	3.77	4.62	(162)	3.28**

Swedish male raters

Attributes	Most men	Most women	(df)	t
Hardworking	2.04	2.93	(163)	2.28*
Sincere	2.31	3.00	(162)	2.37*
Tries to do one's best	2.37	3.26	(163)	2.84**
Warm	3.04	3.70	(163)	2.40*
Subordinates self to others	3.18	3.64	(158)	2.89**

*p < .05
**p < .01
***p < .001

traits that showed gender differences tend to be ones that are not accorded particularly high importance ratings.

Moreover, comparisons for most girls with those for most women, and for most boys with those for most men for each country showed similar results. These data suggest that adults are usually expected to assume greater responsibility than children, although these differences were less marked in Sweden than in the United States. For example, Swedish females rate most girls as reliably more likely to stand up under pressure than most women and most women as more helpful, dominant, and as loving children more than most girls, for a total of four differentiating attributes. Swedish women rate most boys as better looking than most men, and most men as more helpful, more self-confident, harder working, having more leadership abilities, and as loving children more than most boys, a total of six differences. Swedish males consider most girls as kinder, better looking, and more liberated than most women, but most women as taller, shyer, and more likely to subordinate themselves to others than most girls. They think that most boys are more sincere than most men but that most men are more likely to act as a leader, to have social adeptness, to make decisions more easily, and to love children more than most boys. These results are described more fully in Table 6.7.

American females noted a total of 25 differences between most girls and most women and 14 differences between most boys and most men. American men rated 18 traits as differentiating between most girls and most women and 11 traits as differentiating between most boys and most men. In general, both sexes of American respondents agree that most women are more aware of the feelings of others, are more sincere, and are more capable than most girls; most girls are more likely to have blue eyes, to be emotional, tender, eager to soothe hurt feelings, to love children, to be active, humorous, and shy than most women. Most boys are held to be more fun than most men by both sexes of American respondents—other traits differ by the sex of the respondent. American females think that most men are better looking, more likely to subordinate themselves to others, have stronger personalities, and are more eager to soothe hurt feelings than most boys, whereas the American males rated most men as taller, more patriotic, having higher self-esteem, more capable, compassionate, quiet, and as less likely to give up than most boys. Table 6.8 lists the traits showing differences.

The major theme that runs through the differences in ratings assigned to younger and older age groups in both countries is that the older age groups typically are attributed more of the traits that involve taking responsibilities both for selves and for others. Swedish raters tend to see the younger groups as assuming more of these responsibilities than do the American raters, as Tables 6.1–6.4 show.

We are now in a position to consider the first two predictions: Are there distinct cultural gender concepts for girls, boys, women, and men and, if so,

TABLE 6.7
Mean Importance Ratings Showing Significant Differences Between
Most Girls and Most Women

Swedish female raters

Higher ratings for most women than most girls

Attributes	Most women	Most girls	(df)	t
Helpful	2.14	2.28	(180)	2.04*
Loves children	2.18	2.49	(170)	3.25***
Dominant	4.73	5.07	(153)	2.51*

Higher ratings for most girls than most women

Attributes	Most girls	Most women	(df)	t
Stands up under pressure	2.58	2.75	(170)	2.02*

American female raters

Higher ratings for most women than most girls

Attributes	Most women	Most girls	(df)	t
Aware of feelings of others	2.12	3.96	(162)	3.99***
Stands up under pressure	2.15	3.38	(162)	3.68***
Has self-esteem	2.15	3.54	(162)	2.22*
Aggressive	2.50	3.65	(162)	3.82***
Capable	2.58	3.27	(162)	2.62**
Dominant	2.58	3.85	(162)	2.76*

Swedish male raters

Higher ratings for most women than most girls

Attributes	Most women	Most girls	(df)	t
Helpful	2.23	2.41	(149)	2.43*
Shy	4.62	4.87	(145)	2.05*
Subordinates self to others	4.64	4.86	(131)	2.02*

Higher ratings for most girls than most women

Attributes	Most girls	Most women	(df)	t
Kind/nice	1.97	2.15	(150)	2.15*
Good looking	2.79	3.14	(147)	3.11**
Liberated	3.36	3.56	(129)	2.07*

American male raters

Higher ratings for most women than most girls

Attributes	Most women	Most girls	(df)	t
Capable	1.85	3.77	(162)	5.56***
Kind/nice	2.00	3.15	(163)	3.18***
Aware of feelings of others	2.33	3.26	(163)	2.82**
Sincere	2.33	3.29	(163)	2.68**
Gentle	2.56	3.19	(163)	2.45*
Loyal	2.62	3.88	(162)	2.94**

(Continued)

TABLE 6.7
(Continued)

Swedish female raters

Higher ratings for most women than most girls

Attribute	Most girls	Most women	(df)	t
Sincere	2.92	3.77	(162)	2.90***

Higher ratings for most girls than most women

Attributes	Most girls	Most women	(df)	t
Friendly	1.62	3.31	(162)	3.48**
Loves children	1.72	2.72	(161)	3.02**
Eager to soothe hurt feelings	1.88	3.73	(162)	4.27***
Tries to do one's best	1.92	2.73	(162)	2.36*
Creative	1.92	3.34	(161)	3.31**
Active	2.08	2.69	(162)	2.26*
Tender	2.12	3.77	(162)	3.47**
Self-confident	2.23	3.46	(162)	3.30**
Emotional	2.27	3.41	(158)	2.15*
Humorous	2.28	3.60	(161)	3.83***
Cooperative	2.31	3.62	(162)	2.73**
Shy	2.50	3.54	(162)	3.14***
Assertive	2.68	3.80	(161)	2.71**
Tough-minded	2.81	3.81	(161)	2.39*
Thinks one is a good person	2.85	3.92	(162)	2.64**
Athletic	2.88	4.19	(162)	3.13**
Has blue eyes	3.12	4.23	(161)	2.45*
Willing to take a stand	3.24	5.08	(161)	2.83**

Swedish male raters

Higher ratings for most women than most girls

Attribute	Most girls	Most women	(df)	t
Sincere	2.92	3.38	(162)	2.13*
Compassionate / Devotes self completely to others	3.23	4.42	(162)	3.13*

Higher ratings for most girls than most women

Attributes	Most girls	Most women	(df)	t
Active	2.26	3.15	(163)	2.53*
Cooperative	2.31	4.04	(162)	3.94***
Eager to soothe hurt feelings	2.46	3.69	(162)	2.65***
Loves children	2.48	3.70	(163)	2.66**
Humorous	2.48	3.78	(163)	3.76**
Tender	2.65	3.62	(162)	2.63**
Shy	2.67	3.52	(163)	2.31*
Acts as a leader	2.74	3.37	(163)	2.63**
Emotional	2.80	3.56	(161)	2.10*
Has blue eyes	3.89	4.81	(163)	2.15*

*p < .05
**p < .01
***p < .001

TABLE 6.8
Mean Importance Ratings Showing Significant Differences
Between Most Boys and Most Men

Swedish female raters

Higher ratings for most men than for most boys

Attributes	Most men	Most boys	(df)	t
Helpful	2.13	2.31	(181)	2.49*
Loves children	2.30	2.67	(179)	4.12***
Hardworking	2.69	2.86	(177)	2.25*
Self-confident	2.76	2.93	(174)	2.09*
Has leadership abilities	4.60	4.78	(165)	2.00*

Higher ratings for most boys than for most men

Attributes	Most men	Most boys	(df)	t
Good Looking	3.36	3.61	(176)	2.11*

American female raters

Higher ratings for most men than for most boys

Attributes	Most men	Most boys	(df)	t
Strong personality	2.33	3.33	(160)	2.85**
Eager to soothe hurt feelings	2.88	3.48	(161)	2.22*
Good looking	3.24	4.36	(161)	2.09*

Swedish male raters

Higher ratings for most men than for most boys

Attributes	Most men	Most boys	(df)	t
Makes decision easily	2.73	2.94	(145)	2.43*
Loves children	2.90	3.28	(145)	3.68****
Has social adeptness	3.20	3.47	(134)	2.61**
Acts as a leader	3.77	4.10	(146)	2.96**

Higher ratings for most boys than for most men

Attributes	Most men	Most boys	(df)	t
Sincere	2.28	2.46	(148)	2.15*

American male raters

(Continued)

TABLE 6.8
(Continued)

Swedish female raters

Higher ratings for most men than for most boys

	Most boys	Most men	(df)	t
Subordinates self to others	3.29	3.92	(160)	2.08*

Higher ratings for most boys than for most men

Attributes	Most boys	Most men	(df)	t
Kind/nice	1.72	3.04	(161)	3.50**
Aware of feelings of others	1.81	2.38	(162)	2.51*
Helpful	1.85	3.19	(162)	3.54***
Active	2.31	3.65	(162)	3.24***
Fun	2.35	2.85	(162)	2.24*
Generous	2.65	3.27	(162)	2.17*
Tough-minded	2.77	3.65	(162)	2.94***
Humorous	2.81	3.92	(162)	2.36*
Has straight hair	3.58	4.38	(162)	2.10*
Cannot show one's feelings	3.69	4.38	(162)	2.18*

Swedish male raters

Higher ratings for most men than for most boys

Attributes	Most boys	Most men	(df)	t
Compassionate	2.63	3.26	(163)	2.26*
Quiet	2.81	3.77	(162)	3.43**
Patriotic	2.81	4.00	(162)	3.24***
Tall	3.48	4.89	(163)	2.76**

Higher ratings for most boys than for most men

Attributes	Most boys	Most men	(df)	t
Tries to do one's best	2.15	3.31	(162)	3.11**
Fun	2.42	3.31	(162)	2.27*
Lively	2.81	3.35	(162)	2.21*
Whiny	3.96	4.54	(162)	2.59*

*p < .05
**p < .01
***p < .001

do these concepts differ for the two countries? The general answers are clear: Girls and women are accorded more interpersonal, expressive attributes than instrumental ones. Boys are assigned each type about equally. Men vary, depending on their nationality. Swedish men, like Swedish boys, are seen as having both types of traits in equal numbers, whereas American men are assigned more instrumental ones. Thus, these cultural gender concepts show some distinctive age and national characteristics.

They also evince noteworthy similarities. As previously noted, the absence of a statistically significant difference is no guarantee of cross-gender-concept similarities. Such a view would be tantamount to accepting the null hypothesis. If, however, patterns of the data converge on the notion of cross-gender-concept similarities, then such arguments would gain support. Accordingly, we conducted three additional analyses. First, we tabulated the number of the five top-rated traits each of the four stimulus groups shared with each other stimulus group. The results appear in Table 6.9. Consider the top row. The first entry indicates that four of the five top-rated traits were identical for most Swedish girls and most Swedish boys. The next entry indicates that exactly the same traits were rated as highest for most Swedish girls and most Swedish women, and so on. A quick comparison of the upper panel, which presents data for the Swedish respondents, with the lower panel, which presents the same types of data for the American comparisons, indicates clearly the substantial overlap among the top-rated traits for all four of the Swedish groups and the considerably lesser extent of overlap for the Americans. The one exception was for most American girls and most American women, who shared four of the five top-rated attributes.

Also graphically capturing this twin theme of differences against a background of similarities are correlations between overall Swedish and American ratings. The correlations take into account ratings of all 59 traits, in contrast to only the top five, as was done in the preceding analysis. All are statistically significant, although the respondents from the two countries agreed significantly more

TABLE 6.9
Numbers of Five Top-Rated Attributes Shared by the Four Stimulus Groups

	Most boys	Most women	Most men
Sweden			
Most girls	4	5	4
Most boys		5	4
Most women			4
United States			
Most girls	1	4	1
Most boys		0	1
Most women			2

for most girls (.92) and most women (.93) than for most men (.83) or most boys (.54). (The differences among the correlations were tested by converting them to z scores.)

The national differences are consistent with the view that the Swedish policy of gender equality is affecting Swedish cultural gender concepts. This contention is bolstered by several findings. First, the components of cultural gender concepts for most girls, boys, women, and men are more alike in Sweden than in the United States. Second, and more interesting, the contents of the Swedish gender concepts are compatible with basic tenets of the Swedish philosophy described in detail in chapter 2. Two elements integral to the philosophy are individual independence and commitment to their society. The themes that permeate Swedish gender concepts, trying to do one's best and never giving up seem to contribute to both elements, with the other common theme, being kind/nice appearing to make its contribution more to the second element.

These three attributes also are among important ones to most American girls, boys, and women, but they appear to be less important to the gender concept for American men.

Lest the reader conceive of the Swedish cultural gender concepts as a monolithic one, we hasten to add, that, as is true with most American girls and most American women, most Swedish girls and most Swedish women still are accorded more expressive than instrumental traits, overall. The Swedish experience has not abolished all differences in gender concepts, by any stretch of the imagination. One other notable outcome of this research is the strong indication that the cultural gender concepts are complex, with some features distinctive to each sex and others shared by each sex. This view seems to us to more realistic than most models of gender concepts that argue for nonoverlapping characteristics.

Our next set of predictions deal with developmental trends and their possible cross-national manifestations.

DEVELOPMENTAL TRENDS

Very little is known about the development of gender concepts. Most theories of gender concepts (e.g., Bem, 1981, 1985; Freud, 1933/1965; Kohlberg, 1966; Martin & Halverson, 1981) have assumed that these concepts develop during childhood. Although often mute on this point, the models apparently assume that these concepts remain unchanged during adolescence and adulthood, a perspective that seems contraindicated by the dynamic nature of most concepts and by personal experience. Specifically, our view is that gender concepts change in response to exposure to information relevant to gender in one's culture. As young, relatively inexperienced persons, children's views of the world, including the characteristics that discriminate between the sexes should reflect their growing experience with their worlds. Change is an ongoing process, that continues throughout one's lifetime.

What do our data say about developmental changes? Do the contents of gender concepts change with age? To the best of our knowledge, no evidence has systematically addressed this issue.

Again, it is helpful to have some vision of the general contours of the results to act as a structure for incorporating detailed information. The data yield two themes: Some components of cultural gender concepts represent continuity over ages; others show changes. In general, our 11-year-olds had very favorable views of the two sexes, rating nurturing, supportive traits as very important to both sexes in both countries. Many of these views persisted as the age of the respondent increased, although more varied and flexible attributions tended to increase with age. Let us move to more specific information.

In this section, we follow the same procedure as the last. We examine developmental changes for the gender concepts for each of the four stimulus groups for each country.

Most Girls: Changes with Age of Rater.   The three age groups did not differ in their mean importance ratings for 41 of the 59 attributes; they did differ on 18, and these differences included three of the five top-rated attributes (Table 6.1). The 11-year-old Swedish raters accorded a higher mean importance rating (1.77) than the 18-year-old Swedish raters (2.14) to tries to do one's best, $F(2, 409) = 3.94$. Similarly, 11-year-old Swedes considered being gentle, never giving up, being helpful, being eager to soothe hurt feelings, and the like were more important than the 18-year-olds did, but the opposite effects appeared for being warm, tender, affectionate, and being good looking. Puzzlingly, the 14-year-olds considered being liberated more important than the 18-year-olds did. Perhaps, 18-year-olds Swedes take liberation for granted.

Like the Swedish ratings of most girls, American ratings for the three age groups showed some, but fewer differences. Only 8 of the 59 traits yielded statistically significant changes with age, but most of these changes involved top-rated traits. For example, feels good about self, being kind, and being affectionate decreased with age, $F(2, 410) = 4.53$, $F(2, 425) = 3.67$, and $F(2, 418) = 4.61$, respectively. Self-confidence increased, becoming one of the top-rated traits for the 18-year-olds, $F(2, 415) = 3.43$.

A slightly different way of capturing these results is to emphasize the substantial members of attributes that did not show developmental trends (41 for the Swedish ratings and 51 for the American men). Age similarities were more common than age differences.

Most Boys: Changes with Age of Rater.   The same pattern of highly valuing trying to do one's best, never giving up, being kind/nice, sincere, and gentle appeared for all age groups of Swedish respondents as they rated most boys (Table

6.2). Significant age differences appeared on 19 of the 59 attribute ratings. Of the 19, two were among the five traits rated as most important: Both tries to do one's best and never gives up received higher ratings from 11-year-olds than from 18-year-olds, $F(2, 411) = 6.72$, and $F(2, 411) = 7.74$. American ratings of most boys showed an even smaller number of age differences, 13 of 59. The age changes differed from relatively minor fluctuations in the Swedish ratings, because Americans were likely to attach additional importance to the instrumental traits as they aged. Thus, 18-year-olds attributed reliably higher ratings to tries to do one's best and never gives up than did 11-year-olds, $F(2, 413) = 4.53$ and $F(2, 415) = 5.32$. The results of ratings of most girls and most boys showed significant developmental changes for 14% (American girls) to 32% (Swedish boys) of the attributes. These changes affected about half of the most highly rated components of the gender concepts. The most noteworthy change was the increase in ratings accorded instrumental traits for most boys by American raters. Older American raters were more likely to rate instrumental traits as highly important for most boys than younger raters were, consonant with increasing awareness of the importance of competitive, individualism to males within the United States.

Most Women: Changes with Age of Rater.   The rank ordering of the five traits rated most important for defining most Swedish women showed some changes from the 11- to the 18-year-old raters (Table 6.3). Of the 59 traits, 26 showed reliable changes with age, and, in most cases, the ratings of importance declined with the age of the rater. For the 11-year-olds, the top five traits were kind and never gives up (both with mean ratings of 1.84), gentle (1.85), friendly (1.92), and sincere (1.93). For the 18-year-olds, the top five traits were sincere (2.06), willing to take a stand and kind (both 2.11), gentle (2.14), and never gives up and tries to do one's best (both 2.16). As is obvious from an inspection of these mean ratings, the 18-year-old Swedes were not only identifying some different attributes as among the most important for most Swedish women, but they generally rated these traits as less important than the younger groups indicated for their top-rated traits. These results suggest that 18-year-olds perceive most Swedish women in slightly different ways than 11-year-olds do, but that the components of the gender concepts for most women deemed important by the oldest group are less firmly entrenched, perhaps somewhat less salient, or more modifiable than the components of the youngest children's gender concepts for most women. In other words, flexibility of gender stereotypes appears to increase with age.

Overall, then, the major differences were in the ordering of the traits. As with Swedish girls, these top-rated traits are particularly interesting, because they combine expressive-communal traits, such as being gentle, kind, and friendly, with instrumental-agentic traits, such as never giving up, trying to do one's best, and taking a stand. These tendencies increase with the age of Swedish respondents.

The pattern of 18-year-olds' cultural gender concepts being more flexible than those of younger informants appeared again in the assessments for most American women. The top-rated traits for the 11-year-old Americans' ratings of most women ranged from 1.82 for affectionate to 1.90 for aware of feelings of others and warm (tied for fifth). The other top-rated traits were kind/nice (1.84), friendly, and never give up (both 1.86). Being affectionate was still the premier quality for most women in the eyes of American 18-year-olds, with a mean rating of 1.86. The only other attribute that remained among the top five was warm (1.91). The other top-rated components had become sincere (1.93), feels good about self (2.00), and loyal (2.04). Finally, only 9 of the 59 traits showed reliable developmental trends. Note the trend toward evaluation of the attributes as less important as the age of the correspondent increased.

Most Men: Changes with Age of Rater.   The top-ranked traits varied somewhat with age, primarily because willing to take a stand becomes increasingly important. The mean importance ratings for this item for 11-, 14-, and 18-year-olds were 2.32, 2.14, and 2.11, $F(1, 304) = 3.44$. Tries to do one's best, being kind/nice, and never gives up were in the top-rated group from both 11- and 18-year-olds, with somewhat higher (less important) ratings from the 18-year-olds, as Table 6.4 indicates, whereas being friendly and sincere dropped from the roster of highly important components according to 11-year-olds and being willing to take a stand and being gentle emerged among the 18-year-olds' top-rated traits. As further evidence of the greater flexibility of the importance ratings of the 18-year-olds, their ratings ranged for the top five ranged from 2.10 to 2.25; those of the 11-year-olds ranged from 1.72 to 2.02. There was also a trend for 18-year-olds to attribute more instrumental traits (three of the top five), compared to the 11-year-olds (two of the five were instrumental).

No major shifts in the concepts for American men occurred with age across the three ages of respondents. These concepts, the most stable of those we tested, consisted primarily of instrumental components.

The results of the age analyses support the general predictions that some changes in cultural gender concepts may occur with age and add the finding that the general direction of the trend appears to be toward increasing flexibility as the individual matures. That is, the rater appears to become less dogmatic about which traits are extremely important and tends to assign lower importance ratings even to the attributes considered most important. The age analyses also showed, even more persuasively, that many of the components of cultural gender concepts remain constant over age.

Additionally, the developmental trends were quite similar cross-nationally, although occasional minor differences emerged. The general pattern of similarity of age trends suggests to us that, at least within the two countries of the United States and Sweden, which share many characteristics, the rate of change in gender concepts as the holder matures is quite slow, particularly for American males.

We described gender concepts as dynamic. The data indicate that they are indeed inchingly dynamic, roughly akin to molasses!

The importance ratings lend themselves to a different kind of analysis: factor analysis. We consider factor analyses next.

FACTOR ANALYSES

To identify clusters of traits that were rated as highly important components of the cultural gender concepts, factor analyses were performed on the ratings for each of the stimulus groups. These factor analyses were conducted separately for the sex, age, and nationality of the respondents. The data for the 11-year-olds could not be used, however, because some of these respondents omitted one or more ratings. The factor analysis program eliminated all data from any respondent who omitted even a single rating. (Recall that all subjects were told that they could omit any attribute that they did not understand. The 11-year-olds were more likely to exercise this option than the older subjects.)

Scales such as the BSRI and the EPAQ have been factor analyzed before. Theoretically, these scales should yield two factors, one corresponding to the expressive traits typically associated with females and the other corresponding to the instrumental traits often associated with males. A number of investigators have found more than two factors (e.g., Gaa, Liberman, & Edwards, 1979; Pedhazur & Tetenbaum, 1979), although others have found only two (Helmreich et al., 1981). None of these studies has examined factor analyses on data from different age groups in different countries, however.

Like the majority of other experimenters, we found more than two factors associated with most of the analyses. Using only factors with eigenvalues greater than 4.0, two factors emerged for 14-year-old Swedish females rating most girls and for 14-year-old Swedish males rating most boys. Four or more factors surfaced for 14-year-old Swedish males and 18-year-old Swedish females rating most girls, 14-year-old Swedish females rating most women, and all American ratings, regardless of age. The remainder of the ratings yielded three factors. Clearly, most of the analyses indicated the existence of more than two factors. Moreover, as shown in Appendices III–XIII, these factors typically did not account for most of the variance, suggesting that most cultural gender concepts consist of multiple factors. This outcome affirms our previous analysis of individual attributes.

The factors tended to correspond to expressive-instrumental distinctions, with tries to do one's best and never gives up as a separate factor in a number of the analyses. Physical characteristics also occasionally emerged as a separate factor. The factor loadings and the percentage of the variance associated with each factor are given in Appendices III-XIII.

These analyses strongly support our contention that multiple components contribute to cultural gender concepts.

COMPARISONS OF FREE LISTINGS
AND IMPORTANCE RATINGS

The final prediction was that the various measures would yield converging results. Multiple measures of the gender concepts were taken to approach the assessments of these concepts from different perspectives. The free listings tap at least some components that are readily accessible; the importance ratings more systematically require an evaluation of how important each of 59 traits was to cultural gender concepts. To what extent did the two approaches yield converging results? A clear answer to this question is tantalizingly evasive for some obvious reasons. The free listings were just that—spontaneously generated attributes. Although substantial agreement occurred across subjects in most conditions, these listings also were marked by variability and by numerous idiosyncratic responses. The possibilities of such free-wheeling, diverse responses were eliminated from the importance ratings by virtue of the restriction to 59 specific attributes. One qualitative way to assess the extent of overlap is to simply compare the items that received top billing with both approaches, either by contrasting exact attributes or by examining the proportions of expressive/instrumental traits among the five top-rated items.

These evaluations may be supplemented by the more quantitative one of examining the mean importance ratings given to freely listed attributes, wherever possible. Both of these techniques are employed as we attempt to ascertain the convergence of the two measures.

Most Girls: Comparisons of Free Listings and Importance Ratings.   For most Swedish girls, being kind/nice was a highly salient item in both the free listings and in the importance ratings. Moreover, at a very general level, the admired and spontaneously generated attributes were primarily expressive-communal in nature, as were most of the attribute rates as highly important characteristics of most Swedish girls.

At a more specific level, less overlap occurred. Only one attribute emerged near the top of both the free listings and the important ratings: kind/nice. The mean importance rating across all Swedish respondents, 1.93, indicated that these subjects considered kind/nice to be a very important characteristic of most girls. The mean importance rating for the other spontaneously listed traits (assertive, whiny, shy, helpful, good looking, and feels insecure; see Table 6.1) was considerably lower, 4.01, a value that was defined as neither important nor unimportant. These results suggest that some traits that were spontaneously offered as characteristics of most girls were not judged to be particularly important attributes, a pattern that will recur throughout our data.

Similar results appeared for most American girls: Kind/nice was prominent in both approaches, as were generally expressive attributes. At a more detailed level, the one attribute that was rated as both highly important and that was often spontaneously mentioned, kind/nice, had a mean importance rating of 2.20, or "very important," and the mean importance rating for other traits common to both Tables 5.2 (see previous chapter) and 6.1 (shy, athletic, whiny, helpful, active/lively, emotional, and good looking) was 3.66, tending toward "neither important nor unimportant." These curious findings suggest that spontaneously generated items are not necessarily those that are rated as highly important. In other words, the fact that an attribute springs to mind during a retrieval search for characteristics of most girls does not itself imply that the same respondents will necessarily consider that attribute as an important, distinguishing hallmark of the gender concept. This summary may be premature, of course, because, so far, we have examined only the Swedish and American gender concepts for most girls.

Most Boys: Comparisons of Free Listings and Importance Ratings. Comparisons of the freely listed traits and the importance ratings given by Swedish respondents are easy to make, because all of the frequently listed traits of Table 6.2 were rated for importance. The mean importance rating for the five most freely listed attributes of Swedish boys is 4.12, indicating that the spontaneously generated attributes are *not* rated as very important characteristics. More important are two traits not spontaneously mentioned, tries to do one's best and never gives up. Obviously, the fact that some characteristics spring to mind when asked to describe most boys does not necessarily mean that those characteristics are considered important features of boyness. At a general level, both the free listings of traits and the importance ratings showed that instrumental-agentic and expressive-communal traits are associated with boys.

How do American importance ratings compare with the free listings of gender-relevant traits? The mean rating for the freely listed attributes was 2.86, or "important," suggesting substantial overlap. Additionally, the mean ratings on expressive and instrumental attributes did not differ. It is informative to note, however, that there were major differences that highlight the desirability of using multiple measures. Two attributes that received generally high importance ratings for each group, tries to do one's best and never gives up, were *never* mentioned in the free listings.

Most Women: Comparisons of Free Listings and Importance Ratings. Again, kind/nice figured prominently in both measures. It had an overall importance rating of 1.99. Being helpful was both spontaneously generated and considered highly important (2.13) by 11-year-old Swedes; whereas devoting self to others, being ambitious/hardworking, and being liberated were spontaneously generated by the 18-year-old Swedes. The mean importance ratings for these terms was 3.47, a moderate importance level.

The most commonly generated items for most American women were sensitive, compassionate/caring and loving children. Compassionate/caring (2.13) and loving children (2.08) also were highly rated, but sensitive was not rated for importance. Other often generated attributes, whiny in particular, were rated much lower in importance (5.52).

Most Men: Comparisons of Free Listings and Importance Ratings. At a general level, both the freely listed traits and the importance ratings indicated that both instrumental and expressive traits were considered salient for most Swedish men. Of the freely listed traits, kind/nice was rated as highly important ($M = 2.05$), but the other freely listed attributes (strong, acts as a leader, competitive, cannot show feelings, and dominant) had lower mean ratings (3.72, 4.34, 4.29, 4.81, and 4.55, respectively).

The specific traits rated as highly important for most American men typically were not among those most often given as spontaneous descriptions of most men, although at a more abstract level one could argue that most of the acknowledged attributes were instrumental, with a few expressive ones.

How do we interpret these results? Do the cultural gender concepts estimated by freely generated items and by importance ratings agree or disagree? Do they or do they not converge? Both. The results converge for some traits for all four stimulus groups, and they diverge or do not overlap for other traits. This is not really as confusing as it sounds, for a clear pattern emerges. A few attributes, most notably kind/nice, are both frequently generated and rated as highly important. Many other frequently listed attributes are accorded only intermediate levels of importance, and some freely listed attributes were not among the 59 items rated for importance. The data appear to be telling us that the spontaneous generation of an item does not guarantee that it is considered an effective gender differentiator. Indeed, some attributes, such as height, which may function as predictive cues of whether individuals are female or male (see Intons-Peterson, in press), are rated relatively low in importance to the gender concept.

Gender concepts may consist of attributes shared with other gender concepts plus some other that are unique to the specific concepts. Kind/nice is a case in point. This attribute tends to contribute to the gender concepts of most girls, most boys, and most women in both Sweden and the United States. It does not, however, distinguish among the concepts. Other terms, including aggressiveness, may be more differentiating, but they are not rated as high in importance as the shared attributes.

It should be apparent that neither the free listings nor the importance ratings is an ideal indicator of the components of cultural gender concepts. Both measure yield somewhat different, but complementary pictures, and both add to the wealth of information about the gender concepts.

The ratings of importance are extremely rich, and only some of their secrets have been delivered. Nonetheless, this is a good time to compare the results of our importance ratings with those from other gender-role inventories.

COMPARISONS WITH OTHER SEX-
OR GENDER-ROLE INVENTORIES

More specifically, we ask whether the personality traits taken from various sex- and gender-role inventories continue to show gender differences in our American data and whether or not the same traits show gender differences in Sweden. Table 6.10 lists the items taken from two commonly used measures of gender differences, the Bem Sex Role Inventory (Bem, 1974; the BSRI), and the Extended Personal Attributes Questionnaire (Spence et al., 1979; the EPAQ), and the adjectives found by Williams and Best (1977) to be associated with males or females by at least 75% of their American subjects of both sexes. Columns 1–4 list the gender more likely to be associated with each attribute. For example, for the first trait, acts as a leader, Swedish respondents rate most boys (B) as significantly higher than most girls (G) and most men (M) as significantly higher than most women, (W). American respondents do not differentially attribute acts as a leader to most boys versus most girls or to most men versus most women.

Generally, the directions of the differences corroborate previous research using the three scales, although not all of the differences are statistically significant. Some attributes do not show the differences formerly noted. For example, makes decisions easily, assertive, self-confident, stands up under pressure, and strong personality are not associated reliably more often with males than with females nor are gentle, compassionate, loyal, aware of feelings of others, or devotes self completely to others associated more often with females than with males.

Three traits showed crossover effects. Strong personality, classified as a "masculine" trait on the BSRI, is attributed reliably more often to most girls than to most boys by American respondents, just as loyalty, a "feminine" trait on the BSRI, is attributed more often to most men than to most women. In addition, American respondents assign eager to soothe hurt feelings, a "feminine" trait on the BSRI, more often to most men than to most women, but they assign eager to soothe hurt feelings more often to most girls than to most boys, the expected ordering. Swedish respondents show the expected ordering for this adjective in both the most girls–most boys and most women–most men comparisons.

In general, all three of the scales receive partial support. Some, but by no means all, of the attributes used in these measures produce significant sex differences. The failures to find sex differences for some of the attributes may reflect changes in attitudes or concepts, with recognition of gender similarities increasing recently. Or they may result from insensitive measurements, or combinations of these factors. Because there is ample evidence of the sensitivity of the measures, the former alternative seems more plausible. Taken overall, our results suggest the desirability of checking the standardization of the BSRI, the EPAQ, and the Williams–Best adjective checklist.

SUMMARY

The importance ratings of most girls, most boys, most women, and most men

TABLE 6.10
Items from the Bem Sex Role Inventory (BSRI), the Extended Personality Attributes
Questionnaire (EPAQ), and the Adjective Check List
that Showed Reliable Gender Differences

BSRI	Most girls v. most boys		Most women v. most men		Self females v. males		Ideal females v. males	
	Sw. 1	Am. 2	Sw. 3	Am. 4	Sw. 5	Am. 6	Sw. 7	Am. 8
Masculine scale								
Acts as a leader	B		M		M		M	
Competitive	B		M		M		M	
Has leadership abilities	B		M				M	
Aggressive	B	B	M					
Dominant	B	B	M		M		M	
Willing to take a stand				M				
Strong personality		G					F	
Athletic	B			M	M		M	
Makes decisions easily					M			
Assertive					M		M	
Feminine scale								
Gentle							F	
Compassionate								
Tender	G	G	W	W			F	
Affectionate	G	G	W	W			F	
Warm	G	G	W	W			F	
Eager to soothe hurt feelings	G	G	W	M	F		F	
Loves children		G	W		F		F	
Loyal				M			M	
Shy		G			F			
Social desirability scale								
Helpful				W				
Sincere								
Likable	G	G	W	W				
Friendly		G						

EPAQ	Most girls v. most boys		Most women v. most men		Self females v. males		Ideal females v. males	
	Sw.	Am.	Sw.	Am.	Sw.	Am.	Sw.	Am.
M+ scale								
Self-confident					M			
Stands up under pressure					M			

(*Continued*)

TABLE 6.10
(Continued)

	Most girls v. most boys		Most women v. most men		Self females v. males		Ideal females v. males	
	Sw.	Am.	Sw.	Am.	Sw.	Am.	Sw.	Am.
Makes decisions easily					M			
Never gives up				M				
Active			M					
Competitive	B		M				M	
F+ scale								
Gentle							F	
Kind	G	B		W				
Aware of feelings of others					F		F	
Emotional		G	W		F			
F+ scale								
Warm	G	G	W	W			F	
Devotes self completely to others					F			
M-F								
Aggressive	B	B	M					
Dominant	B	B	M		M		M	
F$_{C-}$								
Subordinates self to others			M	W			M	
F$_{VA-}$								
Whiny				W				

Adjectives Associated with Men or Women by at least Three Quarters
of American Subjects of Both Sexes (William & Best, 1975)

Adjectives associated with men								
Aggressive	B	B	M					
Assertive					M		M	
Dominant	B	B	M		M		M	
Strong	B	B	M	M	M			
Adjectives associated with women								
Affectionate	G	G	W	W			F	
Emotional		G	W		F			
Gentle							F	
Whiny				W				

yield systematic answers to the six original questions. First, clusters of attributes were assigned to each of the four groups, as predicted for cultural gender concepts by our model. Respondents from both countries indicate that most girls are kind/nice and friendly and that most boys are kind/nice, try to do their best, and never give up, reflecting some cross-national similarities in gender concepts. Their assignments to most women and most men were more diverse, with Swedish raters attributing more instrumental traits to most women and more expressive traits to most men than the American raters did. Thus, in answer to our second hypothesis, some cross-national differences appeared in the cultural gender concepts. The ratings for Swedish adults were less gender-typed than those for most American adults, as might be expected from the Swedish experience over the last two decades. These findings are consistent with our contention that cross-national differences in gender concepts are predictable from sociocultural and governmental practices. Also interesting was the finding that physical attributes were rated as unimportant gender markers, although they did occasionally differentiate between the sexes.

Perhaps the most striking result is that cross-nationally similar attributes were rated as highly important for each of the four stimulus groups. These results imply that such characteristics as being kind/nice, trying to do one's best, and never giving up are considered to be very important characteristics of all people in both countries, even though the subjects were rating people classified by sex and age. These components appear to be so prominent in the cultural gender concepts for each of the four groups that they are rated as highly important despite their consequent inability to differentiate among the groups.

Third, components of the gender concepts are highly similar for the three age groups. One major effect attributable to increasing age was a tendency for the 18-year-olds to assign lower importance ratings than the younger subjects did and, in some case, the 18-year-olds rated instrumental, agentic traits higher than the younger children did. For the younger children, expressive-communal traits were more likely to be rated important than the instrumental-agentic ones. This pattern suggests that expressive-communal traits are quite salient at young ages, but that the instrumental-agentic ones assume increasing importance with age so that by late adolescence these latter traits are weighted more heavily than the former ones. The other major effect was that Swedish 18-year-olds rated the attributes as generally lower in importance than the Swedish 11- and 14-year-olds did, whereas Americans did not show parallel trends. This outcome, which answers in the affirmative our fourth question about whether developmental trends would show cross-national differences, suggests the intriguing and thought-provoking notion that the concepts of gender equality require years for their development, at least when youngsters' cultural gender concepts contain some different components for females and males. But why should Swedish youngsters have such gender concepts when their nation's espousal of gender equality antedated their births? The most reasonable answer, buttressed by the evidence cited in chapter 2, is that they have been exposed to vestiges of gender inequality, perhaps expressed via parental opinions, experiences with the media, with others, and so on. These observations carry a rather gloomy, although not unexpected message that old attitudes and practices are notoriously different to excise, to eradicate, a pessimistic pronouncement traditionally maintained by social psychologists.

Fifth, the two sexes of respondents show substantial agreement about cultural gender concepts. The important ratings given by males and females of the same age and nationality correlate at a minimum of .97, signaling impressively high agreement. Obviously, both sexes within a culture are aware of the characteristics expected of each sex by the culture. Hence, any adequate model of gender concepts must incorporate the notion that both sexes develop culturally shaped concepts for each of the sexes.

Sixth, the two measures of culture gender concepts considered so far, free listings of attributes and ratings of the importance of attributes do not always coincide. A few attributes were frequently listed and highly rated, such as being kind/nice, trying to do one's best, and never giving up. These persistently valued attributes were so widely acclaimed, regardless of the measure, that they must be considered as essential components of the gender concepts of both Swedes and Americans for all of the stimulus groups. This importance to gender concepts of young and adult females and males was unexpected, and we consider the theoretical implications in greater depth in chapter 10. Suffice it to say that these highly prized attributes appear to function as a core set, as components that are integral to the gender concepts of both females and males although they do not differentiate between gender concepts for the two sexes. Other, seemingly less valued, less highly rated attributes function as gender differentiators. These latter components are the ones whose free listings and importance ratings are less likely to coincide.

Finally, our results parallel standard findings from American inventories of gender concepts in the sense that, in comparison to men, women tend to be assigned more expressive and fewer instrumental traits. Our results challenge previous findings in two ways, however. First, two traits recommended by Swedish informants, trying to do one's best and never gives up, are not typical entries in American gender-role inventories and yet these items were rated as highly important by both nationalities of respondents. These results suggest that extant American inventories may be too limited in their coverage (see also Deaux, 1984; Spence, 1985). Second, the attributes that are included may distinguish between the sexes, as intended, but may not be considered very important to gender concepts, themselves.

Our next topic is the personal or self-gender concept.

7

Personal Gender Concepts: Ratings of Current and Ideal Self

According to our model, people develop a concept of self that contains gender-related information. This concept will overlap with the person's cultural gender concepts for both genders only to the extent that the person believes herself or himself to share gender traits with culturally defined gender concepts. Hence, our model predicts that personal or self-concepts will not always duplicate cultural ones, a view that is at odds with gender schema models proposed by Bem (1981, 1985) and Markus (Crane & Markus, 1982; Markus et al., 1982). These theorists do not distinguish between cultural and personal gender concepts. At least two research projects conducted in the United States support the distinction: Spence et al. (1975) and Intons-Peterson (in press) found differences in the ratings of personality traits ascribed to most women/men and to self, but, until now, no cross-cultural verification has been attempted.

Swedes presumably also develop both cultural and personal gender concepts; if not, our model would have little generality. To explore this prediction, we consider how important our respondents thought the 59 traits were to themselves. Then, to probe further among Swedes, because they had not been tested before, we asked some of the respondents to rate their ideal selves.

Personal gender concepts should show the same effects as cultural gender concepts. That is, we expect the contents of personal gender concepts to differ for girls, boys, women, and men, as cited in Predictions 1 and 3. For our data, these classifications correspond to the self-ratings of 11-year-old girls and boys and to the self-ratings of 18-year-old women and men. The data from the 14-year-olds should constitute intermediate transitions. According to Prediction 2, Swedish and American respondents should characterize themselves somewhat differently, probably in ways that correspond to the national variations noted in chapter 2. Prediction 4 states that these national differences will interact with age, unless developmental trends are similar in the two countries. Prediction 5 holds that females and males should agree about the components of *cultural* gender concepts, and, hence, is not applicable to personal gender concepts, but Prediction 7 posits convergence of the measures. This prediction must be modified to conform to our general expectation that personal gender concepts will not mimic cultural gender concepts in all respects. Indeed, this notion is so central to our model that we include it in our initial treatment of the self ratings.

Thus, we examine the self-ratings as functions of the age, sex, and nationality of the raters, comparing these ratings with those given by the same people when they rated the appropriate stimulus group. For example, we compare the self-ratings of boys with their ratings for most boys of the same country.

PERSONAL GENDER CONCEPTS:
RATINGS OF CURRENT SELF

Table 7.1 presents the mean importance ratings Swedish female and male 11-, 14-, and 18-year-olds assigned to themselves as they currently are. The table also contains American data.

The order of presentation of chapter 7 differs from that of chapter 6. The initial comparisons are made by age for each sex and each country. For example, instead of comparing Swedish and American girls in the initial analysis, Swedish girls are compared with Swedish women. Subsequently, Swedish and American girls are compared. This modification seemed to be more effective in illustrating the developmental changes.

Swedish Girls and Women: Personal Gender Concepts. How do Swedish females describe themselves? They identify loving children (1.74), trying to do their best (1.82), never giving up (1.89), being eager to soothe hurt feelings (2.30), and being kind/nice (2.33) as their five top-valued traits. Except for trying to do one's best (1.78) and loving children (1.72), these traits were not as highly esteemed by Swedish women (the 18-year-olds). They gave their highest ratings to being willing to take a stand (1.87), being emotional (2.01), gentle (2.06), and sincere (2.09). Tries to do one's best and being friendly tied for the fifth spot (2.10). These ratings are very interesting, for they tell us that only one attribute remained of paramount importance across the self-concepts of Swedish girls and women. For the most part, the principal components of Swedish women's personal gender concepts differed from those of Swedish girls, suggesting important developmental changes. Thus, these results support the prediction that personal gender concepts will differ somewhat for different age groups. The data are also interesting in highlighting the favorable role accorded emotionality by Swedish women.

TABLE 7.1

Mean Importance Ratings for Self

Country	Sweden						U.S.A.					
Sex of respondent	Female			Male			Female			Male		
Age Group	11	14	18	11	14	18	11	14	18	11	14	18
Attributes rated												
Tries to do one's best	1.82	1.80	2.10	1.58	1.84	2.17[b]	1.78	1.82	1.80	1.76	1.70	1.73
Never gives up	1.89	2.05	2.28	1.77	1.94	2.05[b]	1.96	1.98	2.00	1.89	2.65	2.82[b]
Willing to take a stand	2.50	2.14	1.87	2.21	2.19	2.18	2.75	2.71	2.73	2.52	2.70	2.64[a]
Friendly	2.45	2.19	2.10	2.12	2.37	2.33	1.80	2.12	2.10	1.42	1.48	1.45[d,e]
Kind/nice	2.33	2.38	2.13	2.21	2.18	2.31[c]	1.98	1.96	2.00	2.20	2.16	2.18
Loves children	1.74	2.12	2.36	2.15	3.08	2.54[a,b,c]	1.72	2.24	2.30	2.08	2.33	2.00
Sincere	2.52	2.49	2.09	2.28	2.29	2.44[c]	2.29	2.25	2.27	1.95	1.87	1.91[a]
Gentle	2.46	2.49	2.06	2.34	2.49	2.38	2.31	2.45	2.55	2.46	2.56	2.36
Cooperative	2.36	2.44	2.52	2.41	2.38	2.55	1.83	2.25	2.73	2.68	2.01	2.27
Active	2.52	2.67	2.53	2.09	2.41	2.48	2.38	2.41	2.40	2.37	2.42	2.36
Helpful	2.53	2.71	2.36	2.25	2.51	2.62	1.69	2.14	2.36	1.80	2.12	2.36
Stands up under pressure	2.48	2.84	2.65	2.33	2.41	2.27[a]	2.54	2.56	2.91	2.23	2.29	2.27[a]
Loyal	3.35	2.57	2.44	2.82	2.41	2.38[b]	2.36	2.44	2.40	2.59	2.31	2.18
Hardworking	2.57	2.57	2.94	2.34	2.38	2.84[b]	1.92	1.88	1.90	2.20	2.01	1.91[d,e]
Emotional	3.02	2.47	2.01	2.71	2.68	2.72[a,c]	3.33	3.29	2.91	2.78	2.83	2.82[a]
Eager to soothe hurt feelings	2.30	2.38	2.51	2.72	3.08	3.24[a]	2.24	2.30	2.60	2.80	2.78	2.27[a,d,e]
Strong personality	2.82	2.79	2.70	2.41	2.51	2.83	2.38	2.43	2.36	2.34	2.35	2.45
Humorous	2.87	2.90	2.53	2.47	2.66	3.03[c]	2.38	2.41	2.70	2.68	2.39	2.45
Capable	2.82	3.00	3.20	2.27	2.55	2.79[a,b]	2.25	2.38	2.45	2.09	2.13	2.18[a,b]
Patriotic	3.00	2.88	2.70	2.60	2.76	2.74	2.68	2.71	2.73	2.59	2.92	2.82
Self-confident	2.56	3.16	3.39	2.27	2.53	2.85[a,b]	2.22	2.26	2.18	1.75	1.71	1.73[a,d]

(Continued)

121

TABLE 7.1
(Continued)

| Country | Sweden | | | | | | U.S.A. | | | | | |
| Sex of respondent | Female | | | Male | | | Female | | | Male | | |
Age Group	11	14	18	11	14	18	11	14	18	11	14	18
Compassionate	2.84	2.67	2.65	2.93	2.88	3.06	2.68	2.52	2.27	2.53	2.58	2.18[d]
Thinks one is a good person	2.74	3.03	3.08	2.51	2.66	2.73[a]	2.76	2.53	2.45	2.02	2.07	2.00[a,d]
Has self-esteem	2.60	3.23	3.00	2.31	2.57	3.07[b]	2.68	2.75	2.73	2.23	2.18	2.09[a]
Has social adeptness	3.20	2.94	2.97	2.92	2.44	2.77[a]	2.78	2.54	2.60	2.38	2.35	2.36[a]
Generous	3.23	2.80	2.69	2.76	2.78	3.02	2.18	2.48	2.55	2.39	2.62	2.09
Aware of feelings of others	2.81	2.68	2.19	3.49	3.25	2.95[a,b]	2.49	2.45	2.27	2.88	2.92	2.27[a]
Fun	3.21	3.03	2.91	2.49	2.57	3.34[a,c]	2.68	2.55	2.40	2.22	2.31	2.18[d]
Warm	3.19	2.79	2.44	3.14	2.82	3.03[b,c]	2.58	2.43	2.27	2.69	2.73	2.09[d]
Liberated	2.78	2.93	3.17	2.82	2.71	3.02	2.79	2.95	3.73	2.86	2.81	3.30
Affectionate	3.34	2.95	2.69	3.03	2.90	2.95[b]	2.30	2.33	2.27	2.32	2.48	2.00[d]
Tender	3.35	2.92	2.43	3.33	2.99	2.88[b]	3.34	2.91	2.45	3.31	2.85	2.45
Makes decisions easily	3.19	3.33	3.28	2.93	2.45	2.93[a]	3.20	3.10	3.00	2.88	2.76	3.18[a]
Likable	3.37	3.36	2.93	2.97	2.96	3.18	3.10	2.82	2.18	2.97	2.95	2.27[d]
Strong	3.58	3.54	3.44	2.66	2.74	3.21[a]	3.38	3.36	2.91	2.88	2.92	3.18[a]
Feels good about oneself	3.16	3.46	3.62	3.03	2.95	3.16[a]	2.32	2.41	2.10	1.60	1.68	1.64[a,d]
Competitive	3.37	3.59	4.28	2.27	3.15	2.82[a,c]	3.67	2.89	2.09	2.66	2.60	2.64[a,d,e]
Creative	3.88	3.39	3.37	3.32	3.22	2.88	3.67	3.22	3.09	3.58	3.52	2.73
Lively	3.42	2.94	3.32	3.13	3.30	3.69	2.59	2.85	2.90	2.65	2.60	2.55[d]
Good looking	3.57	3.88	3.68	3.29	3.26	3.05[a]	3.87	3.58	3.64	3.27	3.31	3.80[a]
Has blue eyes	3.28	3.84	3.89	3.42	3.28	3.36	4.68	4.70	4.82	4.71	4.50	5.45[d]

TABLE 7.1
(Continued)

	Sweden						U.S.A.					
	Female			Male			Female			Male		
Age Group	11	14	18	11	14	18	11	14	18	11	14	18
Artistic	3.11	3.65	4.05	3.72	3.70	3.60[c]	4.13	3.33	4.82	3.68	3.68	3.64
Assertive	3.35	2.92	2.43	3.33	2.99	2.88[b]	2.90	2.85	2.82	2.83	2.80	2.82[d]
Tough-minded	3.98	3.99	3.88	3.49	3.27	3.74[a]	3.96	3.82	2.73	2.88	2.91	3.27[a]
Tall	3.85	4.00	4.21	3.92	3.83	2.79[a]	3.83	4.18	4.36	2.10	2.17	4.82[a,d,e]
Has straight hair	3.63	4.08	4.30	3.55	3.69	3.87	4.86	4.92	5.00	4.72	4.81	5.45[d]
Popular	4.43	3.90	3.60	3.95	3.61	3.29[a,b]	3.31	3.78	3.09	3.34	3.15	3.82
Athletic	3.76	4.36	4.61	3.81	3.38	3.54[a]	3.69	3.50	3.00	3.30	3.27	3.27[a]
Has leadership abilities	4.43	3.99	4.22	4.17	3.39	3.13[c]	3.41	2.88	2.36	2.70	2.85	2.73[d]
Acts as a leader	4.86	4.24	4.46	4.30	3.99	3.48[a,b]	4.88	4.53	2.73	3.02	3.22	2.91[a,d]
Aggressive	4.80	4.33	4.29	3.95	3.88	4.72	1.05	1.01	1.03	1.18	1.26	1.22[d]
Dominant	5.06	4.49	4.72	4.02	3.97	4.07[a]	5.08	4.97	3.27	3.58	3.62	4.00[a,e]
Cannot show one's feelings	4.67	4.63	5.19	4.62	4.35	4.22[a]	5.23	5.01	4.30	4.10	4.08	5.22[a,e]
Quiet	4.57	4.56	4.61	4.69	4.78	4.52[c]	3.91	4.23	4.50	5.32	5.01	4.91
Devotes self completely to others	4.38	4.23	4.80	4.52	4.68	5.26[a,c]	4.01	4.15	4.40	4.38	4.54	4.00[a]
Subordinates self to others	4.42	4.67	5.12	4.40	4.42	4.79[b]	4.13	4.11	4.11	4.19	4.02	4.22
Shy	5.01	3.97	4.20	5.17	4.88	4.66[a,b]	4.21	4.33	4.40	4.22	4.59	4.73[a,b]
Feels insecure	5.28	4.94	4.61	5.49	5.16	5.20	5.31	5.33	5.00	4.67	4.81	4.91[a]
Whiny	4.94	4.97	5.36	5.28	4.87	5.74[b]	5.89	6.01	6.10	5.34	5.96	5.91[a,d]

[a]Significant sex difference
[b]Significant age group difference
[c]Significant sex x age interaction
[d]Significant nationality difference
[e]Significant sex x nationality difference

123

Nonetheless, some general correspondences also appeared. Self-ratings for the Swedish 11- and 18-year-old women were highly correlated (.84). In addition, Swedish girls and women both highly endorsed instrumental and expressive traits, and the comparisons of the mean ratings of these two types of traits did not yield significant differences (see Table 7.2).

American Girls and Women: Personal Gender Concepts. American 11-year-old girls saw themselves as aggressive (1.05), helpful (1.69), loving children (1.72), trying to do their best (1.78), and friendly (1.80), a peculiar combination. Contradictory as this combination seems, it also appears to capture some of the diverse elements that contribute to a stereotypic American persona.

American 18-year-old women rated themselves as being aggressive (1.08) and as trying to do their best (1.80), in concert with American girls, but they added being hardworking (1.90), never giving up (2.00), and being kind/nice (2.00) as the remainder of their five top-rated attributes. Like Swedish females, Americans show developmental changes in some principal components of their self-gender concepts, although also like their Swedish counterparts, American women's ratings of all the attributes correlated highly, .83, with those of American girls.

Swedish Boys and Men: Personal Gender Concepts. Swedish 11-year-old boys rate themselves as trying to do their best (1.58), never giving up (1.77), and as loving children (2.15), three of the attributes cited by Swedish girls as their most important characteristics, suggesting that personal gender concepts of Swedish boys and men are quite similar. Swedish boys also included being active (2.09) and being friendly (2.12) among their six top attributes, whereas Swedish men also included stands up under pressure (2.27) in their top-rated traits.

In contrast to girls and women in both countries, Swedish boys and men describe similar personal gender concepts. What is the significance of these trends? Are females' personal concepts more flexible and susceptible to changes? Are males, regardless of age, treated more similarly and consistently than females, so that their early personal gender concepts are not subjected to disconfirming, change-encouraging evidence as they mature? We return to these possibilities after considering the data from American men.

Before considering American males' ratings as part of our investigation of developmental changes in personal gender concepts, we need to examine more closely the evidence for gender differences among the self-ratings. For example, do these ratings differ among Swedish females and males?

As might be expected from the preceding analyses, the answer is affirmative for young Swedes but not for older men. Swedish girls and boys rate trying to do one's best, never giving up, and as loving children among their five top-rated attributes. To further probe the similarity of the personal gender concepts of

TABLE 7.2
Mean Ratings of Expressive and Instrumental Attributes for Cultural, Personal,
and Ideal Ratings by Swedish Respondents

| Cultural gender concepts | Mean for | | | | | | | | |
| | Female | | | | Male | | | | |
	11	14	18	Av.	11	14	18	Av.	Overall
Swedish girls									
Expressive	6.88	4.01	3.93	5.00	6.27	3.56	3.71	4.67	4.86
Instrumental	6.81	4.21	4.07	5.09	6.20	3.72	4.11	4.81	4.96
		$t(332) = 3.27***$				$t(270) = 4.26***$			
Swedish boys									
Expressive	6.86	3.91	3.84	4.93	6.25	3.75	4.19	4.86	4.90
Instrumental	6.83	4.04	3.92	4.99	6.11	3.71	4.17	4.79	4.90
		$t(332) = 2.23*$				$t(270) = 2.03*$			
Swedish women									
Expressive	6.55	4.09	4.34	5.04	6.86	3.76	3.93	5.03	5.04
Instrumental	6.57	4.29	4.53	5.17	6.78	3.96	4.35	5.19	5.18
		$t(332) = 5.32***$				$t(270) = 4.82***$			
Swedish men									
Expressive	6.64	4.11	4.31	5.07	6.84	3.70	4.09	5.05	5.06
Instrumental	6.66	4.23	4.41	5.15	6.75	3.62	4.06	4.99	5.07
		$t(332) = 2.79**$				$t(270) = 1.99*$			
Personal Gender Concepts (Swedish)									
Expressive	4.91	4.78	4.80	4.83	4.68	4.10	4.75	4.52	4.69
Instrumental	4.68	4.73	5.00	4.79	4.13	3.76	4.56	4.14	4.50
		$t(332) = 1.15$ NS				$t(270) = 10.59***$			
Ideal Gender Concepts (Swedish)									
Expressive	5.94	5.08	5.45	5.49	5.12	4.55	5.52	5.05	5.30
Instrumental	5.80	5.07	5.57	5.47	4.74	4.35	5.50	4.84	5.19
		$t(332) = .63$ NS				$t(270) = 6.15***$			

$*p < .05$
$**p < .01$
$***p < .001$

young Swedes, we correlated the girls' and boys' ratings across all 59 traits. The correlation of .92 was higher than that between the ratings of Swedish girls and women. Additionally corroborating the similarity of the personal concepts of Swedish girls and boys were the nonsignificant differences between the ratings of expressive and instrumental traits the boys assigned to themselves. Our young Swedes showed the first negative result: Personal gender concepts of Swedish girls and boys do *not* show the expected divergences, they overlap instead.

Moreover, Swedish men share self-perceptions with Swedish girls for three at-tributes (tries to do one's best, never gives up, and kind/nice), and they share two with Swedish women (tries to do one's best, willing to take a stand). In-terestingly, the greatest discrepancy among the highest-rated components of per-sonal gender concepts was between Swedish girls and women. This difference apparently stems from Swedish women's greater incorporation of gentleness and emotionality in their self-ratings and from their tendency to assign lower ratings than the other Swedish groups to never gives up and kind/nice.

Further documenting the substantial overlap in the personal gender concepts of Swedish girls, boys, women, and men were the reliable correlations between Swedish men's self-ratings on the 59 attributes and those of Swedish girls (.83), Swedish women (.73), and Swedish boys (.87).

Not only do the results signal extensive overlap among the personal gender concepts of our Swedish respondents, but the nature of the concepts is consis-tent with Sweden's commitment to both gender equality and to pacifism.

We return now to the question of developmental trends among American males. Recall that some changes appeared among the top-rated self-descriptions for Swedish and American girls and women but rarely for Swedish boys and men. Are personal gender concepts of American males also less likely to change than those of American females?

American Boys and Men: Personal Gender Concepts. Like American girls and women, American boys and men identified being aggressive (1.22) as their most important attribute! American boys are rated being friendly (1.42), feels good about self (1.60), self-confident (1.75), and doing one's best (1.76) in their top-rated attributes. American men described themselves as being aggressive (1.22), friendly (1.45), feeling good about themselves (1.64), self-confident (1.73), and as trying to do their best (1.73). This ordering overlapped completely with that of American boys, and, indeed, a correlation of all 59 traits yielded the high figure of .88. Obviously, American boys and American men have very similar self-concepts, suggesting minimal developmental changes in personal gender con-cepts. With the exception of being friendly, the constellation approaches the image of independent individualism to a greater extent than did the cultural gender concepts. Obviously, these respondents did not show the same levels of pacifism that the Swedish raters did. Also contrasting with previous results was the statistically reliable difference between American boys' mean ratings on instrumental (4.13) and expressive (4.68) traits, $t(90) = 4.57$.

At this point, we can support for the developmental prediction and its in-teraction with cross-nationalism. The data afforded partial support for the developmental prediction in that the highest rated components of personal gender concepts changed for females in both countries. Contrariwise, however, the highest rated components of males' personal gender concepts did not show ma-jor developmental shifts in either country. Hence, the predicted interaction emerged, but its specific form was not predicted in advance.

How shall we decipher this puzzle? As previously noted, one possibility is that females' personal gender concepts are more flexible and are more susceptible to change. Another possibility is that the experiences of young males induce the development of personal gender concepts that continue to be fostered as the boy matures. These two possibilities are not mutually exclusive, of course, and we propose that both processes occur, at least in the two countries under question. Specifically, in each country, certain attributes are encouraged and become adopted by many people. Examples are trying to do one's best and never giving up in Sweden and being aggressive in the United States. Other attributes receive more selective attention with age as the experiences of each sex encourage modification of gender concepts.Typical experiences of boys overlap in part with those of men (consider athletic participation, athletic observation, athletic metaphors, for instance). These experiences serve to selectively advance attributes for boys that are similar to those bolstered by male activities. Girls' activities are often considered more diverse, largely because boys tend to be discouraged from playing games usually associated with the other sex to a greater extent than girls are (Fagot, 1978; Jacklin, DiPietro, & Maccoby, 1984; Langlois & Downs, 1980; Price-Bonham & Skeen, 1982).

The fact that minimal developmental changes occurred for males in both countries indicates that the personal gender concepts were similar for boys and men in both Sweden and the United States. In other words, in contrast to the first prediction, personal gender concepts do not differ by age group for males. They do differ, however, for females. What about cross-sex comparisons? The other half of Prediction 1 indicates that gender differences should appear.

As part of the evaluation of the self-ratings for Swedish boys and men, we explored the cross-sex comparisons. In general, the top-rated components of the self-concepts were quite similar, with Swedish women being the most discrepant. Do Americans show the same pattern?

American boys shared trying to do one's best (1.76) with both American girls and American women, and being friendly (1.42) with American girls. Thus, the self-ratings of American boys overlapped with two of the top ratings of American girls and with one of the top ratings of American women, results that suggest greater variation in American than in Swedish self-ratings for boys versus either girls or women. The self-ratings of American men overlapped with three of self-ratings of American girls (aggressive, tries to do one's best, and willing to take a stand) and with two of the self-ratings of American women (aggressive and tries to do one's best). Although the agreement among girls, boys, and men is not quite as marked for Americans as for Swedes, the pattern is similar. And, for both countries, women's self-gender concepts were the most discrepant.

Another way to identify these personal gender concepts is to reiterate their most prominent components. This listing serves the twin purposes of identifying the commonalities that unite the various ages and sexes of respondents in each country and of illuminating cross-national similarities and differences. Swedes, regardless of age or sex, highly rate tries to do one's best. Other attributes highly rated by Swedes except for Swedish women, are being willing to take a stand and being kind/nice, an interesting combination of instrumental and expressive traits. Americans, regardless of age or sex, highly rate being aggressive and tries to do one's best. The other attribute highly rated by all except American women, is being friendly. Again, both instrumental and expressive attributes appear.

As a final check on cross-national similarities and differences, we correlated the self-ratings of Swedish 11-year-old females with those of American 11-year-old females, and so forth for the four groups. The correlations for the girls, women, boys, and men, .75, .76, .66, .66, respectively, suggested more cross-national uniformities during Swedish and American females than among Swedish and American males.

A brief summary is in order before moving to comparisons of personal with cultural gender concepts. In both countries, self-ratings are quite similar for girls, boys, and men but these ratings differ somewhat from those of women. The result is that females, but not males, show developmental changes. Although both countries show roughly the same pattern, the most highly rated components of the personal gender concepts differ, with the exception of the attribute, tries to do one's best. Loosely speaking, the American personal gender concept appears to be more aggressive than the Swedish one. When all of the attributes are considered, substantial cross-national agreement occurred that was greater for girls and women than for boys and men.

COMPARISONS OF PERSONAL
AND CULTURAL GENDER CONCEPTS

Our model differs from those of others (e.g., Bem, 1981, 1985; Crane & Markus, 1982; Markus et al., 1982) in assuming that personal and cultural gender concepts are not necessarily identical. Our view is that one's own concept of self will contain those aspects associated with gender that are important to the self, whereas cultural gender concepts will reflect stereotypic gender associations common in one's culture. Because people are likely to endorse some but not necessarily all of the gender-related attributes typically associated with one's own sex, we must expect incomplete overlap between personal and cultural gender concepts. We do not expect—indeed, the model denies—complete parallelism between the two types of ratings. We are now in a position to test these ideas.

In general, the answer is that the overlap is clearly incomplete. For example, among the Swedish respondents, the 11-year-old girls rated being kind/nice, trying to do one's best, and never giving up among the top five for both themselves and for most Swedish girls, but, for themselves, they added loving children and being eager to soothe hurt feelings, whereas they added being gentle and friendly to the five attributes they considered most important for most Swedish girls. Swedish boys agreed that tries to do one's best and never gives up were traits that were extremely important to them, just as they were to most boys, but they differed for the other top-rated attributes. Swedish women showed an overlap of four traits among the top assignments to themselves and to most Swedish women: tries to do one's best, being gentle, friendly, and sincere; whereas Swedish men agreed on two: tries to do one's best and never gives up. No case yielded complete overlap. As mentioned in chapter 6, the two attributes of tries to do one's best and never gives up seem to be central to the Swedish character, although neither attribute was among the freely listed traits.

These comparisons suggest that similarities, but not identities exist among the top-rated traits for all four of the Swedish stimulus groups. But what about comparisons involving all 59 attributes? Again, we turned to correlations to index the extent of association. As shown in Table 7.3, the correlations were significant, but did not account for most of the variance. Further, analyses of variance showed significant differences between personal and cultural gender ratings for 31 of the comparisons for Swedish girls, 26 of the comparisons for Swedish boys, 30 of the comparisons for Swedish women, and 25 of the comparisons for Swedish men. Further, as shown in Tables 7.4–7.7, in some cases the means were higher for self than for cultural ratings; whereas, in other cases the opposite was true. In other words, it is not possible to make a general statement that self-ratings are always higher than cultural ratings or vice versa. Overall, the data support the prediction that personal gender concepts are not identical to cultural gender concepts, although the two may share some components. The data contradict models that assume identity of the two.

The divergence between personal and cultural gender concepts was even greater for the American than for the Swedish results. Personal and cultural gender concepts for most American girls shared one attribute among the five top-rated ones: being friendly. Ratings for most boys also shared one: tries to do one's best. No overlap emerged for most American women, but three attributes (tries to do one's best, feels good about self, and self-confident) overlapped for most American men. Translated to significant differences between cultural and personal ratings for counterpart groups (e.g., American girls rating themselves and

TABLE 7.3
Correlations between Cultural and Personal Gender Concept Ratings
(all statistically significant)

	Country			
	Sweden		USA	
Comparisons	r	R^2	r	R^2
Most girls vs. 11-year-old females	.84	.70	.75	.56
Most boys vs. 11-year-old males	.86	.74	.90	.81
Most women vs. 18-year-old females	.89	.80	.80	.64
Most men vs. 18-year-old males	.83	.69	.95	.89

most American girls) the numbers of significant differences again exceeded the companion Swedish figures. For most American girls, 22 traits showed reliable differences (Table 7.4). For most boys, 12 traits showed differences (Table 7.5). Fifteen traits differed for most women (Table 7.6), and 11 for most men (Table 7.7).Thus, personal and cultural gender differences emerged for both Swedish and American respondents. Corroborating these results were correlations between the two types of gender concepts. As Table 7.3 indicates, the correlations were high but did not approach identity. Comparisons of the Swedish correlations with counterpart American correlations (using t-tests based on z-transformations of the correlation coefficients) showed that none of the correlations among the Swedish gender concepts differed significantly, whereas the cultural gender concept–personal gender concept correlations for most American men (.95) was reliably higher than that for American women (.80), $t(107) = 3.88$.

More detailed and extensive comparisons of self- (personal) and group (cultural) ratings, can be obtained by contrasting the entries in Table 7.1 with counterpart entries in Tables 6.1–6.4 (see previous chapter). These comparisons reinforce the general findings that personal and cultural gender concepts only partially overlap and that both types of gender concepts and their differences vary by gender and nationality. Clearly, any adequate model of gender concepts must hypothesize the existence of partially overlapping, partially different gender concepts for self and for most others.

Factor Analyses

Factor analyses also were conducted on the self ratings. It seems plausible to assume that if an individual's self concept depends almost exclusively on the person's gender role, then the self ratings will show two factors: one for those attributes deemed important to the person and another for those attributes not considered personally important. The results belied this two-factor assumption, for all of the analyses yielded multiple factors. Indeed, as shown in Appendix XIII, all of the analyses produced three or more eigenvalues of 4.0 or higher. Thus, as with the factor analyses of the cultural ratings, the primary benefit derived from these computations was the evidence that personal gender schemata are multicomponential. Apparently, neither personal nor cultural gender concepts derive from a simple unitary conception of gender roles.

Correspondences with Other Scales

Many of the 59 items were taken from other scales often used in the United States. These scales typically yield gender differences, so it is interesting to ask whether or not those differences emerged among our groups. Accordingly, we tallied separately the number of attributes from the BSRI, EPAQ, and the Adjective Check List that showed gender differences for each nationality. As Columns

TABLE 7.4

Significant Differences Between Mean Importance Ratings
for Self and Those for Most Girls

	Swedish female raters					American female raters			
					Higher ratings for self than for most girls				
Attributes	Self	Most girls	(df)	t	Attributes	Self	Most girls	(df)	t
Loves children	2.08	2.51	(199)	4.10***	Loyal	2.12	4.08	(161)	4.40***
Compassionate	2.57	2.88	(199)	3.00**	Aggressive	2.19	3.65	(162)	3.04**
Loyal	2.60	2.84	(120)	2.22*	Capable	2.23	3.27	(162)	3.10**
Has social adeptness	2.95	3.28	(140)	2.15*	Aware of feelings of others	2.31	3.96	(162)	3.99***
Capable	3.02	3.29	(206)	2.37*	Has self-esteem	2.38	3.54	(162)	2.59*
Lively	3.22	3.81	(200)	5.06***	Strong	2.52	4.28	(161)	4.06***
Strong	3.55	4.11	(207)	4.39***	Has leadership abilities	2.68	3.60	(161)	2.30*
Has blue eyes	3.78	5.95	(208)	10.68***					
Competitive	3.85	4.87	(208)	7.28***					
Popular	3.86	4.13	(209)	2.04*					
Artistic	3.87	4.27	(138)	2.91**					
Tall	3.99	5.29	(216)	9.00***					
Has straight hair	4.06	5.91	(213)	10.39***					
Shy	4.19	4.78	(205)	4.28***					
Has leadership abilities	4.23	5.00	(189)	5.66***					
Aggressive	4.39	5.27	(187)	6.46***					
Acts as a leader	4.53	5.05	(202)	4.40***					
Quiet	4.56	5.07	(204)	3.58***					
Dominant	4.61	5.07	(160)	2.93**					
Whiny	5.07	5.68	(200)	4.65***					

(Continued)

131

TABLE 7.4
(Continued)

Higher ratings for most girls than for self

	Swedish female raters					American female raters			
Attributes	Most girls	Self	(df)	t	Attributes	Most girls	Self	(df)	t
Kind/nice	1.95	2.31	(211)	4.43***	Friendly	1.64	2.40	(161)	2.73*
Gentle	2.04	2.31	(213)	3.12**	Loves children	1.76	3.60	(161)	3.69***
Helpful	2.18	2.56	(217)	4.12***	Affectionate	1.88	2.65	(162)	2.06*
Strong personality	2.52	2.79	(196)	2.63**	Eager to soothe hurt feelings	1.88	3.12	(161)	3.43**
Thinks one is a good person	2.60	2.97	(209)	3.22**	Creative	1.92	3.27	(162)	3.79***
Fun	2.60	3.06	(203)	5.39***	Likable	2.04	3.15	(162)	3.13***
Feels good about oneself	2.75	3.40	(200)	6.66***	Active	2.08	3.64	(161)	2.91***
Has self-esteem	2.82	3.04	(187)	2.38*	Tender	2.12	3.31	(162)	3.10***
Self-confident	2.85	3.13	(201)	2.78**	Humorous	2.25	3.83	(160)	3.65***
Makes decisions easily	2.93	3.31	(210)	3.34***	Emotional	2.32	3.48	(161)	2.46*
Likable	2.96	3.22	(188)	2.48*	Warm	2.42	3.31	(162)	2.61*
					Shy	2.44	3.44	(161)	3.46**
					Feels insecure	2.65	3.62	(162)	3.66***
					Artistic	2.96	4.54	(162)	4.43***
					Whiny	3.48	4.64	(161)	4.22***

*p < .05
**p < .01
***p < .001

TABLE 7.5

Significant Differences Between Mean Importance Ratings for Self and Those for Most Boys

Higher ratings for self than for most boys

	Swedish male raters				American male raters			
Attributes	Self	Most boys	(df)	t	Attributes	Self	Most boys	(df)	t
Active	2.30	2.67	(166)	3.26***	Self-confident	2.00	2.41	(163)	2.10*
Loyal	2.45	2.86	(132)	3.53***	Capable	2.15	3.15	(163)	2.12*
Capable	2.55	3.19	(182)	4.91***	Warm	2.41	3.78	(163)	3.11**
Has social adeptness	2.60	3.29	(144)	6.08***	Never gives up	2.42	2.92	(162)	2.11*
Loves children	2.65	2.93	(181)	2.57*	Patriotic	2.52	4.07	(163)	4.65***
Liberated	2.81	3.17	(139)	3.03**	Loves children	2.69	4.38	(162)	3.18**
Competitive	2.86	3.82	(183)	7.77***	Tall	3.56	4.89	(163)	2.40*
Strong	2.90	3.80	(178)	6.49***					
Has blue eyes	3.23	5.49	(184)	12.31***					
Good looking	3.25	3.90	(178)	4.45***					
Assertive	3.37	3.66	(151)	2.59*					
Lively	3.45	3.99	(179)	4.44***					
Has leadership abilities	3.46	4.08	(172)	4.66***					
Tough-minded	3.55	3.82	(167)	2.17*					
Athletic	3.55	4.02	(118)	2.90**					
Tall	3.56	4.78	(184)	8.05***					
Has straight hair	3.60	5.54	(183)	10.96***					
Popular	3.62	3.98	(180)	2.78**					
Artistic	3.70	4.01	(142)	2.05*					
Acts as a leader	3.90	4.16	(186)	2.26*					
Dominant	4.00	4.25	(154)	2.22*					

(Continued)

133

TABLE 7.5
(Continued)

Higher ratings for self than for most boys

	Swedish male raters				American male raters			
Attributes	Self	Most boys	(df)	t	Self	Most boys	(df)	t
Aggressive	4.16	4.77	(181)	4.52***				
Cannot show one's feelings	4.41	5.01	(176)	3.89***				
Whiny	5.29	5.80	(180)	3.83***				

Higher ratings for most boys than for self

	Swedish male raters				American male raters			
Attributes	Most boys	Self	(df)	t	Most boys	Self	(df)	t
Aware of feelings of others	2.84	3.22	(175)	3.14**	2.04	2.93	(163)	2.30*
Devotes self completely to others	4.56	4.82	(177)	2.47*	2.19	3.30	(163)	4.31***
Has social adeptness					2.22	3.00	(163)	2.07*
Creative					2.22	3.26	(163)	2.09*

*p < .05
**p < .01
***p < .001

TABLE 7.6
Significant Differences Between Mean Importance Ratings for Self and Those for Most Women

Higher ratings for self than for most women

	Swedish female raters					American female raters			
Attributes	Self	Most Women	(df)	t	Attributes	Self	Most Women	(df)	t
Loyal	2.47	2.76	(107)	2.30*	Loyal	2.12	3.48	(161)	2.59*
Compassionate	2.59	2.97	(192)	3.51***	Athletic	2.31	4.19	(162)	5.98***
Lively	3.10	3.91	(189)	6.21***	Feels good about oneself	2.36	2.84	(161)	2.75**
Strong	3.43	3.97	(204)	4.29***	Friendly	2.40	3.36	(161)	2.39*
Artistic	3.64	4.13	(127)	3.43***	Self-confident	2.46	3.46	(162)	2.66**
Has blue eyes	3.66	5.86	(207)	10.81***	Strong	2.52	3.48	(161)	2.65**
Competitive	3.74	4.87	(211)	8.10***	Thinks one is a good person	2.81	3.92	(162)	2.78**
Popular	3.99	4.29	(206)	2.75**	Assertive	2.88	3.77	(162)	2.65**
Tall	4.01	5.36	(215)	9.61***	Willing to take a stand	3.04	5.08	(162)	3.91***
Has leadership abilities	4.03	4.77	(163)	5.14***	Tough-minded	3.12	3.81	(162)	2.51*
Has straight hair	4.08	6.03	(209)	10.59***					
Acts as a leader	4.38	4.91	(194)	4.30***					
Aggressive	4.38	5.33	(181)	6.49***					
Shy	4.40	4.96	(196)	4.18***					
Quiet	4.63	4.92	(196)	2.06*					
Whiny	5.08	5.66	(191)	4.35***					

(Continued)

135

TABLE 7.6
(Continued)

	Swedish female raters					American female raters			
					Higher ratings for most women than for self					
Attributes	Most Women	Self	(df)	t		Attributes	Most Women	Self	(df)	t
Gentle	1.93	2.36	(213)	5.03***		Affectionate	1.54	2.65	(162)	4.00***
Kind/nice	2.00	2.25	(211)	2.46*		Likable	1.77	3.15	(162)	3.07**
Sincere	2.09	2.38	(209)	3.06**		Stands up under pressure	2.15	3.42	(162)	2.46*
Helpful	2.14	2.51	(217)	4.38***		Feels insecure	3.00	3.62	(162)	2.22*
Strong personality	2.47	2.71	(194)	2.65**		Whiny	3.76	4.64	(161)	2.68**
Tender	2.54	2.82	(195)	2.93**						
Humorous	2.55	2.80	(186)	2.51*						
Thinks one is a person	2.55	2.99	(209)	3.87***						
Fun	2.63	3.05	(200)	4.34***						
Has self-esteem	2.66	2.96	(182)	3.04**						
Feels good about oneself	2.71	3.45	(192)	6.80***						
Self-confident	2.76	3.04	(192)	2.39*						
Likable	2.87	3.16	(173)	2.35*						
Makes decisions easily	2.92	3.22	(202)	2.49*						

*$p < .05$
**$p < .01$
***$p < .001$

136

TABLE 7.7

Significant Differences Between Mean Importance Ratings for Self and Those for Most Men

	Swedish male raters					American female raters			
					Higher ratings for self than for most men				
Attributes	Self	Most men	(df)	t	Attributes	Self	Most men	(df)	t
Active	2.33	2.64	(153)	2.80**	Helpful	1.96	2.81	(163)	3.15**
Stands up under pressure	2.34	2.57	(168)	2.10*	Self-confident	2.00	2.41	(163)	2.51*
Loyal	2.45	2.91	(130)	4.04***	Hardworking	2.04	2.93	(163)	2.35*
Capable	2.55	3.15	(168)	4.28***	Tries to do one's best	2.41	3.26	(163)	2.53*
Thinks one is a good person	2.62	2.88	(168)	2.42*	Warm	2.41	3.70	(163)	2.77**
Emotional	2.72	2.95	(161)	2.40*	Fun	2.56	3.30	(163)	2.26*
Competitive	2.74	4.00	(170)	9.19***	Loves children	2.70	3.89	(163)	2.77**
Has social adeptness	2.77	3.18	(140)	3.09**					
Strong	2.84	3.63	(170)	5.74***					
Liberated	2.87	3.39	(126)	3.31***					
Warm	2.89	3.19	(158)	2.54*					
Good looking	3.14	3.67	(164)	3.79***					
Lively	3.34	3.96	(166)	4.80***					
Has blue eyes	3.38	5.45	(168)	9.41***					
Athletic	3.43	4.02	(117)	3.41***					
Tough-minded	3.44	3.83	(168)	3.31***					
Has leadership abilities	3.48	3.90	(162)	2.94**					
Tall	3.49	4.64	(173)	7.69***					
Popular	3.56	3.96	(170)	3.47***					
Artistic	3.66	3.99	(134)	2.23*					
Has straight hair	3.76	5.63	(171)	10.51***					

(Continued)

137

TABLE 7.7
(Continued)

	Swedish male raters				American female raters			
Attributes	Self	Most men	(df)	t	Self	Most men	(df)	t
Higher ratings for self than for most men								
Aggressive	4.24	4.79	(162)	3.97***				
Cannot show one's feelings	4.32	4.84	(163)	2.93**				
Attributes	Most men	Self	(df)	t	Most men	Self	(df)	t
Higher ratings for most men than for self								
Aware of feelings of others	2.81	3.15	(167)	3.16**	1.89	2.52	(163)	2.45*
Devotes self completely to others	4.49	4.83	(165)	3.55*	2.81	3.30	(163)	2.80**
Quiet					2.85	4.07	(163)	2.31*
Shy					2.96	3.63	(163)	2.45*
Has self-esteem					1.89	2.52	(163)	2.45*
Dominant					2.81	3.30	(163)	2.80**

*p < .05
**p < .01
***p < .001

138

5 and 6 of Table 6.9 indicate, any significant differences corresponded to the stereotypic direction, although a number of the traits did not show reliable differences.

These comparisons reinforce the general findings that personal and cultural gender concepts only partially overlap and that both these types of concepts and their differences vary by gender and nationality. By now, the forms of the gender constellations are taking shape. Clearly, personal and cultural concepts each have some unique components, as well as some shared ones. These components differ somewhat for different ages, sexes, and nationalities. For our respondents, overlap is more pronounced among the Swedes than among the Americans, as might be expected from the Swedish policy of gender equality, with tries to do one's best as an attribute that is highly esteemed by children and adults and by females and males alike. Unifying attributes for American respondents were aggression and tries to do one's best. Aggression seemed paramount among personal gender concepts but not among cultural gender ones.

The assessments of personal gender concepts are based on ratings of *current* self. Suppose that we examined a more idealistic situation: ratings of what the respondents would like to be. We undertook this task with our Swedish respondents only, because these kinds of ratings had not been investigated with a Swedish sample.

PERSONAL GENDER CONCEPTS: RATINGS OF THE IDEAL SELF

We made the obvious assumption that the ratings of ideal self would be closer to ratings of current self than to their perceptions of most people (i.e., their cultural gender concepts), regardless of sex.

Ratings of Ideal Self. The two sexes of Swedish respondents rated tries to do one's best, never gives up, and willing to take a stand as the most ideal attributes (Table 7.8). Both sexes added expressive traits to their top-rated set, with Swedish females including kind/nice and gentle and Swedish males adding helpful and sincere.

Nineteen of the attributes showed gender differences, but only one of the top-rated attributes—gentle—did so. As would be expected from previous research, Swedish females considered being gentle to be more important to one's ideal self (1.93) than men did (2.15), $F(1, 386) = 4.69$.

Comparisons of Ideal Self with Current Self-Ratings. The ratings of ideal self correlated highly with ratings of current self: .92. Despite this high correlation, a number of interesting, and statistically significant differences emerged (see Table 7.9). These comparisons are particularly important, because they il-

TABLE 7.8
Mean Importance Ratings for Ideal Self

Country	Sweden					
Sex of respondent	Female			Male		
Age Group	11	14	18	11	14	18
Tries to do one's best	1.76	1.82	1.94	1.52	1.90	2.09[b]
Never gives up	1.78	1.79	1.82	1.79	2.01	2.06
Helpful	1.88	2.04	1.92	1.81	1.99	2.26
Sincere	2.04	1.98	1.81	1.88	2.08	2.14
Willing to take a stand	1.92	1.93	1.94	1.85	2.21	2.10
Kind/nice	2.05	1.78	1.98	1.88	2.18	2.14
Gentle	2.01	1.96	1.81	1.93	2.28	2.24[a]
Friendly	1.94	1.91	2.02	2.10	2.26	2.30
Cooperative	2.16	2.19	2.23	2.23	2.26	2.49
Stands up under pressure	2.10	2.16	2.29	2.49	2.29	2.28
Hardworking	2.24	2.30	2.42	2.04	2.28	2.55
Active	2.30	2.43	2.28	2.06	2.40	2.33
Loves children	2.11	2.31	2.36	2.10	2.70	3.00
Thinks one is a good person	2.36	2.80	2.18	2.24	2.77	2.55
Self-confident	2.19	2.66	2.55	2.20	2.44	2.53
Fun	2.75	2.48	2.60	2.28	2.37	2.74
Strong personality	2.70	2.48	2.35	2.46	2.52	2.74[a]
Has self-esteem	2.45	2.80	2.43	2.27	2.48	2.77
Affectionate	2.39	2.45	2.38	2.79	2.67	2.62[a]
Humorous	2.60	2.55	2.63	2.47	2.62	2.53
Eager to soothe hurt feelings	2.28	2.33	2.69	2.53	2.79	3.28[a,b]
Capable	2.93	2.43	2.89	2.20	2.47	2.89
Generous	2.54	2.71	2.61	2.52	2.71	2.66
Emotional	2.89	2.44	2.23	2.82	2.77	2.81[c]
Aware of feelings of others	2.48	2.34	2.39	2.92	3.06	2.82[a]
Tender	2.99	2.32	2.23	3.20	2.58	2.74[a,b]
Warm	2.92	2.30	2.29	3.19	2.70	2.83[a,b]
Feels good about oneself	2.62	2.62	2.60	2.62	2.74	3.18[a,b]
Loyal	3.58	2.91	2.48	2.96	2.52	2.36[a,b]
Patriotic	2.16	2.19	2.23	2.22	2.26	2.49
Makes decisions easily	2.71	2.71	2.85	2.71	2.79	2.70
Likable	2.84	2.77	2.47	2.96	2.94	2.79
Compassionate	2.84	2.67	2.65	2.93	2.88	3.06
Has social adeptness	3.89	3.74	3.74	3.51	3.28	3.51
Liberated	3.33	2.83	2.64	2.98	3.03	3.08
Good looking	3.56	2.73	3.52	3.02	3.09	2.84[c]
Creative	3.65	3.33	3.29	3.18	3.12	2.74
Artistic	2.95	3.52	3.60	3.09	3.17	3.36
Strong	3.89	3.52	3.50	2.81	2.88	3.68
Popular	4.22	3.30	3.39	3.54	3.18	2.88[a,b]
Assertive	4.29	3.33	3.80	3.45	3.40	3.22[a]
Tough-minded	3.89	3.74	3.74	3.51	3.28	3.51
Eager to soothe hurt feelings	3.79	3.45	3.50	3.68	3.54	3.89
Competitive	3.93	4.32	4.66	2.70	3.32	3.47[a,b]

TABLE 7.8
(*Continued*)

Country	Sweden					
Sex of respondent	Female			Male		
Age Group	11	14	18	11	14	18
Athletic	3.38	4.14	4.41	3.91	3.22	3.64[a]
Has leadership abilities	5.03	4.22	4.55	3.81	3.54	3.20[a]
Acts as a leader	5.00	4.28	4.84	4.15	3.54	3.49[a,b]
Devotes self completely to others	4.21	4.24	4.37	4.01	4.29	4.65
Dominant	5.12	4.29	5.05	3.94	4.16	4.37[a,b]
Subordinates self to others	4.48	4.91	4.89	3.91	4.38	4.48[a]
Tall	5.16	4.89	5.24	4.49	4.28	4.10[a]
Quiet	4.61	5.06	4.92	4.68	4.70	4.87
Aggressive	5.20	4.99	4.97	4.43	4.54	4.94[b]
Cannot show one's feelings	4.72	4.92	4.44	4.68	4.85	5.35
Shy	4.97	4.80	4.75	5.39	5.06	4.98
Has blue eyes	5.38	5.31	5.76	4.55	4.51	5.27
Feels insecure	5.41	5.18	5.15	5.27	5.37	5.55
Has straight hair	5.25	5.83	6.05	4.86	4.91	5.78[a,b]
Whiny	5.51	5.71	5.63	5.40	5.44	5.54

*p < .05
**p < .01
***p < .001

TABLE 7.9

Significant Differences Between Mean Importance Ratings for Current Self and for Ideal Self

Swedish female raters

Higher ratings for current self than for ideal self

Attributes	Self	Ideal	(df)	t
Lively	3.20	3.56	(206)	3.29***
Competitive	3.64	4.29	(209)	5.56***
Has blue eyes	3.64	5.46	(210)	9.59***
Has straight hair	3.95	5.73	(215)	10.31***
Tall	3.99	5.09	(221)	7.56***
Has leadership abilities	4.15	4.51	(184)	3.01**
Aggressive	4.34	5.01	(175)	4.61***
Shy	4.37	4.89	(217)	3.64***
Acts as a leader	4.44	4.68	(198)	2.05*
Quiet	4.56	4.88	(210)	2.19*
Feels insecure	4.89	5.26	(194)	2.91**
Whiny	5.07	5.61	(200)	4.04***

Higher ratings for ideal self than for current self

Attributes	Ideal	Self	(df)	t
Never gives up	1.77	2.04	(210)	3.28***
Willing to take a stand	1.91	2.22	(210)	3.66***
Gentle	1.93	2.40	(216)	5.55***
Friendly	1.94	2.24	(198)	3.45***
Kind	1.94	2.31	(218)	3.86***

Swedish male raters

Higher ratings for current self than for ideal self

Attributes	Self	Ideal	(df)	t
Competitive	2.74	3.11	(193)	3.33***
Lively	3.32	3.69	(186)	3.26***
Has blue eyes	3.35	4.66	(190)	6.98***
Tall	3.56	4.30	(198)	5.61***
Has straight hair	3.75	5.10	(197)	8.26***
Aggressive	4.12	4.59	(175)	3.45***
Cannot show one's feelings	4.43	4.92	(188)	3.65***

Higher ratings for ideal self than for current self

Attributes	Ideal	Self	(df)	t
Helpful	1.98	2.40	(199)	4.95***
Sincere	2.00	2.31	(192)	3.63***
Gentle	2.12	2.33	(192)	2.13*
Fun	2.40	2.67	(191)	3.04**
Humorous	2.46	2.67	(176)	2.37*

TABLE 7.9
(Continued)

	Swedish female raters					Swedish male raters			
Attributes	Self	Ideal	(df)	t	Attributes	Self	Ideal	(df)	t

Higher ratings for ideal self than for current self

Attributes	Self	Ideal	(df)	t	Attributes	Self	Ideal	(df)	t
Sincere	1.95	2.41	(205)	4.96***	Generous	2.60	2.79	(177)	2.06*
Helpful	1.95	2.57	(222)	8.14***	Affectionate	2.69	2.95	(152)	2.22*
Stands up under pressure	2.15	2.67	(207)	5.64***	Feels good about oneself	2.78	3.09	(185)	2.85**
Cooperative	2.18	2.51	(204)	3.89***	Aware of feelings of others	2.96	3.25	(183)	2.44*
Hardworking	2.30	2.69	(211)	4.03***	Good looking	2.98	3.33	(185)	2.91**
Thinks one is a good person	2.30	3.00	(216)	7.27***	Popular	3.26	3.70	(187)	4.06***
Aware of feelings of others	2.40	2.58	(209)	2.10*	Artistic	3.28	3.64	(137)	2.60**
Affectionate	2.40	2.93	(163)	5.02***	Acts as a leader	3.80	4.03	(189)	2.03*
Self-confident	2.44	3.07	(202)	5.91***	Devotes self completely to others	4.26	4.77	(181)	4.33***
Strong personality	2.47	2.77	(195)	3.36***					

*$p < .05$
**$p < .01$
***$p < .001$

143

luminate the areas in which the respondents thought they possessed more of an attribute than was ideal or that they desired to have more of an attribute to satisfy an ideal.

We begin with the attributes that the respondents thought they possessed to an excess, compared to an ideal. Swedish females rated 12 attributes higher for their current selves than for their ideal selves: lively, competitive, has blue eyes, has straight hair, tall, has leadership abilities, aggressive, shy, acts as a leader, quiet, feels insecure, and whiny. Some of these attributes are understandable, because they are often considered socially undesirable, such as being shy, feeling insecure, and being whiny. Others are more difficult to comprehend. The desire to change physical attributes probably reflects some discontent with their current physical appearance and perhaps the desire to appear more distinctive, because Swedish people often have blue eyes, straight hair, and are tall. The remainder of the attributes are instrumental, suggesting that our Swedish female respondents thought the ideal person would not possess these traits to the extent that they did. Remember that, for both sexes of Swedish respondents, the generally admired traits, regardless of sex, were highly expressive.

Buttressing this latter interpretation are the results of the Swedish males. They, too, listed such instrumental traits as competitive, lively, aggressive, and cannot show one's feelings as attributes of their current selves that exceeded the ideal. They also noted the same physical attributes as the females as ones that exceeded their ideal.

Still more support comes from the attributes for which the subjects' current ratings were less than ideal. As the lower panel of Table 7.9 indicates, most of these attributes were expressive—for both sexes. Thus, the Swedish respondents often indicated that they did not have expressive attributes to the extent that they thought was ideal!

But what about changes with age? Do we find children agreeing with adults about the desirability of expressive traits? Do the two sexes agree? As Table 7.8 shows, 12 of the attributes showed reliable differences over the three ages tested. Only one, tries to do one's best, was a top-rated trait. Its importance decreased with age from a mean of 1.64 for the 11-year-olds to a mean of 2.02 for the 18-year-olds. Some attributes that decreased with age were instrumental (e.g., competitive, dominant, aggressive, although eager to soothe hurt feelings, feels good about oneself, and has stright hair also declined); attributes that increased with age often were expressive (e.g., tender, warm, popular, and acts as a leader). Twelve of 59 traits represents a relatively minor number showing changes with age; in most cases, the young respondents agreed with the oldest ones about the desirable traits. Moreover, the two sexes agreed in their ratings for an ideal self to a substantial extent: only 19 of the 59 traits showed gender differences, all of which were in a stereotypical direction, and none of these differences appeared among the top-rated traits. These results indicate solid agreement between the two sexes in their ratings for ideal self. Particularly germane to our thesis, most of the attributes that showed sex or age group differences were ones that were not considered as highly important to ideal selves. Encapulated, the findings inform us that, in Sweden, the ideal person should combine expressive traits with three instrumental ones: tries to do one's best, never gives up, and willing take a stand.

Comparisons of Ideal Self-Ratings with Generally Admired Attributes, Regardless of Sex. The emphasis both sexes of Swedish respondents placed on expressive traits accords nicely with their identical emphasis upon the attributes they admire in all people, regardless of gender. The generally admired attributes did not contain any mention of tries to do one's best, never gives up, or willing to take a stand, however. Apparently, these latter attributes, although rated as highly important to the ideal self, do not spontaneously spring to mind as generally admired traits. These results seem to us to argue that the expressive traits, particularly those of being kind/nice, helpful, and sensitive, are the most salient positive attributes in the culture. This is true for both sexes. The generally admired traits included being honest and having a sense of humor, two traits that are not clearly expressive or instrumental, although our independent raters considered honest to be expressive and having a sense of humor to be instrumental.

Comparisons of Ideal Self-Ratings with Cultural Gender Concepts. In general, the ideal ratings emphasized expressive traits somewhat more than did either the freely listed descriptions or the importance ratings of the four stimulus groups. This was more noticeable when most boys and most men were the target groups. Despite this persistent difference, a stronger theme was that of rating tries to do one's best, never gives up, and willing to take a stand as very important attributes. These attributes tended to be rated a little higher for males than for females and for older than for younger persons, but these attributes contained a major overlap between the components of Swedish cultural gender concepts and those of personal gender concepts, as indexed by ratings of the ideal self, just as they did for ratings of current self.

SUMMARY

The cultural gender concepts showed some cross-national differences with the Swedish versions being less gender-typed than the American counterparts, for both sexes. Similar results have been found with preschoolers (Smetana, 1986). In this work, the children judged male assumptions of female-related appearances and activities to be more serious transgressions than female assumptions of male-related appearances and activities. The cultural gender concepts of the two countries were similar in many other aspects. Most noteworthy was the marked tendency for gender-differentiating traits to be given low ratings, whereas the attributes that were considered highly important for young and adult members of both sexes received high ratings. Would the personal gender concepts parallel these results? Yes. In general, the Swedish personal gender concepts were more similar to their cultural gender concepts than American ones were. Tries to do one's best, never gives up, and being kind/nice were highly rated by our Swedish respondents, regardless of sex, for themselves and for others (the four stimulus groups). Personal gender components were quite similar for Swedish girls, boys, and men, with Swedish women showing more differences. Other top-rated personal attributes differed from top-rated cultural ones, indicating that Swedish personal and cultural gender concepts were similar but not identical.

Americans showed greater divergence between the two types of gender concepts. The top-rated attribute for self, aggression, did not emerge among the five top-rated attributes for any of the stimulus groups. American personal gender concepts also were not markedly gender-typed, with girls, boys, and men assigning high ratings for self to such expressive traits as being kind/nice (females) or friendly (males) along with instrumental traits (aggressiveness) and trying to do one's best (both sexes). Like their Swedish parallels, American women's self-ratings differed somewhat from those of other groups.

We conclude, therefore, that Swedish cultural and personal gender concepts contain more similar components than their American counterparts, and that personal gender concepts contain both expressive and instrumental components for both countries and for both sexes of respondents.

The next issue is whether the attributes rated as most important for self differed for the two sexes in each country. Paralleling the outcomes for cultural gender concepts, the answer is that an interaction appeared, because women differed more from girls (thereby showing developmental changes) than men did from boys.

Only the Swedish respondents assigned importance ratings for their ideal selves. These ratings correlated highly with ratings for current self (.92), hence they are not discussed further. A few differences reflected personal decreases in traits often considered socially undesirable, such as whininess and straight hair!

Our next topic is quite different: We turn from objective ratings of the importance of various attributes within gender concepts to more subjective reactions elicited by asking what their lives would be like if their sex changed.

8

The Change-Sex Story

Suppose that when you waken in the morning, you discover that you have become the other sex. What do you think your life will be like?

Answers to this query were diverse, spanning a vast range of topics. The answers were subjective, unstructured, and imaginative; they seemed at first to defy systematic analysis. More persistent scrutiny showed this impression to be too hasty, for coherent themes soon coalesced. These themes answered most of the questions we framed and added new insights.

In brief, we expected the data to speak to the predictions about gender, cultural, and age differences in gender-role expectations. The responses should provide a window into what the individuals really think about the lives of the other sex. We were particularly interested in whether Swedish respondents would perceive fewer differences between the sexes than Americans did, as would be predicted on the basis of Sweden's 15+ years of commitment to gender equality. Using a similar cue that asked how their lives would change, Baumgartner (see Tavris with Baumgartner, 1983) found that American males were appalled by the notion of becoming a female, whereas females were considerably less negative. Although most of her females were content with their gender roles, many noted advantages of male roles. Translated to our research, we expected to find this asymmetry in both countries, but to be less marked in Sweden than in the United States. This prediction rests on the assumption that Sweden's policies of gender equality contribute to more equal gender expectations for the two sexes than more lax American efforts. It also follows that gender asymmetries should be less pronounced among younger people, whose gender concepts should not be as well developed as those of their elders. As it turned out, the stories yielded information about gender-role expectations, in addition to information about gender attitudes and expectations in each country.

Some of the answers were expected and predicted; others surprised us. In this chapter, we describe the techniques used to analyze the data and then relate the outcomes. Here we give a "sneak preview" of these outcomes as a handy outline for integrating and interpreting the results. First, the overall reactions to the idea of changing from one sex to the other showed the asymmetry we predicted. Men tended to reject the notion, with responses that varied from mild disapproval to extreme rejection. Women were more likely to note positive aspects of the male role, although most of them were content with being females. These asymmetries were more pronounced in the United States than in Sweden, also as predicted. Second, the asymmetries were greater among older respondents than among younger ones, also supporting predictions. Third, in both countries, the male role was clearly valued more than the female role. Fourth, highly specific, gender-stereotypic expectations for each sex emerged in both countries. These expectations were more gender stereotypic than those uncovered by any of the other measures used in our research. The expectations, which included activities, personal appearance, personality attributes, and reactions of others, complemented and extended our insights into the components of gender concepts in the two countries. Fifth, the expectations also illuminated some of the reasons for the persistence of gender inequality in Sweden. We treat each of these topics in turn.

ANALYSES OF THE STORIES

To harness the rich data from the "change-sex" stories, we had raters evaluate (a) the expectations for such characteristics as activities, appearance, behavior, and interactions with other people that would result from the changed gender; and (b) the overall reactions of each person. Included in the judgments of overall affective reactions were the frequencies of comments such as saying that they would have to move within their country or to other countries, change their friends, or commit suicide, and their answers to questions about the likely results of changing sex. All raters were fluent in the language being scored.

One scoring problem was that the respondents often mentioned a negative reaction (surprise, fright) at the beginning of their stories and then went on to indicate adjustment, acceptance, or interest in the role of the other gender. We scored these kinds of responses in terms of the longer range perspective. (A short-range perspective would almost certainly yield evidence of stress and pressures, the expected concomitants of any major change in a person's life. More important for our purposes were the respondents' expectations for their extended future.) The other problem was the assessment of stories citing different expectations for the two genders without offering any affective evaluation. We decided that these responses were most appropriately scored as neutral. All disagreements were settled by discussion with very little difficulty, suggesting that the scoring standards were relatively easy to apply and that the scorers made similar interpretations.

The results are presented both quantitatively and qualitatively to maximize the information from the imaginative stories. In the following sections, the overall affective reaction and then the other results are presented in terms of the predictions for the variables of gender, age, and culture.

OVERALL REACTIONS TO THE IDEA
OF CHANGING ONE'S SEX

Let us begin with the question of whether or not Swedes foretell fewer differences between gender roles than Americans. The answer, a ringing affirmative, comes from the percentages of respondents writing stories with a positive, negative, or neutral reaction about changing sex. Like Baumgartner (Tavris with Baumgartner, 1983), we found that males, more than females found the idea of changing sex repugnant, exclaiming that they would have to commit suicide, that they would have to seek anonymity in a foreign land, that they would suffer a mental breakdown, and the like. Further, as we expected, American males were more resistant than Swedish males. American males were particularly likely to include imagery about the day they died, doomsday, and the day their life ended, and so on. Women, particularly Swedish women, were quite content with their lot, often saying that they were happy as females and did not wish to change. Some women in both countries were enthusiastic about the idea, often noting that they would have greater freedom as males. These responses were considerably more common among American women.

These general conclusions were documented in various ways. Consider first the negative, neutral, and positive stories. Negative stories signal resistance to changing gender or, stated more positively, an affirmation of one's actual gender role, whereas positive stories signal acceptance of a change or at least a partial rejection of one's current gender role. For example, when an 11-year-old American boy writes, "Catastrophe! Hopeless! Hopeless! My life would be ruined," and another prophesies darkly, "I would have to commit suicide," there can be little doubt that they did not relish the idea of trading places with a girl. In contrast, positive reactions, such as, "It would be what I have always wanted," and "Oh good, now I can to to college," as two American girls proclaimed, also were easily interpreted as welcoming a change. Neutral stories presumably index either a balanced presentation of the advantages and disadvantages of the two gender roles or the absence of value judgments. In general, the Swedes wrote more negative stories about changing sex (33%) than the Americans (29%); the Americans wrote more favorable stories about change (17%) than the Swedes (12%). About the same percentages of Swedes (55%) and Americans (54%) wrote neutral stories. These differences were significant, $X^2 = 5.37$. Further examination showed both gender and age trands. More American females (32%) than Swedish females (18%) wrote positive stories and fewer American (11%) than Swedish (27%) females wrote negative stories, $X^2 = 2.30$. By contrast, males from both countries wrote many more negative (40%–60%) stories than positive (3%–6%) ones, $X^2 = 2.5$, NS, implying that males of both countries prefer the gender status quo. Females in both countries find changing gender roles more attractive than males do with the difference being more pronounced in the United States than in Sweden.

The same pattern of strong male preference for the male role, but lesser female attachment to the female role appeared at each age level for each country (see Table 8.1). Moreover, this pattern increased from age 11 to age 14 and then either remained relatively constant to age 18 in Sweden or declined to age 18 in the United States. For example, the percentages of Swedish 11-, 14-, and 18-year-old females who favored a change were 13, 20, and 21. The counterparts for the American females were 30, 48, and 17. The differences were reliable for the 11- and 14-year-olds, $X^2_{11} (2) = 8.66$, and $X^2_{14} (2) = 15.79$, but not for the 18-year-olds, $X^2 (2) = 3.28$, NS. A reliably higher percentage of American (67) than Swedish (35) 11-year-old boys was opposed to changing gender roles, $X^2 = 14.48$. The 14- and 18-year-old males in both countries also were opposed to changes in gender roles, but they did not differ by nationality.

Preference for the male role emerges even more strikingly when the male and female roles are contrasted after excluding neutral stories. These comparisons pit stories favorable to a male role (the frequencies of positive stories written by females plus the frequencies of negative stories written by males) against stories favorable to a female role (the frequencies of positive stories written by males plus the frequencies of negative stories written by females). These comparisons,

TABLE 8.1
Percentages of Stories with Negative, Neutral, and Positive Responses Toward Changing One's Sex Role, by Sex, Age, and Nationality of the Subjects

Sex of Subject	Female			Male		
Affect of Response	−	0	+	−	0	+
11-year-olds						
Swedish	21	66	13	35	62	3
American	11	59	30	67	30	3
14-year-olds						
Swedish	36	44	20	46	45	9
American	15	37	48	51	47	2
18-year-olds						
Swedish	19	60	21	39	58	3
American	9	74	17	20	76	4

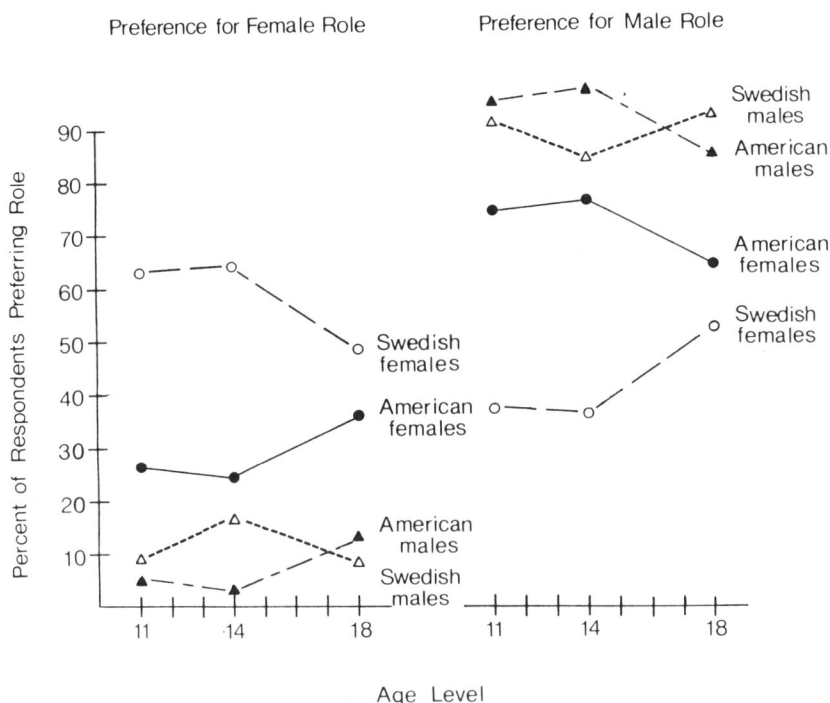

FIG. 8.1. Percentages of Swedish and American females and males preferring female and male roles, by age level.

illustrated in Fig. 8.1, depict the strong preferences of males for the male role in both countries, regardless of age. American females, also regardless of age, prefer the male role, although to a somewhat lesser extent than the males, as do 18-year-old Swedish females (by a slight margin of 52%). Younger Swedish females prefer the female role, however. Table 8.2 presents more detailed evidence.

The data suggest that Swedish women are relatively enthusiastic about the female gender role at ages 11 and 14 but become less enchanted with it by the time they are 18, a pattern that is consistent with the prediction that the Swedish equal opportunity practices may foster the perception of greater equality. As Swedish women mature, they are more likely to encounter evidence of discrepancies between the sexes, with a concomitant change in their attitude about gender roles. American females apparently know, from an early age, that the male role is the culturally preferred and advantaged one.

These views are captured by one Swedish woman, who said, flatly, "I envy all boys." Two American women agreed that, "Life as a boy would be an interesting experience," and that as a boy, one would "get almost any job I want, from coal miner to president, if I worked hard enough." An 18-year-old American male

TABLE 8.2
Frequencies of Gender-change Stories with Negative (−), Neutral (0), and Positive (+) Affect

Country	Age Level	Sex	Frequencies				Percentages			X² (2)
			−	0	+	T	−	0	+	
Sweden										
	11	Female	22	68	13	103	21	66	13	8.18*
		Male	31	55	3	89	35	62	3	
		Totals	53	123	16	192				
	14	Female	42	52	24	118	36	44	20	6.73*
		Male	52	51	10	113	46	45	9	
		Totals	94	103	34	231				
	18	Female	13	40	14	67	19	60	21	11.79**
		Male	24	36	2	62	39	58	3	
		Totals	37	76	16	129				
	Totals	Female	77	160	51	288	27	55	18	24.60***
		Male	107	142	15	264	40	54	6	
		Totals	184	302	66	552				
U.S.A.										
	11	Female	6	33	17	56	11	59	30	39.26***
		Male	36	16	2	54	67	30	4	
		Totals	42	49	19	110				
	14	Female	8	20	26	54	15	37	48	37.11***
		Male	30	28	1	59	51	47	2	
		Totals	38	48	27	113				
	18	Female	5	40	9	54	9	74	17	6.87**
		Male	11	41	2	54	20	76	4	
		Totals	16	81	11	108				
	Totals	Female	19	93	52	164	11	57	32	74.13***
		Male	77	85	5	167	46	51	3	
		Totals	96	178	57	331				

was negative: "All in all, I think it would be hell to be a girl." A Swedish man would use the situation to his advantage: "I would donate my unique body to science for the small sum of 200,000 Swedish Kronor to be left to my descendants"!

Negative reactions occasionally emerged as denials of the change: 2.4% of the Swedish respondents said that they would consider suicide, and 5.0% proposed moving to another community or country to establish a new identity. Still more said that they would go back to sleep to see if the bad dream would disappear! Although these stories suggest maladaptive, drastic ways of coping with a change of sex, most of the respondents thought that they could adapt.

On balance, both sexes would prefer to retain their current sex. One frequently expressed reason for this preference was that they have invested their past lives in the acquisition of one particular gender role. It would be difficult to have to begin again. This sophisticated view was more pronounced among the Swedes than the Americans.

Even though the general reactions to changing sex clearly indicate that the asymmetry of male resistance and slight female acceptance is more pronounced in the United States than in Sweden, it is instructive to note that all age groups, both sexes, and both nationalities showed amazingly stereotypic expectations for the two sexes. Even among Swedish 11-year-olds, the standard expectation was that, compared to Swedish men, Swedish women would have more difficulty obtaining a job, would be more likely to be unemployed, would be primarily concerned about their appearance, would be weak, and so on. The American responses were similar, but more extreme. In short, the stories from both nationalities proclaimed loudly and clearly that the roles of the two sexes differ and that the male sex is the advantaged and valued one.

Perhaps the most striking manifestation of this differential evaluation of the roles of the two sexes was the great difficulty many males expressed in trying to imagine what it would be like to be a female. Many found the task either almost impossible to imagine or too horrifying to contemplate. It is almost as though many of our male respondents viewed female existence as completely foreign, as removed from their ken as the experiences of an entirely different species might be. In contrast, the female respondents did not seem to have this problem, at least not to any great extent. Of course, it is difficult to know how much insight the two sexes had into experiences of the other sex, but the males were the ones who disavowed such knowledge. We could not help but speculate about the meaning of this difference. Are men really unaware of women's activities? Are they unable to imagine women's lives? Are they simply uninterested in the lives of females? It seems surprising that males would express such ignorance when many were occupying the same households as sisters and mothers. Have they been taught that female experience is so devalued that they deliberately ignore it? We return to those problems after considering some other aspects of the data.

A second question asked whether Swedes would show greater gender awareness that both sexes should prepare for shared financial and domestic responsibilities. To our amazement, this answer was strongly negative. For example, in their views of adult occupations, some contended that it is easier for men than for women to get jobs, a view that was more prevalent among Swedes than Americans! Men were perceived as having both greater occupational choice and higher salaries than women; indeed, women were most often relegated to service occupations, including that of homemaker. These patterns appeared for both sexes at all three ages, but increased with age. Even computer-related jobs were considered to be male preserves. Politics and professional jobs certainly were. As one 14-year-old Swedish girl remarked, "As a boy I might become Prime Minister or an executive." Added another, "It would be a good thing as far as jobs are concerned—then I could be a hockey player as I would like to be." Still another said, "As a girl, I want to be a primary school teacher. As a boy I'd want to be a concert pianist."

As mentioned, the values attached to the positions of women and men were quite different. Swedish females stated flatly that their chances of getting jobs would increase if they changed sex and that more choice would be available to them. These opportunities might have costs. Indeed, one Swedish 14-year-old girl viewed the possibility of increased responsibility with alarm: "I would have harder jobs and there would be more demands on me." The values attached to female occupations by males were quite negative. Men mentioned that, as women they would probably be a housewife, an occupation for which they had contempt: An 11-year-old boy announced, "I wouldn't want to be just a typical housewife. It would be so boring." Seconded another, "Standing by the cooker is not my style," and an 18-year-old added, "My life would be tied down by my children." Women, we noted, seemed to share this scorn for housewifery, for they rarely mentioned either that, as a man, they would have to forego the opportunity or that they would miss it.

One 18-year-old Swedish male disagreed with the prevailing negative sentiment against women's roles, arguing that he would have more freedom as a woman, "because women can assume men's roles and be accepted more than men could." No one else voiced this opinion. In fact, the only times male stories attributed occupational successes to women was when the stories portrayed women as photographic models or prostitutes. Indeed, although a few 18-year-olds mentioned career aspirations for women, the only occupations other than housewife mentioned by 11- and 14-year-old Swedes were those of photographic model and prostitute. These results provide insight into Sweden's failure to achieve gender equality. When young children perceive being a housewife and mother as the major occupation of women, they can hardly be expected to realize the importance of educational preparation for women's occupational achievement. Needless to say, failure to prepare educationally can be a substantial occupational handicap, even in the Swedish system, which permits delayed entry into a number of programs.

The stories depicted occupational segregation and discrimination of the sexes as widespread and—surprisingly for Sweden—as rather matter-of-factly accepted. Many Swedish stories stated that women have more difficulty getting jobs, more difficulty obtaining promotions, and lower pay than men. American comments carried the same message, but this is to be expected from the asystematic support for gender equality within the United States.

In both countries, the female role carries greater restriction of personal freedom. Parents are stricter about curfews, less willing to let their daughters go out at night, less willing to let their daughters travel, and the like.

One of the most surprising, and unanticipated cultural differences was the American preoccupation with dieting. One quarter of the women mentioned that, as men, they could eat as much as they wanted, and slightly more men (26%) noted that, as women, they would be dieting constantly. The stories were startlingly graphic. As one 18-year-old American woman wrote, "Now that I am a man, I will get up early enough to eat breakfast. For breakfast, I will have two fried eggs, bacon, orange juice, pancakes, maybe fried potatoes, toast or muffins or bagels. Then I will have cocoa and maybe something else. I'll eat until I'm not hungry any more." The preoccupation with food was astonishing.

American men showed similar awareness of dieting. They often remarked that they would have to watch their weight, they would have to be careful about how much they ate, and that they would have to jog to lose weight. These kinds of responses did not appear in the Swedish stories, although another perspective common to both countries, sexes, and ages was that women are expected to be more concerned about their appearance than men are.

These are general results. Let us turn now to more specific areas, such as activities, behavior, personality, and other expectations.

Activities. The activities mentioned most often by respondents from both countries were that males are more athletic, both as participants and as spectators. For example, most of the respondents from both countries noted that if they changed sex, they would have to change their sports activities or increase them if, as girls, they became boys. Swedish boys, but not the girls, mentioned substituting figure skating for ice hockey. One 11-year-old Swedish boy said woefully, "I could not play ice hockey or show myself to anyone. I would stay indoors and draw horses. I would read quietly and do homework." A few would continue with their current interests. For example, one 14-year-old girl said that she would become a professional jockey, and a 14-year-old male thought that, as a female, he could become a celebrity as a football player. Americans were more likely to talk in terms of increases or decreases in athletic activities.

School activities would change as well. Females were described as more studious than males but males were perceived as more concerned about adult careers than females. Moreover, there was a general agreement that girls get better grades in school. One 14-year-old girl stated that boys cannot be good in school, except in physical education, or they will be teased, and a male classmate saw being a female as an advantage: He "would like to be an excellent scholar." A number of the 18-year-olds said that they would study different courses. Disagreements took several forms. The first was that females do not need as much education. As one 14-year-old Swedish boy said, "I might care less about school if I were just going to stand at the sink." An 18-year-old male indicated that, as a female, he would stop studying and become a photographic model. The second form, unique to Sweden, was that no differences existed. This opinion was represented by one 18-year-old Swedish male, who exclaimed, "Ten years ago I would have had to change courses at school, but not now."

A third activity difference was that of freedom to pursue various activities.

Males were accorded more freedom than females in terms of being less home-bound and as escaping menstruation, contraception, and childbirth. The 18-year-olds often cited other differences in the activities of the two sexes, such as freedom to stay out at night and to travel. Relative to girls, boys are able to stay out later at night, to travel more, and to hitchhike. In addition, boys are expected to do fewer things at home than are girls.

The impressions of female disadvantages were tidily summarized by a 14-year-old girl's proclamation that, as a boy, she would "dare do more things."

Expected Behavior. According to both Swedish and American stories, boys are tougher, more aggressive, more unemotional, more boisterous, and more pugilistic than girls, whereas girls are weaker, kinder, and less able to "stand up" to men and boys. These gender-stereotypic attributes were quite pronounced, but not always admired. One 11-year-old girl remarked, "I wouldn't act tough because I think that's stupid." Boys, in particular, deprecated traits they attributed to females: "If I were hit, I'd (as a girl) shrivel up like a rag." In general, almost twice as many traits were mentioned for males (95) as for females (48), regardless of the value judgment of the trait, $X^2(1) = 28.34$. These results replicate those reported by Best et al., (1977), Broverman, Vogel, Broverman, Clarkson, and Rosenkrantz (1972), Edwards and Williams (1980), and Williams and Best (1982), although dissenting results also have been reported (e.g., Carlsson et al., 1984; Lee & Sugawara, 1982; Tarrier & Gomes, 1981; Trautner et al., 1983). A standard explanation for the more frequent citation of male-defining than female-defining traits is that these citations reflect the preeminence of men in the culture.

Fighting was often assigned to boys. "Boys fight instead of talking," declared one 14-year-old girl. Boys agreed that as girls they would not get "as many beatings." Boys also were characterized as showing off by "swearing, screaming, being naughty, standing outside smoking, drinking to impress their buddies, and bragging about conquests." The relative unemotionality of males was sometimes considered a disadvantage—a facade that covered their true feelings. "Boys don't dare to show their feelings and they don't think they should cry," offered one 14-year-old girl. "Boys can't show their feelings, but they are soft on the inside and think that they have to act hard. I couldn't do that," volunteered an 18-year-old women. One 18-year-old man apparently concurred, for he said that as a girl, "I would relax and be myself more." Comments about the pressures on men to stifle their emotions and to show off increased with age in both countries. Sexual prowess and conquest were common themes, with males being assigned the aggressor role. The American stories, in particular, stressed numbers of conquests rather than intimate liaisons. Once again, these stories ascribe startlingly stereotypic attributes to the two sexes, and the tendencies appear in both countries, although they are more pronounced in the United States. The persistence of these attitudes, even among Swedish youngsters whose entire lives have been lived under Sweden's commitment to gender equality vividly illustrates the difficulty of changing attitudes. It is a testimonial that offers a poor prognosis for the elimination of gender inequality, even in the face of determined governmental and legal onslaught.

Appearance.   Both sexes noted that they would have to change clothes if their gender changed. Girls also assumed that they would change their hairstyles, and boys thought that they would begin wearing makeup. In general, both sexes thought that appearance was more important for girls than for boys and that girls were more concerned about their appearance than boys. These latter perceptions increased with age of the respondents. Three Swedish girls reported that as boys their hair would turn dark and one said that her eyes would turn brown. These surprising comments are consistent with both Swedish (Carlsson, personal communication) and American (Intons-Peterson, in press) results showing that children think that boys have dark hair and girls have blond hair, although these traits typically were rated as low in importance.

In this realm, our Swedish correspondents were even more adamant than the Americans. Physical appearance, the stories announced, is prized, particularly for and by Swedish females. Some comments are illustrative: "Boys always look the same in clothes" (11-year-old girl); "I'd become ugly if I became a boy—no waist and clumsy. Boys with long hair are called sluttish" (11-year-old girl). "I would wear pink trousers, a modern sweater, and nice shoes, wash, and put on makeup" (11-year-old boy). "There is a lot of pressure on girls to look good and fresh. Boys can be ugly and still be popular. Ugly girls never are" (14-year-old girl). "I would have to do my face all the time and wear uncomfortable clothes and shoes" (14-year-old boy). "Looks are more important to women; attractive looks mean more attention" (18-year-old man).

As noted previously, among Americans, the most striking expression of female devotion to appearance burst forth as a concern about a svelte figure: Americans expect females to be thin. Like Swedish females, Americans also expect to spend time applying makeup, curling their hair, and the like. Overall, the preoccupations with physical appearance for females, but far less so for males, reflected yet another gender stereotypis difference.

Will this difference challenge the pursuit of gender equality? It certainly has that potential. Time is, after all, a precious, limited commodity. Time devoted to makeup is time not devoted to one's domestic or financial responsibilities. Why, then, should women, more than men, be expected to allocate more time to what is arguably a nonessential, frivolous activity? This question, ultimately political as well as personal, is not easy to answer, but its answer may well be very important to the achievement of full gender equality.

Treatment by Others.   Most of the subjects expressed concern about their friends' reactions, and many also mentioned their parents' responses. Additionally, many noted the vulnerability of females to attack (rape, murder), and to "passes."

Women were seen as less valued than men: "Women are downrated; boys are valued higher." Stories describing a devaluation of women were considerably more common among Americans, although the same message surfaced in some Swedish comments. As one 18-year-old Swedish male wrote, "Even with equality, my position would deteriorate as a woman."

Males would be listened to more by other people. One 14-year-old girl exclaimed, "Boys are always welcome."

Other males thought that women are more tied to gender roles than men and have less freedom. But being female was assigned the advantages of being hit less, teased less, and even having some omniscient powers: "As a woman one would understand oneself," claimed one 18-year-old male. The older respondents were particularly concerned about breaking off with friends of the other sex and with whether or not they would be attracted to members of their own sex. Most concluded that they wouldn't be.

Other Comments.   Some thought the experience would be interesting and newsworthy, "I would keep a diary," and "I would write a book when I grow up." The adjustments mentioned most often by 11-year-olds involved friends' reactions. The 14-year-olds added problems of bathroom and shower activities, especially those associated with physical education classes at school. The 18-year-olds further extended the list to include problems of sexual preference.

Another common, perspective comment was that is would take time to learn how to be like the other sex. Many thought that their interests and attitudes would change, that they would have to learn how to act, how to dress, and even how to talk. Some indicated that they had spent their lives learning how to be their current sex, so that changes would require both time and effort.

In addition, a number of respondents mentioned that they would have to change their names or redecorate their rooms.

Last, discussions with parents were mentioned by all ages of respondents, suggesting a substantial dependence on their parents even among the oldest students.

QUESTIONS ABOUT THE EFFECTS
OF CHANGING SEX

After writing their story about what their lives would be like as the other sex, the subjects compared their life as the other sex with their real lives, using a scale that ranged from very strongly agree (1) to very strongly disagree (7) to answer each of the five questions presented here.

These responses were assessed by conducting a multivariage analysis of variance (manova) for each nationality. Sex and age of the respondents were the independent variables in each analysis. Across the dependent variables, the five questions, Swedish males rated the change as more negative ($M = 4.51$)

than the females (M = 4.18) did, a difference of .33. Comparable American means were 4.93 and 4.56, a difference of .37. Although the differences for Swedish and American respondents was not statistically significant, the greater American than Swedish asymmetry complemented the substantial differences in the asymmetries found in the stories, themselves. Moreover, disagreement ratings increased with age. Swedish 11-year-olds had an overall mean of 4.21; 18-year-olds had a mean of 4.53. The American means were 4.33 and 4.58. Both manovas yielded significant effects (using Wilks' Lambda) for sex, FSwedish(5, 537) = 8.07, FAmerican(5, 540) = 9.06, and for age group, FSwedish(10, 1074) = 2.16, FAmerican(10, 980) = 2.23, both ps < .05 but not for the interaction. Univariate tests are discussed here.

I would be able to do many more things than I do now. In general, Swedish subjects tended to disagree with this statement, with males (M = 5.06) disagreeing more than females (M = 4.56), F(1, 541) = 14.05. Disagreement also increased with age. Overall, the mean ratings by 11-, 14-, and 18-year-olds were 4.54, 4.86, and 5.12, F(2, 541) = 6.54. American subjects showed an identical pattern, except that American 18-year-old women (5.36) disagreed more than American 18-year-old men, further documenting greater American than Swedish asymmetry.

My new life would become harder than it is now. Swedish males were more likely to agree (3.11) with this statement than Swedish females, (3.78), F(1, 541) = 18.50, as did Americans (males = 2.97; females = 4.02, F(1, 329) = 20.08). These trends did not differ significantly by age or nationality.

My new life would be worse than it is now. Swedish women were more likely to disagree (4.51) with this statement than Swedish men (3.96), F(1, 541) = 12.47. Age had no effect on these views, but 18-year-old American women were somewhat more likely to agree (3.55) than 18-year-old American males (4.82), 18-year-old Swedish women (4.58), or 18-year-old Swedish men (4.16). Other than this interaction, the two nationalities showed the same patterns.

My new life would be more satisfying than it is now. Most subjects disagreed with this statement (the means for the Swedish and American subjects were 5.10 and 4.98), but the disagreements did not differ by sex, age, or nationality.

My new life would be happier. Again, subjects from both countries tended to disagree with this statement, and the extent of the disagreement increased with age. For Swedish subjects, the means for the 11-, 14-, and 18-year-olds were 5.42, 5.52, and 5.98, F(2, 541) = 3.01. Americans showed the same pattern. No sex differences emerged, although women tended to disagree less than men.

Overall, both Swedish and American respondents did not think that their lives would be better, easier, more satisfying, or happier if they changed sex, nor did they think that they would be able to do more things as the other sex. Females tended to be somewhat more favorably disposed toward changing sex, as were younger subjects, effectively supporting the interpretations of the stories.

The stories display highly stereotypical views, suggesting that these views are indeed central to the respondents' cultural gender schemata. Specifically, relative to females, males are assigned more instrumental, socially agentic, and emotionally controlled roles and fewer nurturant, expressive, supportive, and decorative roles. Also significant is the mention of nonpersonality-related gender differentiators in addition to personality traits. Treatment by others was mentioned far more often than personality characteristics.

SUMMARY

The stories written in response to the "change-sex" story yielded rich information about the activities, expected behavior, appearance, and treatment by others accorded each sex. The stories also afforded an overall assessment of the emotional reaction to such a change.

If females became males, they foresaw enjoying more athletics, staying out later at night, and traveling. They would be more interested in career activities and less in studying. If males became females, they would become more studious, more concerned about physical safety, and more burdened by menstruation, contraception, and childbirth. In brief, females seem to be associated with indoor and fairly passive activities, whereas males are seen as pursuing outdoor, vigorous activities. Additionally, males have more career opportunities than females.

Associated with these rather stereotypic views of the activities of the two sexes were equally stereotypic ideas about the expected emotions of the two groups. Females thought that, as males, they would be expected to be more aggressive and unemotional than they are as females. They would have to become more interested in fighting, showing off, and demonstrating sexual prowess. Males thought that as females they would be weaker, kinder, more passive, and more interested in stable sexual alliances than they are as males.

Changing sex also would necessitate changing appearance. Most of the respondents noted that females devote more time to their appearance than males. In addition, Americans, but not Swedes, depict women as preoccupied—even obsessed—with dieting.

Some particularly poignant remarks reflected the ways subjects believe that other people differentially value males. As males, they would receive respect and esteem; as females, they might not.

Overall, most males responded negatively to the prospect of changing sex; females were somewhat more receptive. As expected, these reactions were more extreme among Americans than among Swedes.

In chapter 9, we use still another spotlight to illuminate attributes about gender concepts and their effects upon gender roles. This time, 18-year-olds prophesy their hopes and plans for the future. They also describe the advice they would give to children and the adolescents about future plans and preparations.

9

Lifestyles that 18-Year-Olds Expect for Themselves in 10 Years' Time

What do 18-year-olds expect their lives to be like in 10 years' time? Do both sexes anticipate working outside the home, having families, as the Swedish vision implies? Do Swedish women, themselves, expect to be homemakers or did stories told by Swedish males to the change-sex cues represent primarily a male perspective? This would be a disappointing but telling outcome with respect to discrepancies between the Swedish vision and its realization. It would suggest that the Swedish arguments for the policy of gender equality, that both sexes would benefit from the sharing of financial and domestic roles, have not been fully inculcated by young people, the ones most likely to actualize gender equality.

We sought answers to these puzzles in the prophecies made by 18-year-olds about their future lives. Specifically, 18-year-olds in both countries were asked to predict their activities in 1994, 10 years later. We asked them what they expect to be doing, whether or not they expect to work outside the home, whether or not they plan to be cohabiting, the numbers of children they expect to have, their preferred and disliked occupations. We also asked them to indicate their ideal lives 10 years hence. In short, we wanted to examine the differences between their ideal, highly preferred activities and the activities that they thought were most probable for them, after a decade has passed.

Two further purposes motivated this research. One was to assess students' evaluations of their own educational background with respect to their future plans. If Swedish females have lower occupational goals than Swedish males or even than American females, differences might appear in their educational choices, in addition to their occupational preferences. The final purpose was to obtain the career planning advice that they would give to students who are developing career plans (16-year-olds) and to young students who probably had

not developed serious career plans (8-year-olds). This advice should also illuminate gender discrepancies in career expectations.

Responses to these questions (see Appendix I) are divided into two major
sections: Descriptions of ideal and most likely future plans of 18-year-olds and
an assessment of the career advice they would give to 16- and to 8-year-olds.

FUTURE PLANS

The future plans are further divided into general plans for their lives, educational plans, specific occupational plans, and attitudes that are likely to affect
future planning.

Do both sexes expect to work outside the home? To have families? To answer,
we examined some standard home and employment situations that students think
would be ideal in 10 years' time, as well as the situations they think that they
are likely to be in in 10 years' time. Two questions asked how many hours per
week they would ideally spend in paid employment outside the home in 1994
and how many hours they expected to be spending in paid employment outside
the home in 1994. This item yielded some surprising cultural differences, for,
although 69% of the Americans thought that working a 40-hour week outside
the home would be ideal and only 11% thought that working a 30-hour week
would be ideal, only 35% of the Swedes considered a 40-hour work week ideal
and 30% indicated that a 30-hour week would be ideal! These differences were
significant, X^2 (4) = 14.52, but sex differences were not. All told, 78 of the
women and 72% of the men thought it would be ideal to be working for at least
30 hours per week outside their homes in 10 years' time. Thus, both sexes in
both countries agree that it would be ideal to be employed at least 30 hours
per week, with more Americans than Swedes preferring a 40-hour work week.
What about their perceptions of the most likely scenario in 1994? In this case,
the percentages of Americans and Swedes expecting to work a 40-hour week
were 71 and 64; the percentages expecting a 30-hour work week were 17 and
28. These differences were not significant, X^2 (2) = 1.76. Overall, more men
(93%) than women (89%) thought that they probably would be working at least
30 hours per week outside the home, but this difference was not significant.
Clearly, most respondents of both sexes in both countries expect and want to
be gainfully employed in 10 years' time. These results challenge the "change-
sex" stories told by Swedish males. These stories suggested that they expected
Swedish women to be housewives. Few other occupations were acknowledged.
When Swedish women, themselves, are polled, as in the current questionnaire,
they indicate clear preferences for, and intentions to be in the workplace as adults.

These results may not tell a complete story, however, for Swedish women
have traditionally sought employment in less prestigious, female-dominated occupations. American women show the same tendency, but to a lesser extent,

as discussed in chapter 2. To gain insight into this issue, we turn to occupational preferences.

What occupations do the Swedish students consider most likely? The occupations considered most likely by Swedish women were, in order, sales, hospital worker, and children's caregiver (nanny), with shop assistant, a housewife, or unemployed tied for the next positions. Swedish men expected to be technicians, computer operators, temporarily unemployed, or skilled tradesworkers more often than the other occupations. These distributions differed reliably, X^2 (13) = 25.72. Not only is there no overlap (except for unemployment) between positions considered most likely by Swedish women and men, but both sexes expect to be in reasonably gender-stereotypic positions. Ratings of their *ideal* occupations yielded similar results, although the level of occupational aspiration rose. The five top choices of Swedish women were flight attendant, veterinarian, hospital worker, or children's caregiver, with a tie for the next place between shop assistant, owning a business, being a researcher, a journalist, or a travel agent. Swedish men would like to be technicians, computer operators, engineers, musicians, or have their own business. For the least desired occupations, Swedish women and men agreed that being a priest or being temporarily unemployed would be most undesirable, but, in addition, women considered being a factory worker or a politician undesirable. Men would dislike being a salesperson or a military officer.

In general, Americans expressed higher occupational goals (in terms of educational requirements, likely income and prestige) than the Swedes did. American women prefer to be a doctor/dentist, a psychologist, a chief executive officer of a private company, an attorney, and a business owner. American men's ideal choices were being a chief executive officer in a private business, an attorney, a doctor/dentist, a business owner, or a high school teacher. Note the substantial overlap between the choices of American men and women. Least liked by American women were being a custodian, temporarily unemployed, a factory worker, and a road worker. American men would least like to be temporarily unemployed. After that, they would dislike custodial work, and being a househusband. Obviously, these distributions differ from those given by the Swedish respondents, suggesting some cultural differences in the saliency of occupations in the two countries, although the differences might also be idiosyncratic to our samples. The major similarity is in the general desirability of being highly placed in a business, either as the chief executive officer, or as the owner.

Apparently, Swedish women share a commitment to gainful employment with Swedish men and both sexes of Americans, but their occupational aspirations are somewhat lower than those of the other groups. These lower aspirations may be partly responsible for the failure to achieve full gender equality in Sweden. American women claim occupational aspirations about as high as those of American men, even though statistics would argue that they are less likely to actually join the work force than their Swedish sisters.

Next, we asked the students to indicate the occupations for which they were studying. Again, the distributions for Swedish women and men differed, $X^2 = 28.20$. One third of the Swedish women said that they were studying to become children's caregivers. Another third were almost evenly divided between artist, TV repairer, nurse, air controller, nursing assistant, preschool teacher, and housewife. Apparently, the women perceive their training to be relevant to being a housewife. The remaining third of the women said that they had no idea—another surprising result, because no man said that he had no idea. This is also a telling result, for it is another manifestion of lower occupational goals. Of the Swedish men, 54% were studying to become television repairers, 18% were preparing to be television technicians, and the remainder were equally divided between engineer, technician, and signal repairer. Obviously, the students' marked preferences for certain occupations and dislikes for others often differed from the occupations that they thought they would have in 10 years. For the most part, they are studying for the positions they consider most likely, with the exception of one third of the women, who had no idea about the career for which they are studying.

In contrast, most Americans claimed to be studying for business careers (28% of the women and 35% of the men). Women also were preparing to become psychologists (12%) doctors/dentists (6%). Twelve percent had no idea what they were studying for. After business, men were preparing for a career as an attorney (16%), doctors/dentists (10%). Thirteen percent of American men had no idea.

These three reports (plans to be employed, occupational goals, and educational supports for occupational planning) converge on the conclusion that large numbers of women, like men, in both Sweden and the United States now expect to participate in the workplace, a remarkable testimonial to gender-role change. Even more intriguing, however, is the evidence that Swedish women have lower occupational aims, and associated limitations of education than the other groups. What can explain this perplexing state of affairs? Why should Swedish women have lower goals than American women when more Swedish than American women are in the work force? Part of the answer comes from the substantial number of Swedish women who work part time, a situation that is not as conducive to career commitments as full-time employment. Another part of the answer is that Swedish women seem to view their financial roles as a helper, as one of at least two contributors to the family larder or as a single contributor whose government provides a safety net. In brief, there may be fewer financial incentives for Swedish women to make commitments to careers in the workplace than for their American kin, whose government's largesse is far more limited.

How do other aspects of their anticipated adult lifestyles fit with the occupational goals of Swedes and Americans? Again, we consider both ideal and expected lifestyles. The Swedish respondents' ideal living situation in 1994 would be to live in a house (76% of the women, 75% of the men) with a person of the other sex to whom they were not married (58.3% of both sexes) or their spouse (37.5% of the women and 41.7% of the men) and with one (36% of women, 33.3% of men) or two (28% of women, 41.7% of men) children. The expected housing arrangements included three rooms and a kitchen (50% of women, 41.7% of men). Even though most of the women and men expected to be cohabiting (89%), 8%—all women—expect to be living alone. No man shared this expectation. Women's plans for children ranged from no children (25%) to one child (33.3%) to two children (33.3%) or more (8.4%). Men expected one (54.5%), two (36.4%), or more (9.1%) children. These differences are interesting and probably are in line with current living styles in Sweden. The differences in the distributions were not statistically significant.

Americans think that it would be ideal to be living with their spouse (these views differ reliably from the Swedish ones, $X^2(2) = 37.92$, primarily because Americans, more than Swedes, think that it would be ideal to be married to their cohabitant). Their ideal housing would be a house (88%). They would like to have two children (33%), although a number of respondents preferred one (29%) or no (27%) children. The remainder (11%) preferred to have three or more children. These preferences did not differ for the two countries or for the two sexes.

Both sexes think that they would be contented or very contented if their ideal lives materialized (91% of all of the women and 93% of all of the men). These views did not differ by nationality or sex. Both sexes think that they will be somewhat less contented with their probable lives in 1994 (70% of the women and 80% of the men). Again, these differences were not qualified by nationality or sex.

In general, the responses to these questions about their future lives seem thoughtful, reasonable, and informed. The Swedish indifference to the marital status of their cohabitants and the American preference for marriage indicate that the students are knowledgeable about contemporary living patterns in their respective countries and that they have adopted them. The reader may remember that chapter 2 describes a high rate of marriage in the Swedish nation. That is true—eventually. At the time of marriage, however, more than 90% of the Swedes have cohabited. Clearly, unmarried cohabitation is commonplace during the early years of adulthood, the time frame we were investigating.

In another section, we asked the students to indicate how important they thought various factors were to living a good life. They answered using a 7-point scale that extended from very important (1) to very unimportant (7).

The most important factor was having at least one close friend (1.46), followed by being nice to one another (mean = 1.62). Having self-esteem (1.88), having time for recreation (1.89), having a family (1.97), having many friends (2.29), and doing something well (2.33) were judged next in importance to having a good life. Also rated as important to a good life, although of less importance than the previously cited factors, were working full time to improve one's chances of being promoted and making a good salary (2.47), having money (2.98), and taking risks with the plans for one's life (3.54). Finally, they considered defining full time as 40 hours per week or as 30 hours per week to be still less important to a good life (3.97 and 4.09, respectively).

These data were subjected to a multivariate analysis of variance. In general, only nationality yielded reliable multi- and univariate main effects. Sex produced a single near significant effect for only one question (see later), and the interaction between nationality and sex did not show any reliable differences.

Overall, Americans rated having a family as more important to a good life (1.67) than Swedes did (2.60), $F(15, 190) = 8.26$, and Americans also considered self-esteem to be more important to a good life (1.67) than Swedes did (1.67), $F(15, 190) = 8.17$. In contrast, Swedes rated taking risks with one's life's plans as more important (2.90) than Americans did (3.80), $F(15, 190) = 8.43$, a result that is consistent with the career-planning advice they would give (see later section).

Although the next two questions were rated as lower in importance to a good life than the preceding ones, in each case, the Swedish respondents considered them more important than the Americans did: having full-time jobs defined as 40 hours per week (3.42 and 4.23, respectively) and having full-time jobs defined as 30 hours per week (3.17 and 4.51, respectively). The values of $F(15, 190)$ for these comparisons were 5.58, and 17.77. The single question that showed a trend toward sex differences was the one about redefining 30 hours as a full-time job. In this case, females rated this redefinition as somewhat more important (3.58) than men did (4.01), $F(15, 190) = 2.13$. Swedish women gave this item a higher rating (2.90) than Swedish men (3.45), American women (4.27) or American men (4.76). These results accord with the current debate in Sweden about the possibilities of reducing a full-time work week to 30 hours as a way to provide more time for family and recreational activities. Such possibilities have been discussed in the United States from time to time, but the idea has not attracted as much support as it has in Sweden.

Before considering the career advice the respondents would give to others, it is helpful to examine their own school paths. Males from both countries were more likely than females to take specialized mathematics and science courses, but the differences were reliable for the Swedish students, only. All of the American males, 96% of the American females, and 83% of the Swedish males but only 15% of the Swedish females had taken advanced or specialized courses in mathematics, $X^2(1) = 8.98$. Similarly, all American males, 98% of American females and 92% of Swedish males but only 38% of Swedish females had taken specialized science courses, $X^2(1) = 7.66$. The pattern differed for languages. All Swedish respondents and nearly all Americans (84% of the females and 79% of the males) had studied at least one foreign language. The sexes did not differ significantly when the measure was having studied at least one foreign language.

When the number of languages studied was examined, however, women had studied twice as many languages as men. Overall, the specialized courses in mathematics, science, and languages taken by American respondents of both sexes and the Swedish males should provide them with substantial freedom of choice for selecting either additional training or occupations. Swedish women, with their emphasis on languages, rather than on mathematics and science, presumably would have more constrained opportunities, although their language fluencies also should be marketable.

CAREER AND LIFE-PLANNING ADVICE
FOR 16- AND 8-YEAR-OLDS

What career advice would our respondents give to 16- and to 8-year-olds? For 16-year-olds, they thought that taking special courses was more important for both boys (3.02) and girls (3.10) than deciding on a career by age 16 (5.21 for boys, 5.20 for girls). Indeed, the latter ratings are toward the unimportant end of the continuum, suggesting that the students think it is not particularly important for youngsters to make early decisions about a career track. These are interesting results, because they may reflect the extended educational opportunities for adults now available in both Sweden and the United States. When adults have the opportunity to return for additional training after they have had a chance to learn more about themselves and about career possibilities, young people may not feel as much pressure to make early career decisions.

When we asked what advice they would give 8-year-olds about planning their lives, the option of postponing decisions until they were older also appeared: 75% of the Americans and 62% of the Swedes would advise 8-year-olds to wait before making career decisions. The remainder would advise them to study hard and to get good grades, rather nonspecific advice. For example, one man said, "Be hard on yourself. Don't let anything stand in the way of your plans." Another recommended, "Study hard so that you can get good grades for the future. Work well in any holiday job, if you get one. Devote yourself to whatever you are most interested in." One of the women suggested, "Study for as long as you can. Don't think too much about money. Do what you feel strongly for, but use your head, too." "Learn from your mistakes," counseled others. The general tenor of the remarks was that 8-year-olds should keep their options open, get a good education, and explore various options before making a career choice.

One last result is noteworthy: The advice was similar for girls and boys, with only a few exceptions. The exceptions typically consisted of additional comments for girls, comments that fell into two main categories. The first was that girls should persist in their career goals and not be deterred by their sex (mentioned by one Swedish male and five American females), and the second was that girls should focus on traditional communal enterprises, such as interpersonal skills, marriage (including not getting pregnant while in school). This latter group was cited by one Swedish female, five American males, and three American females.

In general, our 18-year-old respondents from Sweden and the United States would give markedly similar advice to young girls and boys. Both nationalities of respondents would counsel both sexes of 8-year-olds to wait before deciding about a career, to obtain a good education, and to be flexible, advice quite similar to what they would give to adolescents.

SUMMARY

This chapter focused on two areas not investigated by previous parts of the project: expectations for future lifestyles and counsel for younger people. From a number of perspectives, the lifestyles expected by 18-year-old Swedish and American respondents were quite similar. Both females and males expect and want to be working full time in gainful employment in 10 years' time. Swedes, more than Americans, were likely to consider a 30-hour work week as ideal, a view that accords with contemporary debates about a desirable balance between work and family/recreational time in Sweden. The respondents from both countries expect and want to be living in a house or a large apartment with a cohabitant and from 0–2 children. Swedes placed less emphasis on the importance of being married to their cohabitant than Americans did. Both nationalities and both sexes of respondents expected to be contented with their future lives.

The major difference in future plans surfaced in occupational choices. In Sweden, the ideal occupations of the two sexes showed no overlap. Swedish women were interested in service occupations, such as flight attendant, hospital worker, and children's caretaker (nanny), whereas Swedish men cited business-oriented occupations, such as technician, computer operator, engineer, and having their own business. This distribution of ideal occupations mirrors the existing dual labor market in Sweden and is, as noted in chapter 2, likely to impede the achievement of full equality in the country.

The ideal occupations mentioned by Americans showed greater overlap between the sexes, with both females and males listing doctor/dentist, attorney, and chief executive officer of own business among their top choices. There were some differences among the occuptions most disliked by respondents from the two countries, but all agreed that being temporarily unemployed was undesirable.

What are the chances that the respondents will achieve their occupational desires? Without a follow-up study (which would be impossible, because all identifying information has been destroyed), we cannot answer this question with certainty, but some information can be obtained from the career for which they are studying. One third of the Swedish women were studying to be children's caretakers, one third were studying for other occupations (they explicitly included housewife), and one third had no idea. This distribution contrasts with that for Swedish men, none of whom said that they had no idea, and with those for Americans, most of whom were studying for business or professional careers. About 12% of the Americans had no idea about how their studies related to an eventual occupation. These results highlight the educational–occupational discrepancies between the sexes that exist in Sweden. The educational differences in Sweden also were noticeable in the specialized courses that have been taken. Almost all Americans of both sexes and Swedish males but fewer Swedish females reported that they had taken specialized courses in mathematics and science, an educational difference that would be expected to limit somewhat the educational and occupational opportunities open to Swedish females. In contrast, although most respondents from both countries had studied at least one foreign language, females, particularly those from Sweden, had studied more foreign languages. Presumably, the respondents with specialized language training would be able to capitalize on their background. Such plans were surprisingly few in the listings of ideal occupations, however.

Several cautious implications can be drawn from these data. In each case, we need to remain skeptical, however, because the data represent speculations about future lifestyles. There is also the possibility that, despite the sizable numbers of respondents, our subjects were not representative of their compatriots.

In their "change-sex" stories, Swedish males depicted Swedish women as primarily homemakers, an image that appears to reflect a male, but not a female perspective. Apparently, Swedish males still envision housewifery as a central and appropriate role for women. Employment is not so viewed. In contrast, Swedish females expect to combine the two, although they evinced a lesser commitment to full-time careers than American women, perhaps because of the greater support from the state in Sweden. Succinctly stated, in the United States, one's own efforts may well be more likely to produce financial stability than reliance on the government. This is true in Sweden, as well, but to a lesser extent.

These results suggest some reasons for failures to achieve the goal of gender equality espoused by Sweden. If men hold specific, stereotypic expectations for women, such as staying at home, women are likely to be pressured to conform, even though they may not share the expectations. One way to resolve the discrepancy is to modify career aspirations to part time, rather than full time. Another way is to aim for occupations with lower educational requirements. Because the governmental safety net for the unemployed is more erratic and undependable in the United States than in Sweden, American women had not have the luxury of aiming for part-time employment. Part-time employment is not as common in the United States as in Sweden, and welfare recipients are not given the same educational and employment opportunities as they are in Sweden.

These results also illuminate components of adult gender roles. Adult occupation is prominent as a component in cultural gender concepts, at least, in both sexes in both countries, but is apparently stronger in males than in female concepts, at least in Sweden. Family roles also contribute to cultural gender concepts in both countries.

Other aspects of this questionnaire dovetail with the preceding analysis. For example, the expected and desired lifestyles of the respondents from the two countries were quite similar with respect to personal plans. The major differences were associated with occupational choices and previous courses, for which Swedish females recorded more traditionally circumscribed choices.

In addition, the major advice that the respondents would give to younger people was to wait, to not make early or hasty decisions about career goals. They would counsel the students to obtain a good education and to be flexible. The advice recommended for females and males by females and males was remarkably similar, with the minor exceptions that girls, more than boys, would occasionally be told to persist in their goals, deterred by their sex, or to develop interpersonal affiliations, including marriage. These results are consistent with the extended educational opportunities now available to both sexes in both countries.

10

Conclusions and Discussion

What story do our many response measures tell? Do we find support for the notions of distinct cultural gender concepts for females and males? Do these concepts really represent the culture in the sense that they describe perceptions of each sex held by both sexes in the culture? Do personal gender concepts differ from cultural gender concepts and should they be considered as separate? Are components of the gender concepts unique to individual countries (and are appropriately considered as cross-nationally similar components)? Do the components differ (and may be labeled as cross-national differences)? Are these similarities and differences consistent with distinguishing characteristics of the two countries, particularly Sweden's commitment to gender equality? Have we gained anything from using different measures? What are the implications? These are the issues that drive the research; these are the issues that we now address.

Most of the questions just raised are restatements of the predictions introduced at the end of chapter 4. In the first section, we evaluate the support for each prediction. We then turn to interpretations and implications of the results.

SUPPORT FOR THE PREDICTIONS

According to the first prediction, if we hold distinctive cultural gender concepts for most girls, most boys, most women, and most men, we will assign somewhat different constellations of attributes to each of these stimulus groups. Such constellations emerged. But just as conspicuously, some components did *not* differ: Some were shared by two or more of the stimulus groups. Before trying to reconcile this seeming paradox, we review the data.

Most Swedish girls, our data tell us, are kind/nice, friendly, and concerned with their appearance. Most American girls share these attributes. They also are described as playful. In general, most of the personality adjectives applied to most girls were expressive-communal in nature. Most boys also are kind/nice. They try to do their best; they never give up. They are athletic and competitive, an intriguing combination of expressive and instrumental attributes. Thus, most girls and boys are seen as kind/nice, but their other attributes differ. In brief, the distinguishing, distinctive characteristics of each gender concept is its particular *conjunction* of features. This is true for most women and most men, as well, although these conjunctions are both more complex and more nationally specific.

Most (Swedish) women are kind/nice, concerned about their appearance, gentle, friendly, and helpful, according to 11-year-old Swedish respondents. Older Swedes concurred, adding being ambitious, hardworking, patriotic, and liberated to the list. The gender concept for American women differs. For example, no American respondent freely listed "liberated" as an attribute of most American women. American women are rated by American women as affectionate, warm, loyal, sincere, sensitive, and compassionate and by American men as feeling good about themselves, self-confident, and as trying to do their best. American men also included some instrumental traits, along with expressive ones, but American women attributed primarily expressive-communal attributes to most women.

Note that in both countries, most women, like most girls and most boys, are kind/nice and have other expressive-communal attributes, but the conjunctions are distinctively different. Most men also are considered kind/nice, mainly by 11-year-old Swedish respondents. The 14-year-old Swedish respondents thought that most men were strong and that they acted as leaders; the 18-year-olds described most men as competitive, not showing their feelings, and dominant.

Most Swedish males leaven the instrumental-agentic traits ascribed to most men of trying to do their best and never giving up with such expressive qualities as being kind/nice, gentle, and helpful. The inclusion of the expressive traits was more pronounced with younger than with older Swedish subjects. American males suggest that men are self-confident and feel good about themselves, in addition to trying to do their best and never giving up. Thus, most American men were accorded somewhat more instrumental traits than were most Swedish men.

These descriptions, loosely collated from the various measures, certainly look like constellations of traits, like cultural gender concepts. Our informants had no difficulty characterizing most girls, most boys, most women, and most men in their countries; the attributes seemed to spring quickly to mind.

But to evaluate support for the first prediction we need to ask some other questions. Are these concepts *gender* concepts? Clearly they are. Marked differences distinguish among the concepts associated with females and those associated with males.

Are the gender concepts cultural? The acid test of a cultural influence on gender concepts is cross-sex concurrence on the nature of the concepts referring to females and those referring to males.

The impressive evidence of within-culture agreement about the contents of the cultural gender concepts suggests that cultural gender concepts not only exist but are quite well defined. Female and male respondents alike mentioned very similar conjunctions of attributes when asked to freely list those that they thought characterized most girls, most boys, most women, and most men in their culture. Female and male respondents also showed substantial agreement in the importance ratings they assigned to the traits applied to each of the four stimulus groups and to the characteristics they attributed to each sex in their change-sex stories. In brief, for these three quite different measures, the response patterns from the two sexes were highly similar, and this result held for both countries. The results also were similar across age groups within a country, although some developmental changes emerged. These findings are consistent with the view that members of a culture develop concepts for most girls, most boys, most women, and most men that correspond to those held by most other members of the culture. Note that these results argue against the contention that individuals may be divided into those who possess a single gender concept (e.g., Bem, 1981, 1985) and may be considered gender schematic versus those who do not hold this schema and are, therefore, gender aschematic. The results are more consistent with the perspective that separate gender schemata develop for the two genders associated with the two sexes (see Crane & Markus, 1982; Markus et al., 1982).

In essence, the presence of cultural gender concepts for females and males means that any adequate model of gender concepts must assume that both sexes within a culture will develop knowledge about societally held expectations for both sexes, as our model contends. Our model provides for a third gender concept, a personal gender concept. Is this assumption supported? Again, the answer is ringingly affirmative, for the self-ratings described in chapter 7 identified a number of attributes that differentiated between the sexes. Most impressive among these differences was the Americans' claims to be aggressive themselves, although they did not rate aggressiveness as very important for most Americans, including most American men. Thus far, we find general support for the first prediction stated in chapter 4.

The second prediction, that of cross-cultural differences, was emphatically documented by all of our measures. Many of these differences were described previously, such as greater differences between the sexes (asymmetry) in the United States than in Sweden. Overall, the cultural gender concepts, be they for males or females, show some cross-national differences, just as the personal gender concepts did (e.g., the differences in self-ascribed aggressiveness). The "change-sex" stories further emphasized cultural differences. Most of the differences were expected and showed that Swedish respondents both accepted their own gender roles and the possibility of assuming gender roles of the other sex with more equanimity than Americans, but a few differences were unexpected. For example, although the Swedish stories frequently noted that females devote more time to their appearance than males, a factor that also emerged in the American stories, the American, but not the Swedish, stories dwelt on the need for American females to watch their weight. To be more precise, the American stories almost seemed fixated on the subject of eating/dieting.

From a slightly different perspective, the data suggest that the gender concepts generated for most females and most males in one culture (cultural gender concepts) are insufficient to explain one's own gender-related self-assignments. Instead, these self-assignments, or what we have labeled *personal gender concepts*, differ significantly from the cultural gender concepts, although, as with cultural gender concepts, some components were shared by the various concepts. The evidence for personal gender concepts affirmed the views advanced by Martin and Halverson (1983) and by Spence et al. (1975) but deviates from the views of Bem (1981, 1982) and Markus (Crane & Markus, 1982; Markus et al., 1982). In general, the differences are less pronounced among Swedes, as we might expect for inhabitants of a country that has pursued an active policy of equality for more than a decade, and this pattern was found for both cultural and personal gender concepts.

Fortunately, not all attributes showed cross-national differences. Those appearing to be treated similarly in the two countries serve two useful functions. The first is to suggest that the differences were not due solely to subjects from one country interpreting the tests very differently from subjects from the other country. The second is to document the areas in which the people from the two countries share views. If the measures are indeed sensitive, they should mirror cultural similarities, as well as differences. In fact, cultural similarities turned out to be far more numerous than cultural differences, an unsurprising result, given the numerous parallels between the two countries in terms of economy, democratic structures, standard of living, and widespread literacy.

At this point, then, the model is faring well. The evidence for cultural gender concepts for each sex and for personal gender concepts is robust, as is the evidence for cross-national effects. According to the model, the gender concepts develop from the child's experiences, which are societally influenced. This hypothesized relation, coupled with the proposed dynamic nature of the gender concept acquisition process led to the third and fourth predictions that gender concepts would show developmental changes and that these changes would differ for the two countries. We actually had two ways to assess these predictions: differences in the components of gender concepts shown by raters of the three ages (11-, 14-, and 18-year-olds) and differences in the gender attributes assigned to younger (most girls, most boys) versus older (most women, most men) age groups.

Both sets of data yield supporting findings. As noted in connection with the first prediction, girls and boys are generally ascribed more active and expressive traits than women and men, and this is particularly true in Sweden, but the major differences among the four stimulus groups were those for gender and its interaction with country. Developmental changes across the age categories emerged more often for Swedes than for Americans. One striking example is that, although Swedish females and males, and American women to a somewhat lesser extent, showed some changes in their personal gender concepts, American males did not. In fact, 11- and 18-year-old American males agreed completely in the attributes they rated as most important to themselves! The simplest explanation for these results seems to be that the American cultural gender concepts for males, regardless of age, are relatively clear, constant, and consistently reinforced from an early age through adulthood. More than the other gender concepts in either the United States or Sweden, the American perception of maleness seems monolithic and relatively impervious to change.

What about younger versus older age groups? Again, some differences emerged. Most girls and most boys were seen as more active/lively and somewhat more gentle than most men. In general, however, the differences were more pronounced between females and males than between younger and older age groups. The interactions with country were intriguing, for, in keeping with the prevailing pattern of fewer Swedish than American gender differences, Swedish women shared substantial components with Swedish men, whereas American women resembled American girls more than American men.

The fifth prediction stated simply that female and male correspondents from the same culture would agree on the contents of cultural gender concepts. The support accorded the fifth prediction was noted in connection with discussions of the prediction that cultural gender concepts would emerge. Even though this support was robust at a general level, finer grained analyses illuminated one of the most intriguing aspects of our data, the widespread sharing of components by the gender concepts for most girls, most boys, most women, and most men. In other words, some attributes are freely listed or rated as highly important to more than one of the four stimulus groups, indicating partial overlap in the cultural gender concepts for these groups. These tantalizing findings suggest that both sexes share attributes considered highly related to each gender, just as age groups do, and that the shared attributes differ somewhat for the two countries. Most important, the attributes rated as important were less likely to distinguish between the two sexes than were attributes rated less important! How should these results be interpreted? We return to this perplexing issue after considering the support for the sixth prediction, that the results of the various measures would show at least partial convergence.

The measures did converge on the now-familiar theme of some similarities and some differences. The various measures afforded both advantages and disadvantages. What, if anything, was gained from each measure?

Our first measure was the listing of generally admired traits, regardless of sex.

We thought that some traits might function as cultural imperatives, as attributes typically expected of all citizens within a country. Not so. Although 11-year-olds from both countries often admired being kind/nice, at last one third of the respondents chose other attributes that they admired most. Similarly, most, but by no means all, 18-year-olds admired honesty. These listings yielded greater cross-national similarity than any of the others. They have the distinct disadvantage of *not* assessing gender-related admiration.

When most girls, most boys, most women, and most men were freely characterized some different attributes were used. For example, honesty almost disappeared, and cross-national differences increased. The major benefit of the free listings was that they indicated the most accessible attributes associated with each of the four stimulus groups. These orderings could then be compared with the importance ratings to assess correspondences. Additionally, we planned to use this measure to catch gender- and culture-distinctive attributes we failed to include in the importance ratings. And some appeared, such as being playful for youngsters. Generally speaking, we did not find significant attributes that had been overlooked—indeed, the evidence went in the opposite direction. There were attributes rated as highly important that did not surface among the freely listed traits. Two outstanding examples are tries to do one's best and never gives up.

As a measure, the free-wheeling appeal of the free listings was compromised by substantial numbers of idiosyncratic responses. This result, expected to be sure, severely limits its use as a single instrument for assessing gender concepts. It is best used in conjunction with other, more systematic measures for gaining information.

The importance listings afforded systematic ratings by almost all of the respondents (a few raters, primarily 11-year-olds, occasionally ignored words that they did not understand, as they had been instructed to do). The utility of importance ratings is largely determined by the particular attributes that are rated, of course, and we were pleased that we had taken promising items from a number of American scales for assessing gender roles and gender attitudes.

As Deaux and Lewis (1984) suggest, the components of the concepts contain attributes other than personality characteristics, including physical characteristics. Interestingly, subjects did not rate physical characteristics as very effective gender differentiators, although previous work (Carlsson, personal communication; Intons-Peterson, in press) have shown that physical attributes are important, just as are occupations and activities (e.g., Deaux & Lewis, 1984; Intons-Peterson, in press). Despite their relatively low importance ratings, physical characteristics were among the attributes that Swedes would change to achieve an ideal self. For example, Swedish women would like to be shorter and to have less straight hair! Taken collectively, the results suggest that research focusing solely on personality differences may miss contributing and differentiating components of the gender concepts. Personality traits certainly play a role, however, and our data are generally consistent with results of earlier studies that focused solely on these traits, using such instruments as the BSRI, EPAQ, and ACL.

Serious disadvantages of importance ratings are that they are tedious, subjects may use only the middle ranges of responses, and when asked to apply the attributes to different stimulus groups, some subjects may try to use the same response for an adjective without thinking of how suitable the reponse is. The "change-sex" stories yielded the richest information, but they are difficult to score and magnify the problems of idiosyncratic responding. A similar problem occurs with advice 18-year-olds would give to others. Finally, the information about lifestyle plans of the 18-year-olds, obtained objectively, nicely rounded out the picture of our respondents' expectations for the future. Those expectations turned out to be markedly gender specific.

In brief, the measures yielded some converging and complementary evidence and some unique information. No single measure seemed to us to be sufficient to handle all of the tasks of identifying the components of gender concepts.

HIGHLY IMPORTANT AND CHARACTERISTIC GENDER COMPONENTS ARE NOT DISTINCTIVE GENDER DIFFERENTIATORS

The data delivered a challenging puzzle: Some attributes are rated as highly important to both cultural and personal gender concepts and are cited quite often in the free descriptions, yet these attributes rarely show gender differences. Thus, we have the interesting paradox that when respondents identify the most important characteristics of "girlness," they tend to use some of the same traits they use to characterize "boyness." The same is true for the adult comparisons. In brief, some attributes contribute significantly to more than one gender concept. The differentiating aspects, although typically less salient and rated as less important, function to render each concept qua concept unique. Figure 10.1 illustrates these relations for cultural gender concepts.

Figure 10.1 was constructed from the attributes with the 10 highest importance ratings for each of the four stimulus groups and from attributes that frequently emerged in the free listings of traits. A few other attributes that distinguished one group from others also were included. Those attributes rated as highly important to all four groups—and that did not differentiate among the groups—were assigned to the intersection of the four concepts. Attributes that were reliably associated more often with one group (say "competitive" with most men for the Swedish concepts) are assigned to nonoverlapping portions of the concept.

Although largely restricted to the most important attributes, the tentative results graphically depict some of our central findings. First, all four stimulus groups shared more attributes in the Swedish than in the American data, and second,

AMERICAN CULTURAL GENDER SCHEMATA

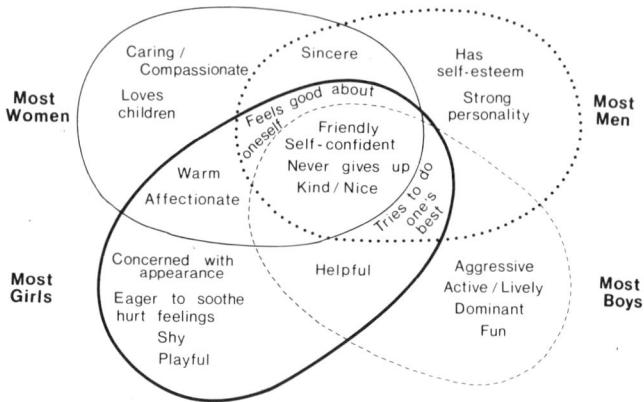

SWEDISH CULTURAL GENDER SCHEMATA

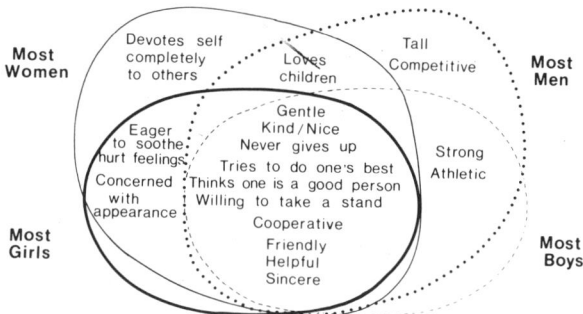

FIG. 10.1   Schematic American and Swedish cultural gender concepts

no attributes reasonably unique to most girls and to most boys were observed in the Swedish data although they were in the American data. These results again emphasize the greater androgyny of Swedish cultural gender concepts, and they suggest that gender-differentiating attributes are more likely to appear in Swedish concepts for adults than for children.

The most interesting aspect of the nondifferentiating components is their importance. Clearly, these attributes were typically rated as more important and were freely cited more often than the gender-differentiating attributes. Being kind/nice, trying to do one's best, never giving up, and being willing to take a stand are important aspects of one's own self-ratings. To remove these components from the gender concepts would be to remove essential aspects. For example, boys who do not try to do their best, who give up easily, and so on, would not fit the cultural gender concept for most boys as well as boys who display these traits even though the two groups are otherwise matched in terms of the stereotypic gender-differentiating traits that they possess. These attributes may not distinguish one gender concept from another but they are powerful, conjunctive, components of their gender concepts. They seem to function as the essence, the fundamental core of the cultural concepts that is then embellished and rendered sexually distinctive by the addition of other attributes.

The same approach was used to diagram personal cultural concepts for the two countries. As Fig. 10.2 shows, the results paralleled those of cultural gender concepts in the sense that female and male concepts shared more attributes for the Swedish results than for the American ones. Moreover, the personal and cultural gender concepts differ in a number of ways. Swedish males describe themselves as being more helpful, active/lively, and as standing up under pressure than they think most Swedish males possess. American males describe themselves as being more willing to take a stand, as a better person, as more sincere, and

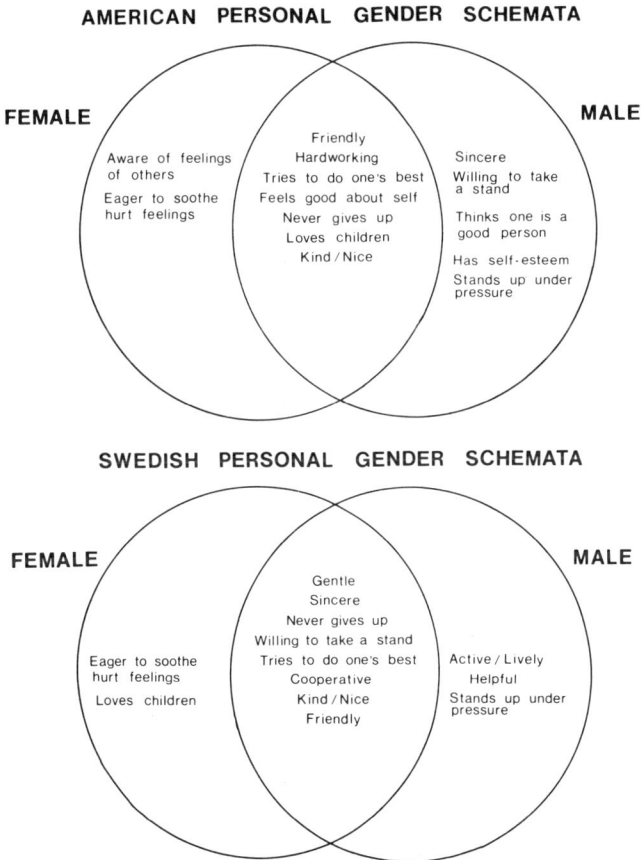

AMERICAN PERSONAL GENDER SCHEMATA

FEMALE — MALE

Aware of feelings of others
Eager to soothe hurt feelings

Friendly
Hardworking
Tries to do one's best
Feels good about self
Never gives up
Loves children
Kind / Nice

Sincere
Willing to take a stand
Thinks one is a good person
Has self-esteem
Stands up under pressure

SWEDISH PERSONAL GENDER SCHEMATA

FEMALE — MALE

Eager to soothe hurt feelings
Loves children

Gentle
Sincere
Never gives up
Willing to take a stand
Tries to do one's best
Cooperative
Kind / Nice
Friendly

Active / Lively
Helpful
Stands up under pressure

FIG. 10.1 Schematic American and Swedish personal gender concepts

as more likely to stand up under pressure than they think characterize most American males. The personal and cultural concepts for women show fewer differences.

A number of questions arise about these relations. Why should the overlapping attributes be considered as components of the gender concepts at all? It might be more sensible to consider them as part of a "national" schema. This is a reasonable possibility that we must entertain. The major countervailing argument is that the attributes often are rated as highly important characteristics of each stimulus group, including self, and this is true in both countries. The ratings convey the impression that the respondents consider it highly important for both most women and most men (and for most girls and most boys) to have certain (identical) attributes. These groups also have other characteristics that distinguish among them, although these latter attributes are less important to their essential qualities than the nondifferentiating ones.

SWEDEN'S POLICIES OF GENDER EQUALITY
AFFECT GENDER CONCEPTS—SLOWLY

Because many of the cross-national similarities are consistent with similar economic and governmental practices in the two countries, it is tempting to ascribe the cross-national differences to Sweden's program of gender equality. The differences, themselves, are fully compatible with what might be expected from Sweden's systematic program of equality. The cultural gender concept for most Swedish women contained more instrumental-agentic traits than its American counterpart, just as the concept for most Swedish men contained more expressive-communal traits than that for most American men. In other words, the American gender concepts, particularly those for adults, could be described as more traditionally gender stereotyped than those of Swedes.

Further support is provided by the "change-sex" stories. American women, more than Swedish women, were likely to favor the idea of changing sex, whereas American men and Swedish men alike rejected the notion of changing sex. Swedish respondents, more than American ones, occasionally said that changing sex would not have a major effect upon their lives, other than the inconvenience of buying new clothes, learning "how" to be the other gender, and so forth.

As captured by the change-sex results, another conclusion is warranted. A preference for the male role continues to exist in both countries. The male role is accorded a privileged status. This is not to say that the female respondents in both countries all envied the male role. Indeed, many of the respondents, particularly younger Swedish females, were content with the female role and wrote disparaging stories about the male role, but they also noted that males had more opportunities of various kinds. Our scorers received the distinct impressions that many of the women were resigned to some inequities, and that they have "made their peace" with the situation by focusing on negative and hazardous aspects of the male role and on positive aspects of the female role.

Swedish 11- and 14-year-old females were quite content with their roles. The Swedish 18-year-olds were more favorable than the younger subjects to changing sex, perhaps because they, more than their younger compatriots, had become aware of the restricted avenues open to them. These women were likely to note that it was easier for men to get jobs, that men could go out more at night and generally had fewer fears about personal safety, and other related points. Most striking, however, was the general acceptance of their current roles shown by Swedish females and males compared to that of American females. Clearly, the views are far more symmetric in Sweden than in the United States, and the most reasonable explanation is that the systematic Swedish policy and its legal implementation has produced the perception of greater equality than exists in the United States.

The perception of greater equality in Sweden than in the United States accords with various statistics. For example, in 1981, 85% of Swedish women aged 25–54 but only 67% of American women the same age were in the labor force. Moreover, the salaries of Swedish women are roughly 90% of those of men, in contrast to the comparable figure of 63% in the United States. These figures depict a more advantageous economic position for Swedish than for American women. They also document, it must be noted, the continuing relative advantage of men, even in Sweden. Presumably, these disparities are more likely to be realized by older, rather than younger, Swedish women, and may, in turn, cause some discontent with the female gender role, just as it does in the United States. It is also possible that Swedish women realize how many changes have been made in the last few decades and are appreciative of them. Progress of American women has been slower.

THEORETICAL IMPLICATIONS

Other Models.   The results argue forcefully that adequate models of gender concepts must encompass both cultural and personal gender concepts and their development. Such a model must accommodate the influences of society, a requirement met by virtually all theories of gender development, with the likely exception of biologically based models, such as those of Freud (1933/1965) and his followers, and the newer cerebral lateralization models (Buffery & Gray, 1972; Harshman & Remington, 1976). These models have been severely challenged conceptually and empirically (Bleier, 1987; Intons-Peterson, in press).

Models that place greater emphasis on the person's social environment, and the acquisition of knowledge about seemingly gender-related aspects seem more promising. More than any other theorist, Bem (1981, 1985) has focused attention on the development of a schema for gender. Her pioneering paper (1981) heralded a new approach to theories of gender development. It is not surprising, therefore, that it did not include all of the characteristics that we now know to be important, such as provisions for cultural gender concepts for each of the two sexes or for the differentiation between cultural and personal gender schemata. Serbin and Sprafkin (1986) combined features of Bem's model with Kohlberg's (1966) cognitive developmental approach. They assume that the child cognitively classifies gender-related information into dichotomies that subsequently lead to the development of "sex-role" concepts. They then predict that "the salience of gender as a dimension for classification should be greatest just before sex rates are learned and should decline as they are mastered conceptually" (p.1189), a perplexing prediction given that the original gender-related information should subsume the sex role-related information. (This point also illustrates the ambiguity of use of the terms *gender* and *sex*).

The views of Markus (e.g., Crane & Markus, 1982; Markus et al., 1982) make allowances for cultural and personal gender concepts but do not detail developmental aspects. Closest to our view is Martin and Halverson's (1981) model, although they couched their predictions in terms of "in-group" (same sex) and "out-group" (other sex). It seems clearer to use terms that are more descriptive, such as "same sex," where appropriate. Unfortunately, Martin and Halverson did not accord as much significance to cultural influence as we considered important; hence, we opted to define our own model.

Our Model.   The results have been encouraging, and we conclude that our model is useful. In addition, the data highlight theoretical implications that inform our model. Basically, as presented in chapter 1, we hypothesize that people form gender concepts in much the same way that they develop concepts for other complexes of related concepts and actions. The maturing child associates certain objects, actions, traits, opinions, and related concepts with femaleness or maleness, and these associations function as the components of the concepts. Because the components are related to the experiences of the child, they are subject to change as the child ages. Simultaneously, the child develops a concept about self that includes elements related to gender. These elements may, but do not necessarily, overlap with those contained in the child's concept for most females or for most males.

As our data proclaim, substantial numbers of components function in the concepts for most males and most females as well as in the self-concept. Not all components of either cultural or personal gender concepts distinguish one gender from the other. Indeed, our results suggest that the most salient and important components do not differentiate, although they seem to be integral to the concepts.

As described so far, the model does not address the question of how the components of gender concepts are learned. We propose that, like other concepts, gender concepts function as classification systems, as devices for sorting people (or other things) into categories. Such systems typically have been explained in one of three ways (Medin & Smith, 1984; Smith & Medin, 1981): classical, probabilistic, or exemplar views. Classical models assume that each concept or category has necessary and sufficient defining features. Cast in terms of our research, this view predicts that each person has a set of necessary and sufficient features for each gender concept, a prediction obviously at odds with our findings of concept-overlapping features. The only way to reconcile the results with the assumptions of necessary and sufficient defining features is to posit that the subjects define their concepts to include both sexes, both ages, or sexes plus ages. This is so because the subjects frequently use the same adjective to define more than one of the four stimulus groups. The difficulty with this argument is that not all of the adjectives followed this pattern; some attributes differentiated between the sexes or the age groups. Hence, some attributes could not have been necessary and sufficient designators of the gender concepts.

According to the second type of classification model, a probabilistic or prototypic one, a concept corresponds to the central tendency of the properties (features, dimensions) of its instances. These properties are probabilistically related to the summary representation, an assumption that means that not all features or attributes associated with a concept need appear for an instance to be considered an exemplar of the concept. As typically construed, the features or dimensions actually present in an instance are summed or acknowledged in some way. Moreover, some features or dimensions are weighted more heavily (are more important) than others. To make classificatory decisions, the weighted features are summed. If the weighted sum exceeds a criterion, the instance is classified with the concept. It is this assumption that fits uneasily with our data, for a standard view is that the most relevant (read most differentiating) attributes are weighted the most heavily, and yet we found that the attributes with heavy weights were unlikely to be uniquely associated with any one concept. In fact, the attributes that were most likely to be distinguished between the concepts had relatively low weights in terms of both free listings of the traits and the importance ratings. These patterns were as characteristic of individual subjects as they were of the averages. The generic prototypic models are not definitely excluded by our data, of course, but they are rendered far less plausible and attractive as explanations for the underlying structures that configure the concepts.

A third classification model, the exemplar view, argues that a concept is nothing more than the separate characteristics of each of its exemplars. No single summary representation of the concept exists. Because this model obviously is the most promising candidate for explaining our results, we go into greater detail about its assumptions than we did for the first two perspectives. As Smith and Medin (1981) stated, an exemplar is categorized as an instance of a concept, say most women, if and only if the exemplar activates a criterial number of the features in instances of most women before activating a criterial number of features associated with instances of other concepts, say most men. They proposed further that the probability that an instance activates an exemplar of the concept is directly related to the similarity between the instance and another exemplar.

This view seems to accommodate our findings more readily than the two other views. It permits substantial overlap among the features activating or associated with particular concepts. Overlapping features simply would not be determinative; the gender-discriminating features with relatively low weights would be.

When adapting the exemplar model of classification to our preliminary model, we posit that the weights of the exemplars vis-à-vis particular concepts would change with age. This assumption is consistent with our developmental data, given the qualifications that the rate of change with age is slow indeed.

Taking all of these factors into account, a fuller description of our revised model is that, as they mature, individuals associate various attributes, features, or dimensions with girlness, boyness, womanness, manness. Some of the attributes are associated with more than one concept, but a few are unique to one. These attributes may refer to personality characteristics, occupations, activities, physical characteristics, and so on. When the total weight of the features retrieves a criterial number of exemplars associated with one gender concept, say girls, then the person, activity, event or other stimulus source of the features will be assigned to girls. The features associated with a particular gender concept will be determined by the experience of each individual, some of which presumably differ with gender, age, and culture. Similar processes occur with personal gender concepts.

SOCIAL POLICY AND GENDER CONCEPTS

Can gender-related social policy affect gender concepts? We must conclude that the answer seems to be yes. Gender-related attitudes in Sweden show fewer gender-related differences than gender-related attitudes in the United States. But are these differences due to Sweden's policy of gender equality? We cannot be certain, for the research offers inferential support, at best. The results are impressive, however, in their consistency with what would be expected from Sweden's policies. Swedish women are described both expressive and instrumental. They are considered liberated, an adjective never used to characterize American women. This does not mean that no American women are liberated. Rather, it means that being liberated is not an attribute that occurred to our respondents when they thought about most American women. Swedish men are instrumental, just as American men are, but they are also seen as expressive. This moving together of the components of Swedish gender concepts for women and men parallels what we would expect from Sweden's policies.

Perhaps nowhere is this clearer than when we consider as aspect of the Swedish experience that deviates from full participation in the Swedish plan, Swedish women's economic contribution, and Swedish men's domestic contribution. Although attitudes seem to be changing more in Sweden than in the United States, gender stereotypoic attitudes still persist, even among the 11-year-olds, probably fostered by their parents, other adults (remember the males in Trost's, 1983, study who disapproved of paternity and child-care leaves), and various institutions (Trost also noted greater support for the gender equality program within the government than the public sector) in the Swedish nation. The influence of these forces surfaced most pronouncedly in the "change-sex" stories and in the occupational–educational plans of 18-year-olds. In their stories about changing sex, the males expected females to play domestic roles. Significant economic roles were simply not part of their scenarios. Although Swedish women did not really affirm their domestic roles in the "change-sex" stories, neither did they lay claim to ambitious careers. This almost laissez-faire attitude toward employment continued in Swedish 18-year-old females' very modest occupational and educational aspirations. According to their "change-sex" stories, Swedish males often explicitly denied domestic interests, although their future expectations typically included cohabitation and children.

These attitudes are surely encouraged by continuing sources of gender discrimination. They are likely to perpetuate gender-differentiating attitudes in both sexes and militate against a complete achievement of the Swedish vision.

The moral is clear. In a quest for gender equality, changing practices may be effective ways of changing attitudes. Without a change in attitudes, however, the practices probably will not effect full gender equality. Thus, a feedback loop develops, with the practices contributing to modifications of the components of gender concepts, which, in turn, affect espousal of the practices.

Note that our data indicate that the rate of change in gender concepts is slow, even when bolstered by monumental governmental and legal provisions. After all, the Swedish policies have been in effect since 1968 or so, longer than some of our respondents had been alive. Moreover, social change in a heterogenous society probably is more difficult and sluggish, an ominous prospect for the United States or any other country that embarks on such a program.

In the course of our investigation of the components of the gender concepts of Swedish and American 11-, 14-, and 18-year-olds we found some surprising similarities as well as differences. One of the most interesting results was that attributes that were listed frequently as characteristic of most girls, most boys, most women, or most men also were rated as highly important to the stimulus groups. These attributes did *not* differentiate among the groups, however. The attributes that differentiated among the groups were not listed as often and were rated as less important than the nondifferentiating ones. These results, which fit nicely into an exemplar model of gender concept development, provide new insights into gender-role development. The results also indicated that the male role is still valued more highly than the female role, although this discrepancy has been moderated somewhat in Sweden, which has pursued a program of equal opportunity for more than a decade.

REFERENCES

Anderson, J. L. (1986). *Scandinavian humor & other myths*. Minneapolis, MN: Nordbook.

Andersson, T., Magnusson, D., & Duner, A. (1983). *"Basdata-81"; Livssituationen i tidig vuxenalder*. Individ, Utreckling och Miljo, Rapport No. 49, Department of Psychology, University of Stockholm, Stockholm, Sweden.

Bakan, D. (1966). *The duality of human existence*. Chicago: Rand McNally.

Barry, H. III, Bacon, M. K., & Child, I. L. (1957). A cross-cultural survey of some sex differences in socialization. *Journal of Abnormal and Social Psychology, 55*, 327–332.

Basow, S. A. (1986). *Gender stereotypes: Traditions and alternatives* (2nd ed.). Monterey, CA: Brooks/Cole.

Baude, A. (1979). Public policy and changing family patterns in Sweden: 1930–1977. In J. Lipman-Blumen & J. Bernard (Eds.), *Sex roles and social policy* (pp.145–176). Beverly Hills, CA: Sage.

Bem, S. L. (1974). The measurement of psychological androgyny. *Journal of Consulting and Clinical Psychology, 42*, 155–162.

Bem, S. L. (1981). Gender schema theory: A cognitive account of sex typing. *Psychological Review, 88*, 354–364.

Bem, S. L. (1982). Gender schema theory and self-schema compared: A comment on Markus, Crane, Bernstein, and Siladi's "Self-Schemas and Gender." *Journal of Personality and Social Psychology, 43*, 1192–1194.

Bem, S. L. (1985). Androgyny and gender schema theory: A conceptual and empirical integration. In T. B. Sonderegger (Ed.), *Nebraska symposium on motivation, 1984: Psychology and gender* (pp.179–226). Lincoln, NE: University of Nebraska Press.

Bem, S. L., & Bem, D. J. (1976). Case study of a nonconscious ideology: Training the woman to know her place. In S. Cox (Ed.), *Female psychology: The emerging self* (pp.180–190). Chicago: Science Research Associates.

Berry, J. W. (1969). On cross-cultural comparability. *International Journal of Psychology, 4*, 119–128.

Best, D. L., Williams, J. E., Cloud, J. M., Davis, S. W., Robertson, L. S., Edwards, J. R., Giles, H., & Fowles, J. (1977). Development of sex-trait stereotypes among young children in the United States, England, and Ireland. *Child Development, 48*, 1375–1384.

Bieri, J., Bradburn, W., & Galinsky, M. (1958). Sex differences in perceptual behavior. *Journal of Personality, 26*, 1–12.

Bleier, R. (1987, February). *Sex differences research in the neurosciences*. Paper presented at the American Association for the Advancement of Science Symposium "Bias in sex differences research," Chicago.

Block, J. H. (1973). Conceptions of sex roles: Some cross-cultural and longitudinal perspectives. *American Psychologist*, 512–526.

Broverman, I. K., Vogel, S. R., Broverman, D. M., Clarkson, F. E., & Rosenkrantz, P. S. (1972). Sex-role stereotypes: A current appraisal. *Journal of Social Issues, 28*, 59–78.

Buffery, A. W. H., & Gray, J. A. (1972). Sex differences in the development of spatial and linguistic skills. In C. Ownsted & D. C. Taylor (Eds.), *Gender differences: Their ontogeny and significance* (pp.128–157). Baltimore, MD: Williams & Wilkins.

Campbell, D. T. (1964). Distinguishing differences of perceptions from failures of communication in cross-cultural studies. In F. S. C. Northrop & H. H. Livingston (Eds.), *Cross-cultural understanding: Epistemology in anthropology* (pp.308–336). New York: Harper & Row.

Carlsson, M. (1981). Note on the factor structure of the Bem Sex Role Inventory. *Scandinavian Journal of Psychology, 22*, 123–127.

Carlsson, M., Andersson, K., Berg, E., Jaderquist, P., & Magnusson, E. (1984). Opinions of typical female and male sex-role behavior in Swedish children. *Scandinavian Journal of Psychology, 25*, 276–283.

Coffman, R., & Levy, B. I. (1972). The dimensions implicit in psychological masculinity-femininity. *Educational and Psychological Measurement, 32*, 975–985.

Cole, M., Gay, L., Glick, J. A., & Sharp, D. W. (1971). *The cultural context of learning and thinking: An exploration in experimental anthropology.* New York: Basic Books.

Constantinople, A. (1973). Masculinity-femininity: An exception to a famous dictum. *Psychological Bulletin, 80*, 389–407.

Crane, M., & Markus, H. (1982). Gender identity: The benefits of a self-schema approach. *Journal of Personality and Social Psychology, 43*, 1195–1197.

Deaux, K. (1984). From individual differences to social categories: Analysis of a decade's research on gender. *American Psychologist, 39*, 105–116.

Deaux, K., & Lewis, L. L. (1983). Components of gender stereotypes. *Psychological Documents, 13*, 25 (Ms. No. 2583).

Deaux, K., & Lewis, L. L. (1984). Structure of gender stereotypes: Interrelationships among components and gender label. *Journal of Personality and Social Psychology, 46*, 991–1004.

Edwards, A. L., & Ashworth, C. D. (1977). A replication study of item selection for the Bem Sex-Role Inventory. *Applied Psychological Measurement, 1*, 501–507.

Edwards, J. R., & Williams, J. E. (1980). Sex-trait stereotypes among young children and young adults: Canadian findings and cross-national comparisons. *Canadian Journal of Behavioural Science, 12*, 210–220.

Ember, C. R. (1981). A cross-cultural perspective on sex differences. In R. H. Munroe, R. L. Munroe, & B. B. Whiting (Eds.), *Handbook of cross-cultural human development* (pp. 531–580). New York: Garland.

Fact Sheets on Sweden (1982–1984). Stockholm: The Swedish Institute.

Fagot, B. (1978). The influence of sex of child or parental reactions to toddler children. *Child Development, 49*, 462.

Foa, U. G., Anderson, B., Converse, J. Jr., Urbansky, W. A., Cawley, M. J., III, Muhlhausen, S. M., & Tornblom, K. Y. (1987). Gender-related sexual attitudes: Some cross cultural similarities and differences. *Sex Roles, 16*, 511–519.

Freud, S. (1965). Femininity. In J. Strachey (Trans. and Ed.), *New introductory lectures on psychoanalysis* (pp. 112–135). New York: Norton. (Originally published, 1933)

Frijda, N., & Jahoda, G. (1966). On the scope and methods of cross-cultural research. *International Journal of Psychology, 1*, 109–127.

Gaa, J. P., Liberman, D., & Edwards, T. A. (1979). A comparative factor analysis of the Bem Sex Role Inventory and the Personal Attributes Questionnaire. *Journal of Clinical Psychology, 35*, 592–598.

Gonzalez, A. (1982). Sex roles of the traditional Mexican family: A comparison of Chicano and Anglo-students' attitudes. *Journal of Cross-Cultural Psychology, 13*, 330–339.

Gough, H. G. (1966). A cross-cultural analysis of the CPI femininity scale. *Journal of Consulting Psychology, 30*, 136–141.

Gough, H. G., & Heilbrun, A. B., Jr. (1965). *Adjective check list manual.* Palo Alto, CA: Consulting Psychologists Press.

Gough, H. G., & Heilbrun, A. B., Jr. (1980). *Adjective check list manual.* Palo Alto, CA: Consulting Psychologists Press.

Haas, L. (1982). Parental sharing of childcare tasks in Sweden. *Journal of Family Issues, 3*, 389–412.

Haas, L. (1986). Wives' orientation toward breadwinning. *Journal of Family Issues, 7*, 358–381.

Harbison, F. H., & Myers, C. A. (1959). *Management in the industrial world: An international analysis.* New York: McGraw-Hill.

Harshman, R. A., & Remington, R. (1976). *Sex, language, and the brain, part I: A review of the literature on adult sex differences in lateralization.* (UCLA Working Papers in Phonetics). Los Angeles: Phonetics Laboratory, University of California, Los Angeles.

Helmreich, R. L., Spence, J. T., & Wilhelm, J. A. (1981). A psychometric analysis of the Personal Attributes Questionnaire. *Sex Roles, 7*, 1097–1108.

Hofstede, G. (1980). *Culture's consequences.* Beverly Hills, CA: Sage.

Hwang, C. P. (1987). The changing role of Swedish fathers. In M. E. Lamb (Ed.), *The father's role* (pp. 115–138). Hillsdale, NJ: Lawrence Erlbaum Associates.

Hyde, J. S. (1981). How large are cognitive gender differences? A meta-analysis using $w2$ and d. *American Psychologist, 36*, 892–901.

Information please: Almanac, atlas, & yearbook (40th ed.). (1987). Boston: Houghton Mifflin.

Intons-Peterson, M. J. (in press). *Children's concepts of gender.* Norwood, NJ: Ablex.

Jacklin, C. N., DiPietro, J. A., & Maccoby, E. E. (1984). Sex-typing behavior and sex-typing pressure in child/parent interaction. *Archives of Sexual Behavior, 13*, 413–425.

Kaplan, A. G. (Ed.). (1979). Psychological androgyny: Further considerations. *Psychology of Women Quarterly, 3*(3), (special issue).

Kohlberg, L. (1966). A cognitive-developmental analysis of children's sex-role concepts and attitudes. In E. E. Maccoby (Ed.), *The development of sex differences* (pp. 82–173). Stanford, CA: Stanford University Press.

Langlois, J. H., & Downs, A. C. (1980). Mothers, fathers, and peers as socialization agents of sex-typed play behaviors in young children. *Child Development, 51*, 1217–1247.

Lederer, W. J., & Burdick, E. (1958). *The ugly American.* New York: Norton.

Lee, J. Y., & Sugawara, A. I. (1982). Awareness of sex-trait stereotypes among Korean children. *Journal of Social Psychology, 117*, 161–170.

Levin, J., & Karni, E. S. (1971). A comparative study of the CPI femininity scale: Validation in Israel. *Journal of Cross-Cultural Psychology, 2*, 387–389.

Lindblom, P. (1986). *The Swedish family: Problems, programs, and prospects.* The Swedish Institute, Stockholm, Sweden, No. 347.

Lonner, W. J. (1980). The search for psychological universals. In H. C. Triandis & W. W. Lambert (Eds.), *Handbook of cross-cultural psychology* (Vol. 1, pp. 143–204). Boston: Allyn & Bacon.

Maccoby, E. E., & Jacklin, C. N. (1974). *The psychology of sex differences.* Stanford, CA: Stanford University Press.

Major, B., Carnevale, P. J. D., & Deaux, K. (1981). A different perspective on androgyny: Evaluations of masculine and feminine personality characteristics. *Journal of Personality and Social Psychology, 41*, 988–1001.

Malinkowski, B. (1922). *Argonauts of the western Pacific.* London: Routledge.

Maloney, P., Wilkof, J., & Dambrot, F. (1981). Androgyny across two cultures: United States and Israel. *Journal of Cross-Cultural Psychology, 12*, 95–102.

Marks, E. (1968). Personality factors in the performance of a perceptual recognition task under competing incentives. *Journal of Personality and Social Psychology, 8*, 69–74.

Markus, H., Crane, M., Bernstein, S., & Siladi, M. (1982). Self schemas and gender. *Journal of Personality and Social Psychology, 42*, 38–50.

Martin, C. L., & Halverson, C. F., Jr. (1981). A schematic processing model of sex-typing and stereotyping in children. *Child Development, 52,* 1119–1134.

Medin, D. L., & Smith, E. E. (1984). Concepts and concept formation. In M. R. Rosenzweig & L. W. Porter (Eds.), *Annual review of psychology* (pp. 113–138). Palo Alto, CA: Annual Reviews, Inc.

Morgenthaler, E. (1979, January 29). Sweden offers fathers paid paternity leaves: About 10% take them. *Wall Street Journal,* p. 1.

Munroe, R. L., & Munroe, R. H. (1975). *Cross-cultural human development.* Monterey, CA: Brooks/Cole.

Murray, H. A. (1938). *Explorations in perso .ality.* New York: Oxford University Press.

Myers, A. M., & Gonda, G. (198 ?). Empirical validation of the Bem Sex-Role Inventory. *Journal of Personality and Social Psychology, 43,* 304–318.

Nash, S. C. (1979). Sex role as a mediator of intellectual functioning. In M. A. Wittig & A. C. Petersen (Eds.), *Sex-related differences in cognitive functioning* (pp. 263–302). New York: Academic Press.

Orlofsky, J. L. (1981). Relationship between sex role attitudes and personality traits and the Sex Role Behavior Scale: A new measure of masculine and feminine role behaviors and interests. *Journal of Personality and Social Psychology, 40,* 927–940.

Osgood, C. E., May, W. H., & Miron, M. S. (1975). *Cross-cultural universals of affective meaning.* Urbana, IL: University of Illinois Press.

Pedhazur, E. J., & Tetenbaum, T. J. (1979). Bem Sex Role Inventory: A theoretical and methodological critique. *Journal of Personality and Social Psychology, 37,* 996–1014.

Peters, T. J., & Austin, N. (1986). *A passion for excellence.* New York: Random House.

Pike, K. (1954). *Language in relation to a unified theory of the structure of human behavior* (Part I). Glendale, CA: Summer Institute of Linguistics.

Price-Bonham, S., & Skeen, P. (1982). Black and white fathers' attitudes toward children's sex roles. *Psychological Reports, 50,* 1187–1190.

Price-Williams, D. R. (1975). *Explorations in cross-cultural psychology.* San Francisco: Chandler & Sharp.

Ringer, R. J. (1977). *Looking out for number one.* Beverly Hills, CA: Los Angeles Book Corp.

Rosaldo, M. Z. (1980). The use and abuse of anthropology: Reflections on feminism and cross-cultural understanding. *Signs, 5,* 389–417.

Runge, T. E., Frey, D., Gollwitzer, P. M., Helmreich, R. L., & Spence, J. T. (1981). Masculine (instrumental) and feminine (expressive) traits: A comparison between students in the United States and West Germany. *Journal of Cross-Cultural Psychology, 12,* 142–162.

Schau, C. G., Ein, P. L., & Tremaine, L. (1977). The development of gender-stereotyping of adult occupations in elementary school children. *Child Development, 48,* 507–512.

Scott, H. (1982). *Sweden's "right to be human" sex role equality: The goal and the reality.* Armonk, NY: M. E. Sharpe.

Serbin, L. A., & Sprafkin, C. (1986). The salience of gender and the process of sex typing in three- to seven-year-old children. *Child Development, 57,* 1188–1199.

Servan-Schreiber, C. (1973, February). Think about our government . . . Now think about Sweden's policy. *MS,* pp. 88–93, 113.

Smetana, J. G. (1986). Preschool children's conceptions of sex-role transgressions. *Child Development, 57,* 862–871.

Smith, E. E., & Medin, D. L. (1981). *Categories and concepts.* Cambridge, MA: Harvard University Press.

Spence, J. T. (1985). Gender identity and its implications for the concepts of masculinity and femininity. In T. B. Sonderegger (Ed.), *Nebraska symposium on motivation, 1984: Psychology and gender* (pp. 35–66). Lincoln, NE: University of Nebraska Press.

Spence, J. T., & Helmreich, R. L. (1978). *The psychological dimensions of masculinity and femininity: Their correlates and antecedents.* Austin: University of Texas Press.

Spence, J. T., & Helmreich, R. L. (1980). Masculine instrumentality and feminine expressiveness: Their relationships with sex-role attitudes and behaviors. *Psychology of Women Quarterly, 5,* 147–163.

Spence, J. T., Helmreich, R. L., & Holahan, C. K. (1979). Negative and positive components of psychological masculinity and femininity and their relationships to neurotic and acting out behaviors. *Journal of Personality and Social Psychology, 37,* 1673–1682.

Spence, J. T., Helmreich, R. L., & Stapp, J. (1975). Ratings of self and peers on sex-role attributes and their relation to self-esteem and conceptions of masculinity and femininity. *Journal of Personality and Social Psychology, 32*, 29–39.

Spence, J. T., & Sawin, L. L. (1984). Images of masculinity and femininity: A reconceptualization. In V. O'Leary, R. Unger, & B. Wallston (Eds.), *Sex, gender, and social psychology* (pp.35–66). Hillsdale, NJ: Lawrence Erlbaum Associates.

Stewart, V. M. (1973). Tests of the 'Carpentered' world hypothesis by race and environment in America and Zambia. *International Journal of Psychology, 8*, 83–94.

Strodtbeck, F. L. (1964). Considerations of meta-method in cross-cultural studies. *American Anthropologist, 66*, 223–229.

Sunar, D. G. (1982). Female stereotypes in the United States and Turkey: An application of functional theory to perception in power relationships. *Journal of Cross-Cultural Psychology, 13*, 445–460.

Sundström-Feigenberg, K. (1983, June) Parenthood education—A reform to support the family. *Current Sweden* (No. 304). Stockholm: The Swedish Institute.

Tarrier, N., & Gomes, L. F. (1981). Knowledge of sex-trait stereotypes: Effects of age, sex, and social class on Brazilian children. *Journal of Cross-Cultural Psychology, 12*, 81–93.

Tavris, C., with Baumgartner, A. I. (1983, February). How would your life be different if you'd been born a boy? *Redbook*, 99.

Taylor, M. C., & Hall, J. A. (1982). Psychological androgyny: Theories, methods, and conclusions. *Psychological Bulletin, 92*, 347–366.

Tellegen, A., & Lubinski, D. (1983). Some methodological comments on labels, traits, interaction, and types in the study of "femininity" and "masculinity": Reply to Spence. *Journal of Personality and Social Psychology, 44*, 447–455.

Thompson, S. K. (1975). Gender labels and early sex role development. *Child Development, 46*, 339–347.

Trautner, H. M., Sahm, W. B., & Stevermann, I. (1983, August). *The development of sex-role stereotypes and classificatory skills in children.* Paper presented at the Seventh Biennial Meeting of the International Society for the Study of Behavioural Development in Munich.

Tremaine, L. S., Schau, C. G., & Busch, J. W. (1982). Children's occupational sex-typing. *Sex Roles: A Journal of Research, 8*, 691–710.

Trost, J. (1983, June). Parental benefits—A study of men's behavior and views. *Current Sweden* (No. 306). Stockholm: The Swedish Institute.

Williams, J. E., & Bennett, S. M. (1975). The definitions of sex stereotypes via the Adjective Check List. *Sex Roles, 1*, 327–337.

Williams, J. E., & Best, D. L. (1977). Sex stereotypes and trait favorability on the Adjective Check List. *Educational and Psychological Measurement, 37*, 101–110.

Williams, J. E., & Best, D. L. (1982). *Measuring sex stereotypes.* Beverly Hills, CA: Sage.

Wistrand, B. (1981). *Swedish women on the move.* Uddevalla, Sweden: The Swedish Institute.

World Fact Book (1986). Washington, DC: Government Publications Office, U.S. Central Intelligence Agency.

APPENDIX I

The English Version of the Test Booklets

BOOKLET 1 (FOR GIRLS)

Fill in the following:

Name _____

School _____

Birthdate _____ Age _____

Grade _____

Now we want you to think about something unusual. You might have thought about what it would be like to be a boy (girl). Think a little more about that. Think that when you waken in the morning, you discover that you are a boy (girl). What do you think your life would be like? We want you to write a little story about how you think your life would be if you are a boy (girl). Use this side of the page and the reverse side if you need it. Begin by thinking first about what your life would be like and then start to write.

_____

_____

_____

How do you think your new life as a girl would be compared to your life as a boy? Below are five statements. Read each statement carefully. Then you are to decide if you very strongly agree, strongly agree, agree, are in between, disagree, strongly disagree, or very strongly disagree with each statement. Let us take an example. The first question reads: "I would be able to do many more things than I do now." If you strongly disagree with the statement, draw a ring around number 6. If you very strongly agree you would circle 1, and so forth. Raise your hand if you have any questions.

	Very strongly agree	Strongly agree	Agree	In between agree and disagree	Disagree	Strongly disagree	Very strongly disagree
I would be able to do many more things than I do now.	1	2	3	4	5	6	7
My new life would become harder than it is now.	1	2	3	4	5	6	7
My new life would become worse than it is now.	1	2	3	4	5	6	7
My new life would become much more satisfying than it is now.	1	2	3	4	5	6	7
My new life would become much happier than it is now.	1	2	3	4	5	6	7

BOOKLET 2 (FOR BOTH SEXES)

Now that you have finished writing your story and answering the first questions you are to go back to being your own self. In the rest of the experiment you should answer the questions as your own self.

Fill in the following:

Name _____

Age _____

Please write about men on this page. Write some adjectives that describe most men.

_____

_____

_____

What first name best describes a person with the qualities you described above?

_____

Please write about girls on this page. Write some adjectives that describe most girls.

_____

_____

_____

What first name best describes a person with the qualities you just described above?

_____

Please write about boys on this page. Write some adjectives that describe most boys.

_____

_____

_____

What first name best describes a person with the qualities you described above?

_____

Please write about women on this page. Write some adjectives that describe most women.

_____

_____

_____

What first name best describes a person with the qualities you just described above?

_____

What are 10 characteristics that you admire most in people? If you cannot think of 10 characteristics, write as many as you can.

1. _____
2. _____
3. _____
4. _____
5. _____
6. _____
7. _____
8. _____
9. _____
10. _____

In this part, we want you to decide *how important* you think it is for girls to have the characteristics that are listed. Draw a circle around the number that is closest to what you think. Here is an example: Suppose that you see the word "contented." If you think that it is extremely important for girls to be contented, draw a cricle around number 1, because 1 means extremely important. If you think that being contented is unimportant, but not very unimportant, you would draw a circle around 5, and so forth. Hold up your hand if you have any questions.

Are there any words that you do not understand?

Put a cross in from of the word you do not understand, like this: X contented

	Extremely Important	Very Impor- tant	Impor- tant	Neither important nor unim- portant	Unimpor- tant	Very unimpor- tant	Extremely unimpor- tant
Helpful	1	2	3	4	5	6	7
Tall	1	2	3	4	5	6	7
Acts as a leader	1	2	3	4	5	6	7
Gentle	1	2	3	4	5	6	7

(Continued)

	Extremely Important	Very Important	Important	Neither important nor unimportant	Unimportant	Very unimportant	Extremely unimportant
Has straight hair	1	2	3	4	5	6	7
Has social adeptness	1	2	3	4	5	6	7
Competitive	1	2	3	4	5	6	7
Patriotic and feeling loyal to other citizens of one's country	1	2	3	4	5	6	7
Kind	1	2	3	4	5	6	7
Feel insecure	1	2	3	4	5	6	7
Aware of feelings of others	1	2	3	4	5	6	7
Good looking	1	2	3	4	5	6	7
Thinks one is a good person	1	2	3	4	5	6	7
Popular	1	2	3	4	5	6	7
Sincere	1	2	3	4	5	6	7
Liberated	1	2	3	4	5	6	7
Has blue eyes	1	2	3	4	5	6	7
Has leadership abilities	1	2	3	4	5	6	7
Creative	1	2	3	4	5	6	7
Aggressive	1	2	3	4	5	6	7
Dominant	1	2	3	4	5	6	7
Willing to take a stand	1	2	3	4	5	6	7
Subordinates self to others	1	2	3	4	5	6	7
Strong	1	2	3	4	5	6	7
Emotional	1	2	3	4	5	6	7
Has a strong personality	1	2	3	4	5	6	7
Self-confident	1	2	3.	4	5	6	7
Athletic	1	2	3	4	5	6	7
Has self-esteem	1	2	3	4	5	6	7
Cooperative	1	2	3	4	5	6	7
Capable	1	2	3	4	5	6	7
Artistic	1	2	3	4	5	6	7
Stands up under pressure	1	2	3	4	5	6	7
Tough-minded	1	2	3	4	5	6	7
Compassionate	1	2	3	4	5	6	7
Makes decisions easily	1	2	3	4	5	6	7
Tender	1	2	3	4	5	6	7
Assertive	1	2	3	4	5	6	7
Likable	1	2	3	4	5	6	7
Generous	1	2	3	4	5	6	7

(Continued)

	Extremely Important	Very Impor- tant	Impor- tant	Neither important nor unim- portant	Unimpor- tant	Very unimpor- tant	Extremely unimpor- tant
Affectionate	1	2	3	4	5	6	7
Warm	1	2	3	4	5	6	7
Eager to soothe hurt feelings	1	2	3	4	5	6	7
Feels good about oneself	1	2	3	4	5	6	7
Likes (loves) children	1	2	3	4	5	6	7
Friendly	1	2	3	4	5	6	7
Hard-working	1	2	3	4	5	6	7
Tries to do one's best	1	2	3	4	5	6	7
Never gives up	1	2	3	4	5	6	7
Active	1	2	3	4	5	6	7
Loyal	1	2	3	4	5	6	7
Cannot show one's feelings	1	2	3	4	5	6	7
Quiet	1	2	3	4	5	6	7
Lively	1	2	3	4	5	6	7
Devotes self com- pletely to others	1	2	3	4	5	6	7
Whiny	1	2	3	4	5	6	7
Humorous	1	2	3	4	5	6	7
Fun	1	2	3	4	5	6	7
Shy	1	2	3	4	5	6	7

In this part, we want you to decide *how important* you think it is for boys to have the characteristics that are listed. Draw a circle around the number that is closest to what you think. Here is an example: Suppose that you see the word "contented." If you think that it is extremely important for boys to be contented, draw a circle around number 1, because 1 means extremely important. If you think that being contented is unimportant, but not very unimportant, you would draw a cricle around 5, and so forth. Hold up your hand if you have any questions.

Are there any words that you do not understand?

Put a cross in front of the word you do not understand, like this: X contented.

	Extremely Important	Very Impor- tant	Impor- tant	Neither important nor unim- portant	Unimpor- tant	Very unimpor- tant	Extremely unimpor- tant
Helpful	1	2	3	4	5	6	7
Tall	1	2	3	4	5	6	7
Acts as a leader	1	2	3	4	5	6	7
Gentle	1	2	3	4	5	6	7
Has straight hair	1	2	3	4	5	6	7
Has social adeptness	1	2	3	4	5	6	7
Competitive	1	2	3	4	5	6	7

(Continued)

	Extremely Important	Very Impor- tant	Impor- tant	Neither important nor unim- portant	Unimpor- tant	Very unimpor- tant	Extremely unimpor- tant
Patriotic and feeling loyal to other citizens of one's country	1	2	3	4	5	6	7
Kind	1	2	3	4	5	6	7
Feel insecure	1	2	3	4	5	6	7
Aware of feelings of others	1	2	3	4	5	6	7
Good looking	1	2	3	4	5	6	7
Thinks one is a good person	1	2	3	4	5	6	7
Popular	1	2	3	4	5	6	7
Sincere	1	2	3	4	5	6	7
Liberated	1	2	3	4	5	6	7
Has blue eyes	1	2	3	4	5	6	7
Has leadership abilities	1	2	3	4	5	6	7
Creative	1	2	3	4	5	6	7
Aggressive	1	2	3	4	5	6	7
Dominant	1	2	3	4	5	6	7
Willing to take a stand	1	2	3	4	5	6	7
Subordinates self to others	1	2	3	4	5	6	7
Strong	1	2	3	4	5	6	7
Emotional	1	2	3	4	5	6	7
Has a strong personality	1	2	3	4	5	6	7
Self-confident	1	2	3	4	5	6	7
Athletic	1	2	3	4	5	6	7
Has self-esteem	1	2	3	4	5	6	7
Cooperative	1	2	3	4	5	6	7
Capable	1	2	3	4	5	6	7
Artistic	1	2	3	4	5	6	7
Stands up under pressure	1	2	3	4	5	6	7
Tough-minded	1	2	3	4	5	6	7
Compassionate	1	2	3	4	5	6	7
Makes decisions easily	1	2	3	4	5	6	7
Tender	1	2	3	4	5	6	7
Assertive	1	2	3	4	5	6	7
Likable	1	2	3	4	5	6	7
Generous	1	2	3	4	5	6	7
Affectionate	1	2	3	4	5	6	7
Warm	1	2	3	4	5	6	7
Eager to soothe hurt feelings	1	2	3	4	5	6	7

(Continued)

	Extremely Important	Very Impor- tant	Impor- tant	Neither important nor unim- portant	Unimpor- tant	Very unimpor- tant	Extremely unimpor- tant
Feels good about oneself	1	2	3	4	5	6	7
Likes (loves) children	1	2	3	4	5	6	7
Friendly	1	2	3	4	5	6	7
Hard-working	1	2	3	4	5	6	7
Tries to do one's best	1	2	3	4	5	6	7
Never gives up	1	2	3	4	5	6	7
Active	1	2	3	4	5	6	7
Loyal	1	2	3	4	5	6	7
Cannot show one's feelings	1	2	3	4	5	6	7
Quiet	1	2	3	4	5	6	7
Lively	1	2	3	4	5	6	7
Devotes self com- pletely to others	1	2	3	4	5	6	7
Whiny	1	2	3	4	5	6	7
Humorous	1	2	3	4	5	6	7
Fun	1	2	3	4	5	6	7
Shy	1	2	3	4	5	6	7

In this part, we want you to decide *how important* you think it is for men to have the characteristics that are listed. Draw a circle around the number that is closest to what you think. Here is an example: Suppose that you see the word "contented." If you think that it is extremely important for boys to be contented, draw a circle around number 1, because 1 means extremely important. If you think that being contented is unimportant, but not very unimportant, you would draw a cricle around 5, and so forth. Hold up your hand if you have any questions.

Are there any words that you do not understand?

Put a cross in front of the word you do not understand, like this: X contented.

	Extremely Important	Very Impor- tant	Impor- tant	Neither important nor unim- portant	Unimpor- tant	Very unimpor- tant	Extremely unimpor- tant
Helpful	1	2	3	4	5	6	7
Tall	1	2	3	4	5	6	7
Acts as a leader	1	2	3	4	5	6	7
Gentle	1	2	3	4	5	6	7
Has straight hair	1	2	3	4	5	6	7
Has social adeptness	1	2	3	4	5	6	7
Competitive	1	2	3	4	5	6	7
Patriotic and feeling loyal to other citizens of one's country	1	2	3	4	5	6	7
Kind	1	2	3	4	5	6	7

(Continued)

	Extremely Important	Very Impor- tant	Impor- tant	Neither important nor unim- portant	Unimpor- tant	Very unimpor- tant	Extremely unimpor- tant
Feel insecure	1	2	3	4	5	6	7
Aware of feelings of others	1	2	3	4	5	6	7
Good looking	1	2	3	4	5	6	7
Thinks one is a good person	1	2	3	4	5	6	7
Popular	1	2	3	4	5	6	7
Sincere	1	2	3	4	5	6	7
Liberated	1	2	3	4	5	6	7
Has blue eyes	1	2	3	4	5	6	7
Has leadership abilities	1	2	3	4	5	6	7
Creative	1	2	3	4	5	6	7
Aggressive	1	2	3	4	5	6	7
Dominant	1	2	3	4	5	6	7
Willing to take a stand	1	2	3	4	5	6	7
Subordinates self to others	1	2	3	4	5	6	7
Strong	1	2	3	4	5	6	7
Emotional	1	2	3	4	5	6	7
Has a strong personality	1	2	3	4	5	6	7
Self-confident	1	2	3	4	5	6	7
Athletic	1	2	3	4	5	6	7
Has self-esteem	1	2	3	4	5	6	7
Cooperative	1	2	3	4	5	6	7
Capable	1	2	3	4	5	6	7
Artistic	1	2	3	4	5	6	7
Stands up under pressure	1	2	3	4	5	6	7
Tough-minded	1	2	3	4	5	6	7
Compassionate	1	2	3	4	5	6	7
Makes decisions easily	1	2	3	4	5	6	7
Tender	1	2	3	4	5	6	7
Assertive	1	2	3	4	5	6	7
Likable	1	2	3	4	5	6	7
Generous	1	2	3	4	5	6	7
Affectionate	1	2	3	4	5	6	7
Warm	1	2	3	4	5	6	7
Eager to soothe hurt feelings	1	2	3	4	5	6	7
Feels good about oneself	1	2	3	4	5	6	7
Likes (loves) children	1	2	3	4	5	6	7
Friendly	1	2	3	4	5	6	7

(Continued)

	Extremely Important	Very Impor- tant	Impor- tant	Neither important nor unim- portant	Unimpor- tant	Very unimpor- tant	Extremely unimpor- tant
Hard-working	1	2	3	4	5	6	7
Tries to do one's best	1	2	3	4	5	6	7
Never gives up	1	2	3	4	5	6	7
Active	1	2	3	4	5	6	7
Loyal	1	2	3	4	5	6	7
Cannot show one's feelings	1	2	3	4	5	6	7
Quiet	1	2	3	4	5	6	7
Lively	1	2	3	4	5	6	7
Devotes self com- pletely to others	1	2	3	4	5	6	7
Whiny	1	2	3	4	5	6	7
Humorous	1	2	3	4	5	6	7
Fun	1	2	3	4	5	6	7
Shy	1	2	3	4	5	6	7

In this part, we want you to decide *how important* you think it is for women to have the characteristics that are listed. Draw a circle around the number that is closest to what you think. Here is an example: Suppose that you see the word "contented." If you think that it is extremely important for women to be contented, draw a circle around number 1, because 1 means extremely important. If you think that being contented is unimpor- tant, but not very unimportant, you would draw a cricle around 5, and so forth. Hold up your hand if you have any questions.

Are there any words that you do not understand?

Put a cross in front of the word you do not understand, like this: X contented.

	Extremely Important	Very Impor- tant	Impor- tant	Neither important nor unim- portant	Unimpor- tant	Very unimpor- tant	Extremely unimpor- tant
Helpful	1	2	3	4	5	6	7
Tall	1	2	3	4	5	6	7
Acts as a leader	1	2	3	4	5	6	7
Gentle	1	2	3	4	5	6	7
Has straight hair	1	2	3	4	5	6	7
Has social adeptness	1	2	3	4	5	6	7
Competitive	1	2	3	4	5	6	7
Patriotic and feeling loyal to other citizens of one's country	1	2	3	4	5	6	7
Kind	1	2	3	4	5	6	7
Feel insecure	1	2	3	4	5	6	7
Aware of feelings of others	1	2	3	4	5	6	7
Good looking	1	2	3	4	5	6	7

(Continued)

	Extremely Important	Very Important	Important	Neither important nor unimportant	Unimportant	Very unimportant	Extremely unimportant
Thinks one is a good person	1	2	3	4	5	6	7
Popular	1	2	3	4	5	6	7
Sincere	1	2	3	4	5	6	7
Liberated	1	2	3	4	5	6	7
Has blue eyes	1	2	3	4	5	6	7
Has leadership abilities	1	2	3	4	5	6	7
Creative	1	2	3	4	5	6	7
Aggressive	1	2	3	4	5	6	7
Dominant	1	2	3	4	5	6	7
Willing to take a stand	1	2	3	4	5	6	7
Subordinates self to others	1	2	3	4	5	6	7
Strong	1	2	3	4	5	6	7
Emotional	1	2	3	4	5	6	7
Has a strong personality	1	2	3	4	5	6	7
Self-confident	1	2	3	4	5	6	7
Athletic	1	2	3	4	5	6	7
Has self-esteem	1	2	3	4	5	6	7
Cooperative	1	2	3	4	5	6	7
Capable	1	2	3	4	5	6	7
Artistic	1	2	3	4	5	6	7
Stands up under pressure	1	2	3	4	5	6	7
Tough-minded	1	2	3	4	5	6	7
Compassionate	1	2	3	4	5	6	7
Makes decisions easily	1	2	3	4	5	6	7
Tender	1	2	3	4	5	6	7
Assertive	1	2	3	4	5	6	7
Likable	1	2	3	4	5	6	7
Generous	1	2	3	4	5	6	7
Affectionate	1	2	3	4	5	6	7
Warm	1	2	3	4	5	6	7
Eager to soothe hurt feelings	1	2	3	4	5	6	7
Feels good about oneself	1	2	3	4	5	6	7
Likes (loves) children	1	2	3	4	5	6	7
Friendly	1	2	3	4	5	6	7
Hard-working	1	2	3	4	5	6	7
Tries to do one's best	1	2	3	4	5	6	7
Never gives up	1	2	3	4	5	6	7
Active	1	2	3	4	5	6	7
Loyal	1	2	3	4	5	6	7

(*Continued*)

	Extremely Important	Very Important	Important	Neither important nor unimportant	Unimportant	Very unimportant	Extremely unimportant
Cannot show one's feelings	1	2	3	4	5	6	7
Quiet	1	2	3	4	5	6	7
Lively	1	2	3	4	5	6	7
Devotes self completely to others	1	2	3	4	5	6	7
Whiny	1	2	3	4	5	6	7
Humorous	1	2	3	4	5	6	7
Fun	1	2	3	4	5	6	7
Shy	1	2	3	4	5	6	7

Next, we want you to describe yourself as you are right now. Again, simply draw a circle around the number that best shows how important the trait is to you—that is, how well the trait describes you right now. Do you have any questions? Be sure to put a cross next to any word you do not understand.

	Extremely Important	Very Important	Important	Neither important nor unimportant	Unimportant	Very unimportant	Extremely unimportant
Helpful	1	2	3	4	5	6	7
Tall	1	2	3	4	5	6	7
Acts as a leader	1	2	3	4	5	6	7
Gentle	1	2	3	4	5	6	7
Has straight hair	1	2	3	4	5	6	7
Has social adeptness	1	2	3	4	5	6	7
Competitive	1	2	3	4	5	6	7
Patriotic and feeling loyal to other citizens of one's country	1	2	3	4	5	6	7
Kind	1	2	3	4	5	6	7
Feel insecure	1	2	3	4	5	6	7
Aware of feelings of others	1	2	3	4	5	6	7
Good looking	1	2	3	4	5	6	7
Thinks one is a good person	1	2	3	4	5	6	7
Popular	1	2	3	4	5	6	7
Sincere	1	2	3	4	5	6	7
Liberated	1	2	3	4	5	6	7
Has blue eyes	1	2	3	4	5	6	7
Has leadership abilities	1	2	3	4	5	6	7
Creative	1	2	3	4	5	6	7
Aggressive	1	2	3	4	5	6	7
Dominant	1	2	3	4	5	6	7

(Continued)

	Extremely Important	Very Important	Important	Neither important nor unimportant	Unimportant	Very unimportant	Extremely unimportant
Willing to take a stand	1	2	3	4	5	6	7
Subordinates self to others	1	2	3	4	5	6	7
Strong	1	2	3	4	5	6	7
Emotional	1	2	3	4	5	6	7
Has a strong personality	1	2	3	4	5	6	7
Self-confident	1	2	3	4	5	6	7
Athletic	1	2	3	4	5	6	7
Has self-esteem	1	2	3	4	5	6	7
Cooperative	1	2	3	4	5	6	7
Capable	1	2	3	4	5	6	7
Artistic	1	2	3	4	5	6	7
Stands up under pressure	1	2	3	4	5	6	7
Tough-minded	1	2	3	4	5	6	7
Compassionate	1	2	3	4	5	6	7
Makes decisions easily	1	2	3	4	5	6	7
Tender	1	2	3	4	5	6	7
Assertive	1	2	3	4	5	6	7
Likable	1	2	3	4	5	6	7
Generous	1	2	3	4	5	6	7
Affectionate	1	2	3	4	5	6	7
Warm	1	2	3	4	5	6	7
Eager to soothe hurt feelings	1	2	3	4	5	6	7
Feels good about oneself	1	2	3	4	5	6	7
Likes (loves) children	1	2	3	4	5	6	7
Friendly	1	2	3	4	5	6	7
Hard-working	1	2	3	4	5	6	7
Tries to do one's best	1	2	3	4	5	6	7
Never gives up	1	2	3	4	5	6	7
Active	1	2	3	4	5	6	7
Loyal	1	2	3	4	5	6	7
Cannot show one's feelings	1	2	3	4	5	6	7
Quiet	1	2	3	4	5	6	7
Lively	1	2	3	4	5	6	7
Devotes self completely to others	1	2	3	4	5	6	7
Whiny	1	2	3	4	5	6	7
Humorous	1	2	3	4	5	6	7
Fun	1	2	3	4	5	6	7
Shy	1	2	3	4	5	6	7

(Continued)

NAME	STUDENT NUMBER

We are interested in what young people think that they will be doing in 10 years—in 1995. Ten years is a long time and you may not be sure about your plans, so we want you to answer some questions in two ways. First answer on the basis of your top choice—what you would do if you could satisfy your highest wish. Write the number of the alternative under the label "Highest wish." Then answer on the basis of what you think you are most likely to be doing. Write the number of the alternative under the label "Most likely." Here is an example:

	Highest wish	*Most likely*
In 1987 I would like to be in 1) the USA 2) Sweden, 3) Finland 4) Algeria 5) Switzerland	_____	_____

If you would really like to be in Algeria you would write number 4 under the heading "Highest wish." Then consider where you think you are most likely to be. Write its number under the heading "Most likely." The two numbers can be the same, or different, depending on what you would ideally like to do and what you think you are most likely to do.

	Highest wish	*Most likely*
1. In 1995 I expect to have paid employment outside the home 1) not all all (I will work only at home). 2) about 10 hours per week 3) about 20 hours per week 4) about 30 hours per week 5) about 40 hours per week	_____	_____
2. In 1995 I will have 1) no children 2) one child 3) two children 4) three children 5) four or more children	_____	_____
3. In 1995 I will live in 1) one room with a kitchen (efficiency apartment) 2) apartment with two rooms and a kitchen 3) apartment with three rooms and a kitchen 4) apartment with 4-6 rooms and a kitchen 5) a house	_____	_____
4. In 1995 I will live 1) alone 2) with my husband/wife		

	Highest wish	*Most likely*
3) with another unmarried person		
4) in a collective of some kind		
5) in some other type of housing (student dorm, etc.)	_____	_____

5. In 1995 I will have completed
   1) some college
   2) an undergraduate degree
   3) a masters degree
   4) a professional degree (e.g., in law, business, medicine)
   5) a Ph.D.   _____   _____

6. How contented do you think that you will be with your life?
   1) Not at all contented and I will think about making a drastic change.
   2) A little discontented, but I will not make many changes.
   3) Occasionally I will be discontented and occasionally I will be contented, but I will not make major changes.
   4) Mostly contented.
   5) Very contented, and I will not change it even a little.   _____   _____

Now, please look at page 3. Here you will see listed a number of occupations. You are to indicate the occupations that you would most like to have in 1995. Write the number 1 for the occupation that would be your top choice under the heading "Most like to have." Then write the number 2 next to the occupation that would be your second highest choice. This number also goes under the heading "Most like to have." Continue in this way under the "Most like to have" heading until you have indicated your five top choices.

Next, you are to do the exercise over again, but this time, you are to indicate the five occupations that you would *least* like to have in 1995. Use the number 1 for the occupation that you would *least* like to have. Then, use the number 2 for the next most disliked, and so on, until you have indicated your five most unwanted or disliked occupations. Remember, the most disliked will have the number 1 by it.

Do you have any questions? Please raise your hand if you have questions.

	Most like to have	*Least like to have*
Shop assistant	_____	_____
Architect	_____	_____
Children's nurse (nanny)	_____	_____
Construction worker	_____	_____
Manager of state agency	_____	_____

	Most like to have	Least like to have
Chief executive office, private industry	——————	——————
Chauffer	——————	——————
Computer operator	——————	——————
Doctor/dentist	——————	——————
Owner of a small business	——————	——————
Factory worker	——————	——————
Pilot/flight attendant	——————	——————
Researcher	——————	——————
Preschool teacher	——————	——————
Author	——————	——————
Sales	——————	——————
Insurance agent	——————	——————
Housewife/husband	——————	——————
Engineer	——————	——————
Attorney	——————	——————
Journalist	——————	——————
Artist	——————	——————
Cook (chef)	——————	——————
Office worker (other than secretary)	——————	——————
Skilled tradesperson (carpenter, painter, etc.)	——————	——————
Custodian	——————	——————
Elementary school teacher	——————	——————
High school teacher	——————	——————
Machinist	——————	——————
Military officer	——————	——————
Musician	——————	——————
Politician	——————	——————
Police officer	——————	——————
Psychologist	——————	——————
Minister, priest,...	——————	——————
Secretary	——————	——————
Waiter/waitress	——————	——————
Hospital worker (other than doctor)	——————	——————
Social worker	——————	——————
Technician	——————	——————
Temporarily unemployed	——————	——————
Official in federal agency	——————	——————
Professor	——————	——————
Veterinarian	——————	——————
Road worker	——————	——————
Other (Fill in) _____	——————	——————
Other (Fill in) _____	——————	——————

21. Which occupation are you studying for now? _____

We are interested in the opinions that young people have about certain matters that can influence their lives. Please answer the following questions using the scale:

1 = Extremely important
2
3
4
5
6
7 = Extremely unimportant

For example, consider the following questions. How important do you think it is for people to be up-to-date? If you think that it is extremely important for people to be up-to-date, you would write a number 1. If you think that it is not so very important, you would write number 5 or 6.

22. _____ How important do you think it is for people to be nice to one another?
23. _____ How important do you think it is for you to have many friends?
24. _____ How important do you think it is for you to have at least one close friend?
25. _____ How important do you think it is for boys to decide about an occupation as early as possible (at least by 16 years of age)?
26. _____ How important do you think it is for one to take risks with the plans for one's life?
27. _____ How important is money to having a good life?
28. _____ How important is a family to having a good life?
29. _____ How important do you think it is for one to do something well to have a good life?
30. _____ How important is self-esteem to having a good life?
31. _____ How important do you think it is to have time for recreation?
32. _____ How important do you think it is for girls to decide about an occupation as early as possible (at least by 16 years of age)?
33. _____ How important do you think it is for one to work full time if one wants to be promoted and to earn a good salary?
34. _____ How important do you think it is for most full-time jobs to be defined as 30 hours per week even if the pay is a little less than for a 40-hour work week?
35. _____ How important is it that full-time jobs be defined as 40 hours per week?
36. _____ How important is it for girls to have special courses in mathematics, to speak several languages, or to take science courses in case they continue in these areas?
37. _____ (Same as 36, but for boys.)

List the mathematics courses you have taken _____

What other courses in mathematics do you wish that you had taken? _____

List the science courses that you have studied _____

What other science courses do you wish that you had taken? _____

What languages do you speak? _____

What other languages do you wish that you had studied? _____

What advice would you give to an 8-year-old boy who asked you how he should plan his life? _____

_____

What advice would you give to an 8-year-old girl who asked you how she should plan her life? _____

_____

APPENDIX II

Part of the Swedish Version of the Test Booklets

Fyll i följande:

namn _____

skola _____

kön _____

födelsedatum _____   ålder _____

stad _____

Nu tänker vi be dig göra något som kanske känns lite ovanligt till en början. Du har kanske funderat någon gång hur det skulle vara om du var en flicka. Tänk lite mer på det
här. Tänk dig, att när du vaknar i morgon, så upptäcker du att du är en flicka. Hur tror
du ditt liv skulle bli då? Vi vill att du skriver en liten berättelse om hur du tror att ditt
liv skulle vara om du var en flicka. Använd resten av sidan, och även baksidan om du
behöver det. Men börja med att tänka efter ett tag innan du börjar skriva.

_____

_____

_____

Hur tror du att ditt nya liv som flicka skulle kunna jämföras med ditt liv som pojke?
Vad som följer är fem påståenden. Läs varje påstående omsorgsfullt. Sedan får du bestämma
om påståendet stämmer med vad du tycker, eller om det inte stämmer, och hur mycket
eller lite påståendet stämmer med vad du tycker. Låt oss ta ett exempel. Första påståendet
lyder: "Jag skulle kunna göra många fler saker än jag gör nu." Om detta inte stämmer
med vad du tycker, så kanske du ritar en cirkel runt 6. Stämmer det inte alls kanske
du ritar en cirkel runt 7, osv. Räck upp handen om du har några frågor.

	stämmer helt med vad jag tycker	*stämmer ganska mycket*	*stämmer lite grann*	*mitt emellan*	*stämmer inte särskilt mycket*	*stämmer inte*	*stämmer inte alls med vad jag tycker*
Jag skulle kunna göra många fler saker än jag gör nu.	1	2	3	4	5	6	7
Mitt nya liv skulle bli svårare än vad det är nu.	1	2	3	4	5	6	7
Mitt nya liv skulle bli mycket värre än vad det är nu.	1	2	3	4	5	6	7
Mitt nya liv skulle bli mycket mer tillfredsställande än det är nu.	1	2	3	4	5	6	7
Mitt nya liv skulle bli mycket lyckligare än vad det är nu.	1	2	3	4	5	6	7

Nu när du skrivit klart din berättelse och svarat på de första frågorna kan du gå tillbaks till att vara dig själv igen. Under resten av lektionen skall du svara på frågorna som dig själv.

Fyll i följande:

Namn _____

Ålder _____

APPENDIX III

*Factor Analyses of Importance Ratings
of Most Girls by Swedish Respondents*

| | Females | | | | | Males | | | | | | | |
| | 14-year-olds n = 33 | | 18-year-olds n = 38 | | | 14-year-olds n = 36 | | | | 18-year-olds n = 44 | | |
	1	2	1	2	3	1	2	3	4	1	2	3
Helpful	.70	-.11	.35	-.06	.14	.32	.18	.16	-.13	.24	.16	.17
Tall	-.39	.50	-.18	-.66	.09	-.03	.08	.08	.01	.00	.20	.30
Acts as leaders	.04	.03	-.27	.65	-.15	-.33	-.19	.33	.07	-.19	.09	-.17
Gentle	.42	-.23	.83	-.34	.32	.36	-.06	.01	-.31	.75	-.18	.14
Straight hair	-.01	.50	-.08	.61	-.17	-.24	.07	.09	.29	-.23	-.09	.21
Socially adept	-.10	-.12	.10	.12	.10	.12	.11	.11	-.20	-.03	.15	.25
Competitive	-.16	.34	-.28	.67	-.23	-.10	-.02	.69	-.15	-.24	.13	-.05
Patriotic	-.04	-.76	.71	-.16	.33	.28	.00	.07	-.23	.17	-.04	.04
Kind	.63	-.16	.65	-.33	.05	.46	-.05	.04	-.13	.59	-.09	.05
Insecure	-.09	.26	-.09	.22	-.09	-.11	.47	-.41	.52	-.12	-.30	-.05
Aware of feelings of others	.29	-.37	.60	-.15	.21	.64	.14	.03	-.05	.59	-.03	.29
Good looking	.24	.16	-.23	.14	-.22	.04	.22	.26	-.06	.63	.27	.36
Good person	.62	-.09	-.11	.23	-.13	.35	.30	.30	.02	.15	.12	.14
Popular	.36	.40	-.09	.30	-.14	.16	.56	.38	-.12	.26	.41	.19
Sincere	.20	.02	.16	-.03	.01	.21	.11	.23	-.18	.40	-.06	.24
Liberated	.38	-.30	-.01	.05	.12	.39	.23	.02	.17	.24	-.11	.12
Blue eyes	-.02	.29	-.08	.34	-.20	.11	.51	-.11	-.05	.06	.05	.33
Has leadership qualities	.03	.18	-.09	.79	-.02	-.06	.06	.08	-.09	-.09	.08	.01
Creative	.06	.20	.55	-.01	.51	.23	.17	.31	-.15	-.11	.08	.12
Aggressive	.00	.20	.00	.30	.00	.02	.85	-.02	.19	-.12	.15	-.01
Dominant	-.12	.83	-.13	.38	-.17	-.04	.00	.05	.21	-.32	.09	-.17
Willing to take a stand	.20	-.44	.22	.06	.10	.45	.01	.20	-.18	.09	.20	-.10
Subordinates self to others	-.04	.20	-.08	.21	-.33	-.13	.59	-.26	.42	-.22	.02	-.11

(Continued)

	Females						Males						
	14-year-olds n = 33		18-year-olds n = 38			14-year-olds n = 36				18-year-olds n = 44			
	1	2	1	2	3	1	2	3	4	1	2	3	
Strong	.10	.39	.07	.17	-.18	.28	.46	.10	-.14	.00	.33	.06	
Emotional	.30	-.20	.47	-.51	.00	.63	-.02	.15	-.12	.32	.02	.41	
Strong personality	.25	-.20	.27	-.02	.45	.40	.14	-.06	-.23	.07	.09	.36	
Self confident	.27	.13	-.09	.16	.22	.33	.41	.39	-.20	-.15	.47	.09	
Athletic	.17	.60	.02	.33	-.11	.22	.44	.00	-.03	.02	.15	-.06	
Self-esteem	.41	.06	.60	.14	.38	.11	.60	.44	-.04	-.18	.57	-.03	
Cooperative	.09	-.07	.91	-.12	.41	.33	.10	.22	-.23	.05	.42	-.02	
Capable	.61	.21	.08	-.04	.30	.48	.31	.40	-.18	.07	.58	.25	
Artistic	.23	.09	.12	.02	.10	.70	.18	.18	-.14	-.03	-.03	.19	
Stands up under pressure	.20	-.36	.26	-.01	.67	.29	.13	.42	-.18	.07	.37	.34	
Tough-minded	.40	.33	-.03	.32	-.15	.49	.14	.18	-.10	.18	.48	.12	
Compassionate	.31	.02	.40	.04	.09	.41	.05	.01	-.19	.12	-.05	.83	
Decides easily	.15	-.08	.18	.20	-.01	.47	.07	.24	-.13	.16	.85	.06	
Tender	.77	-.09	.27	.03	-.24	.86	.12	.21	.02	.84	.17	.14	
Assertive	.23	.18	-.20	.32	-.09	.13	.64	-.12	.10	.19	.54	-.01	
Likable	.82	-.17	.30	.00	.21	.50	.26	.17	-.29	.76	.05	.37	
Generous	.34	-.13	.38	.15	.38	.85	-.01	.11	-.28	.37	.10	.19	
Affectionate	.73	-.23	.32	-.02	.25	.88	-.04	.03	-.27	.39	.15	.17	
Warm	.59	-.10	.21	.02	-.29	.78	.04	.17	-.03	.86	.26	.18	
Soothes hurt feelings	.62	.06	.41	-.03	-.05	.40	.06	-.07	-.05	.35	-.06	.67	
Feels good about self	.47	-.09	.21	.27	.20	.39	.35	.20	-.10	.12	.14	.31	
Loves children	.24	-.09	-.03	.06	-.08	.13	.02	.06	-.02	.09	.06	.08	
Friendly	.36	.07	.61	-.29	.13	.36	.09	.25	-.22	.30	.11	.13	

(Continued)

	Females					Males						
	14-year-olds n = 33		18-year-olds n = 38			14-year-olds n = 36				18-year-olds n = 44		
	1	2	1	2	3	1	2	3	4	1	2	3
Hardworking	.45	.11	.05	.19	.44	.10	-.24	.46	.06	-.10	.16	.01
Tries to do one's best	.13	-.14	.36	-.11	.91	.17	-.25	.25	.21	-.06	.42	.03
Never gives up	.27	-.04	.30	.04	.89	.18	-.35	.43	.12	.00	.47	-.10
Active	.16	.11	.43	.31	.50	.18	.03	.89	.05	.06	.63	.02
Loyal	.44	-.55	.63	.01	.41	.17	-.22	.41	.05	.04	.12	.11
Doesn't show feelings	-.08	.37	-.30	.16	-.18	-.28	.04	-.23	.83	.04	.02	.23
Quiet	.11	.19	-.09	.29	-.12	-.02	.02	.10	.53	-.14	-.46	.08
Lively	.09	.09	-.11	.11	-.06	.16	-.13	.30	.13	-.05	.22	-.04
Devotes self to others	.01	.02	.03	.21	-.27	.05	.28	.02	.56	-.06	-.11	.12
Whiny	.04	.19	-.13	.10	-.40	.00	.26	.12	.81	-.18	-.08	-.11
Humorous	.33	-.28	.23	.19	.12	-.10	.03	.42	.01	.18	.11	-.18
Fun	.33	-.03	.28	.49	.10	-.15	-.02	.23	-.10	.24	.22	.04
Shy	.11	.04	.03	-.07	.07	-.21	-.09	-.06	.80	.10	-.13	.09
% of Variance	28.4	14.7	20.4	17.9	10.4	26.5	13.0	10.7	8.9	20.5	16.2	8.6
	43.2		48.8			59.1				45.3		
Factor Correlations												
1		-.04		-.15	.27		.09	.10	-.10		.02	.21
2					-.02			.00	.07			.00
3									-.07			

APPENDIX IV

Factor Analyses of Importance Ratings of Most Boys by Swedish Respondents

	Females						Males				
	14-year-olds n = 29			18-year-olds n = 36			14-year-olds n = 38		18-year-olds n = 40		
	1	2	3	1	2	3	1	2	1	2	3
Helpful	.79	-.07	.05	.52	-.24	.36	.36	.05	-.05	-.13	.08
Tall	-.10	.78	-.08	.05	.18	.06	-.09	.22	-.05	.28	.11
Acts as leaders	-.10	.56	.28	-.21	.91	-.01	.00	.93	-.26	.41	-.14
Gentle	.75	-.19	-.14	.42	.00	.07	.28	.01	-.10	.24	.14
Straight hair	-.27	.14	-.09	-.10	.11	.01	-.01	.19	-.36	.17	.06
Socially adept	-.05	.16	.11	.20	.09	-.19	.25	.13	-.02	.24	-.25
Competitive	-.25	.59	-.01	-.04	.62	-.08	.15	.69	-.03	.43	-.17
Patriotic	.15	-.18	.08	.28	.18	-.05	.39	-.04	.32	-.26	.23
Kind	.69	-.10	-.19	.45	-.17	.37	.43	-.09	.30	-.13	.05
Insecure	-.12	-.02	.12	-.15	-.09	.18	-.14	-.07	-.03	-.71	-.01
Aware of feelings of others	.46	-.12	.12	.15	-.02	.52	.63	.07	.55	-.30	.26
Good looking	.05	.80	-.29	.05	.02	.10	.24	.24	-.24	.15	.24
Good person	.28	-.06	.33	-.05	-.29	.17	.41	.23	.28	.56	-.10
Popular	.01	.34	.10	-.03	.29	-.10	.27	.24	-.34	.62	-.04
Sincere	.37	-.01	-.14	.08	-.08	.12	.68	.05	.54	-.18	.15
Liberated	.17	.12	.02	.14	.05	.08	.59	.10	.18	.16	.23
Blue eyes	-.03	.23	-.04	-.04	.02	.19	-.03	.16	-.42	.22	.13
Has leadership qualities	-.26	.69	.17	-.22	.82	.06	-.01	.80	-.41	.39	-.30
Creative	-.05	-.12	.91	.21	.08	.18	.51	.11	-.07	.10	.14
Aggressive	-.19	.19	.20	-.48	.32	.04	-.13	.18	-.20	.28	-.05
Dominant	-.01	-.06	-.11	-.39	.55	.05	.04	.42	-.17	.30	.09
Willing to take a stand	.17	-.01	.39	.14	.00	.16	.57	.10	.44	-.17	.04
Subordinates self to others	-.15	.00	-.16	-.12	.44	.17	-.12	-.04	-.32	-.03	.03

(Continued)

| | Females | | | | | | Males | | | | | |
| | 14-year-olds n = 29 | | | 18-year-olds n = 36 | | | 14-year-olds n = 38 | | | 18-year-olds n = 40 | | |
	1	2	3	1	2	3	1	2	1	2	3
Strong	.11	.57	-.45	.20	.61	.15	-.07	.46	-.19	.61	.14
Emotional	.60	-.10	.16	.39	-.35	.56	.65	.09	-.03	.32	.77
Strong personality	.38	.17	.48	.19	-.03	.26	.61	.07	.30	.16	.26
Self confident	.38	.01	.50	-.20	.27	.23	.24	.24	.14	.37	-.13
Athletic	-.10	.68	-.38	.12	.54	.01	.11	.42	.03	.49	.25
Self-esteem	.15	-.05	.49	.02	.27	.05	.32	.12	.01	.49	.47
Cooperative	.54	-.10	.02	.25	-.02	.27	.83	-.06	.43	-.07	-.02
Capable	.35	.14	-.13	.19	.32	.34	.52	.22	-.23	.83	.14
Artistic	.25	.64	-.32	.31	.20	-.06	.53	.15	.12	.29	.28
Stands up under pressure	.22	.07	.42	-.05	.13	.23	.62	-.01	.01	.41	.26
Tough-minded	.07	.65	.00	.21	.64	-.08	.16	.75	-.01	.52	.24
Compassionate	.35	.07	.04	.16	.05	.88	.59	.28	.09	.05	.88
Decides easily	.65	-.01	.24	.35	.23	.10	.28	.38	-.11	.57	.19
Tender	.73	.10	-.01	.84	-.25	.30	.32	.15	.25	-.04	.25
Assertive	.17	-.01	.28	.02	.51	.01	.01	.33	-.08	.82	.16
Likable	.63	.06	.09	.63	-.08	.25	.42	.06	.40	-.09	.22
Generous	.42	.16	.13	.40	-.06	.18	.63	.02	.43	.05	-.03
Affectionate	.64	.07	-.11	.57	-.33	.21	.54	.08	.38	-.16	.41
Warm	.52	.23	-.13	.84	-.36	.21	.40	-.06	.40	-.17	.35
Soothes hurt feelings	.35	.03	.00	.64	.03	.60	.52	.00	.58	-.08	.40
Feels good about self	.09	-.06	.46	.31	.11	-.12	.52	.04	-.03	.57	.43
Loves children	.29	-.09	.05	.35	.08	.47	.28	-.12	.78	.04	-.02
Friendly	.45	.18	.09	.74	-.36	.36	.55	-.04	.64	-.06	.07

(Continued)

	Females						Males						
	14-year-olds n = 29			18-year-olds n = 36			14-year-olds n = 38		18-year-olds n = 40				
	1	2	3	1	2	3	1	2	1	2	3		
Hardworking	.34	-.08	-.04	.11	.04	.33	.37	-.05	.15	.35	-.25		
Tries to do one's best	.14	-.26	.14	.01	-.18	.18	.54	-.21	.50	.08	-.06		
Never gives up	.50	.02	.18	.14	.00	.17	.52	-.16	.48	.20	-.10		
Active	.12	-.03	-.10	-.03	-.06	.37	.15	.18	.06	.69	.26		
Loyal	.03	.01	.50	.06	.04	-.06	.64	-.16	.24	.20	.13		
Doesn't show feelings	-.02	.25	-.11	-.24	-.10	.29	-.06	-.25	-.72	.19	-.24		
Quiet	-.07	-.20	.13	-.29	-.14	.15	.06	-.10	-.24	-.07	.22		
Lively	.24	.54	.26	.00	.28	.03	.05	.05	-.13	.25	.26		
Devotes self to others	-.15	.06	.41	-.01	.15	.44	.00	.01	-.08	-.05	-.19		
Whiny	-.11	.08	-.02	-.27	.10	.27	.07	.06	-.48	.09	.99		
Humorous	.60	-.08	.17	.58	.15	.12	.47	-.11	.15	-.01	-.05		
Fun	.54	.00	.10	.66	.05	.27	.67	-.23	.18	.02	-.06		
Shy	.15	-.06	-.09	.03	.02	.13	-.13	.17	-.12	-.11	.15		
% of Variance	27.3	14.1	9.1	24.4	16.8	12.2	41.5	13.1	31.7	18.2	9.6		
		50.6			53.4			54.6					
Factor Correlations													
1		-.02	-.05		-.10	.13		.05		-.02	.13		
			-.09			-.02					.09		

APPENDIX V

*Factor Analyses of Importance Ratings
of Most Women by Swedish Respondents*

| | Females | | | | | | | Males | | | | | |
| | 14-year-olds n = 27 | | | | 18-year-olds n = 28 | | | 14-year-olds n = 33 | | | 18-year-olds n = 41 | | |
	1	2	3	4	1	2	3	1	2	3	1	2	3
Helpful	.35	.08	.31	.00	.50	-.11	-.19	.44	.10	.12	.27	-.06	-.15
Tall	-.32	.40	.16	.21	.25	.49	.26	-.22	.24	.22	-.12	.14	.05
Acts as leader	-.15	.71	.25	.23	-.14	.38	.43	-.10	.37	.01	-.51	.25	.19
Gentle	.29	.24	.54	-.14	.22	-.07	-.25	.69	-.04	-.20	.83	-.15	-.21
Straight hair	-.16	.40	.09	.03	.22	-.03	-.09	-.09	.27	.32	-.45	-.07	-.04
Socially adept	.25	.29	.76	-.19	.12	.31	.44	.48	.07	-.43	.10	-.13	.06
Competitive	-.03	.50	.5-	.02	-.09	-.31	.20	.47	.52	-.03	-.14	.46	-.06
Patriotic	.22	-.05	.90	-.04	.15	-.19	.03	.30	-.13	-.03	.10	-.01	-.03
Kind	.33	.32	.41	-.04	.16	.25	-.70	.90	.06	-.25	.84	-.05	-.18
Insecure	-.05	.22	.06	.02	.49	-.05	.10	-.10	.32	-.11	-.30	.00	-.01
Aware of feelings of others	.34	-.11	.53	.09	.49	-.05	-.18	.32	-.13	-.23	.19	.04	-.30
Good looking	.10	.92	.04	.14	.24	.55	.09	.04	.20	.30	.15	.04	-.17
Good person	.05	-.03	.45	.08	.00	-.26	-.07	.17	-.03	.21	.15	.26	.29
Popular	-.03	.88	.09	.09	.34	.57	-.04	.01	.39	.65	-.44	.22	-.21
Sincere	.09	-.03	.13	.14	.33	.24	-.10	.40	-.12	.12	.50	-.10	.01
Liberated	-.02	.02	.56	.06	.20	.06	-.04	.78	.09	-.11	.14	-.12	-.57
Blue eyes	-.03	.45	.15	.02	.66	-.01	-.35	-.21	-.11	.78	-.36	.00	-.14
Has leadership qualities	.00	.18	.44	.03	-.01	.37	.51	.27	.01	-.19	-.34	.35	-.24
Creative	.07	-.27	-.04	.02	.06	.00	-.04	.31	.26	-.10	.09	.24	.04
Aggressive	-.07	.40	-.02	.39	.25	.72	.19	-.15	.53	.03	-.18	.34	.15
Dominant	-.11	.06	.18	.60	.10	.56	.25	-.02	.09	-.11	-.53	.37	.01
Willing to take a stand	.27	-.08	.07	.00	-.08	-.08	-.02	.22	.12	.16	.51	.16	-.10
Subordinates self to others	.33	.57	.08	.17	.39	.29	-.38	-.20	.23	.40	-.22	.24	.01

(Continued)

219

| | Females | | | | | | | Males | | | | | |
| | 14-year-olds n = 27 | | | | 18-year-olds n = 28 | | | 14-year-olds n = 33 | | | 18-year-olds n = 41 | | |
	1	2	3	4	1	2	3	1	2	3	1	2	3
Strong	-.06	.23	-.38	.51	.03	.29	.52	.05	.06	-.11	-.12	.11	.25
Emotional	.20	-.10	.17	.04	.40	.01	-.43	.20	-.13	.21	.39	.02	-.47
Strong personality	.54	.14	.09	-.23	.18	.20	-.03	.02	-.23	.13	.10	-.24	-.22
Self confident	.62	.30	.33	-.45	.30	.10	.11	.20	-.03	.25	.12	.74	.14
Athletic	.20	.18	.11	.75	.31	.41	.06	.04	.15	.43	-.28	.10	.23
Self-esteem	.13	-.03	.22	.13	.33	.09	.05	.34	-.06	.13	-.07	.67	-.05
Cooperative	.56	-.05	.09	.06	.49	.20	.06	.51	-.24	.24	.23	.23	-.30
Capable	.48	.02	-.28	-.21	.35	.25	-.03	.09	.16	.77	-.25	.45	.06
Artistic	.12	.19	.02	.73	.18	.27	-.14	.27	.10	-.10	-.15	.00	-.27
Stands up under pressure	.39	-.11	.16	-.03	.27	.11	.21	.22	-.11	.05	.23	.43	-.48
Tough-minded	.14	.26	.15	-.17	-.10	.90	.22	.20	-.13	-.35	.09	.62	-.13
Compassionate	.38	-.05	.18	-.28	.93	.14	-.26	.47	.14	-.07	.09	-.07	-.83
Decides easily	.68	-.25	.20	-.16	.28	.43	-.14	.28	.18	.06	-.34	.79	.08
Tender	.81	-.10	.05	-.08	.19	.13	-.18	.30	.29	-.11	.25	.02	-.39
Assertive	.14	.07	.12	.00	.18	.23	.17	-.14	-.03	-.11	-.39	.74	-.19
Likable	.73	.13	.46	.18	.51	-.20	-.23	.17	.04	-.04	.38	.28	-.60
Generous	.77	.18	.28	.05	.53	-.15	-.42	.33	.00	-.24	.19	.17	-.43
Affectionate	.46	.18	.42	-.05	.29	-.10	-.12	.45	.05	-.38	.61	.17	-.31
Warm	.83	.17	.01	-.01	.36	-.01	-.26	.71	.11	-.06	.56	.35	-.48
Soothes hurt feelings	.72	.02	.20	.03	.33	-.22	-.65	.69	-.03	.22	.10	.10	-.84
Feels good about self	.15	-.10	.02	-.08	-.07	.03	-.11	.21	.12	.49	.01	.09	-.21
Loves children	.50	-.03	.30	-.03	.22	.03	-.35	.68	.10	-.10	.19	.16	-.24
Friendly	.38	-.04	.09	.04	-.02	-.40	-.24	.51	-.11	-.04	.51	.11	-.22

(Continued)

| | Females | | | | | | | Males | | | | | |
| | 14-year-olds n = 27 | | | | 18-year-olds n = 28 | | | 14-year-olds n = 33 | | | 18-year-olds n = 41 | | |
	1	2	3	4	1	2	3	1	2	3	1	2	3
Hardworking	.30	.22	-.03	-.05	.58	.00	-.20	.00	.05	.26	-.23	.24	.20
Tries to do one's best	.37	-.24	.14	-.21	.05	-.17	.27	.23	-.12	.00	.44	.06	.21
Never gives up	.49	-.06	-.06	-.04	-.09	-.04	.25	.30	-.10	.00	.15	.10	.02
Active	.40	.20	-.07	.15	.35	.06	-.20	.42	.00	.04	-.10	.52	.08
Loyal	.47	-.18	.05	-.24	.04	-.18	-.26	.55	.13	-.06	.13	-.02	.17
Doesn't show feelings	-.13	.03	-.03	.26	-.21	.39	-.16	.02	.83	-.13	-.16	-.04	-.01
Quiet	.00	.33	.07	-.19	-.03	.21	-.01	.17	.71	.04	.01	-.46	-.08
Lively	.38	.21	-.14	-.12	.22	.39	-.24	.36	.44	.13	.02	.16	.08
Devotes self to others	.20	-.04	.04	-.53	.21	.01	-.87	.01	.65	.33	-.17	-.17	-.24
Whiny	-.16	.42	.29	.17	.01	.21	.11	-.05	.92	.09	-.43	.11	.02
Humorous	.22	.13	-.03	.01	.41	-.22	-.09	.33	-.21	.10	.15	-.02	.21
Fun	.31	.05	-.34	-.25	.52	-.03	-.19	.27	-.35	.09	.23	.01	.07
Shy	.10	-.02	.18	-.74	.18	-.06	-.36	-.29	.09	.14	-.06	-.13	.16
% of Variance	27.6	14.8	11.0	7.9	23.3	13.5	12.2	32.4	12.3	11.0	21.5	16.5	9.6
		61.4				49.1			55.7			47.5	
Factor Correlations													
1		.07	.11	-.08		.07	-.19		.08	-.10		-.05	-.12
			.15	.11			.18			.06			.00
				-.02									

APPENDIX VI

Factors Analyses of Importance Ratings of Most Men by Swedish Respondents

| | Females | | | | | | Males | | | | | |
| | 14-year-olds n = 32 | | | 18-year-olds n = 34 | | | 14-year-olds n = 35 | | | 18-year-olds n = 41 | | |
	1	2	3	1	2	3	1	2	3	1	2	3
Helpful	.17	-.11	-.17	.76	.06	.07	.22	.26	-.18	-.01	.12	.07
Tall	-.18	.39	.06	-.02	.80	.12	.06	.32	.16	-.48	.34	.20
Acts as leader	-.06	.82	.03	.11	.17	-.18	-.13	.85	.09	-.46	.69	-.38
Gentle	.62	.11	-.35	.50	.03	.16	.43	.17	-.38	-.04	-.10	.00
Straight hair	-.16	.37	.12	.14	.49	.19	-.06	.15	-.06	-.33	.31	-.21
Socially adept	.14	.02	-.11	.11	.12	-.28	.20	.17	-.16	.21	-.05	-.01
Competitive	.09	.18	-.32	.41	.53	-.29	.08	.50	-.17	-.28	.43	-.51
Patriotic	.30	-.06	-.56	.41	-.05	-.25	.26	.20	-.42	.89	-.29	.36
Kind	.76	-.13	-.30	.60	.00	.10	.43	.27	-.33	.73	-.22	.22
Insecure	-.13	.43	.20	.11	.38	.40	.13	.07	.16	-.22	-.11	.09
Aware of feelings of others	.47	.02	-.24	.31	-.07	.02	.23	.29	-.35	.47	-.36	.47
Good looking	-.10	.49	.16	.22	.81	.35	.01	.13	.17	-.46	.37	.35
Good person	-.03	.24	-.28	.11	.33	.28	.17	.77	-.14	.22	.19	.14
Popular	.06	.50	-.06	.21	.84	-.01	.16	.72	.14	-.17	.81	-.15
Sincere	-.02	-.19	.02	.58	-.06	-.02	.31	.31	-.41	.50	-.25	.39
Liberated	-.03	.36	-.31	-.02	-.04	-.63	.06	.35	-.24	.17	.09	.13
Blue eyes	.08	.49	-.10	.24	.44	.29	-.25	.26	-.04	-.54	.36	.04
Has leadership qualities	-.23	.88	-.17	.15	.26	-.24	-.04	.90	-.10	-.45	.78	-.29
Creative	-.15	-.08	-.03	-.02	.20	-.24	-.06	.41	-.21	-.29	.16	.03
Aggressive	-.31	.31	.17	-.13	.28	-.05	-.22	.30	.22	-.32	.28	-.18
Dominant	-.10	.23	.40	-.22	.45	-.06	-.26	.65	.15	-.34	.50	-.14
Willing to take a stand	.18	-.15	.11	.20	-.03	.18	.09	.12	-.45	.48	-.32	.23
Subordinates self to others	.05	.45	.21	.26	.15	.06	-.24	.23	.42	-.30	.33	-.12

(Continued)

| | Females | | | | | | Males | | | | | |
| | 14-year-olds n = 32 | | | 18-year-olds n = 34 | | | 14-year-olds n = 35 | | | 18-year-olds n = 41 | | |
	1	2	3	1	2	3	1	2	3	1	2	3
Strong	.02	.17	.26	.02	.29	-.04	-.68	.22	.11	-.16	.62	-.35
Emotional	.53	-.23	-.05	.42	-.20	.14	-.35	.06	-.41	.30	-.03	-.07
Strong personality	.34	-.06	-.01	.16	-.15	-.08	-.05	.14	-.29	.32	-.17	.23
Self confident	.25	.12	-.17	.19	-.08	-.34	-.04	.12	-.18	.20	.22	.19
Athletic	.23	.19	.16	.23	.41	-.31	-.04	.75	.10	-.37	.51	-.29
Self-esteem	.04	.11	-.16	.07	.04	-.28	-.01	.55	-.20	-.11	.22	-.02
Cooperative	.33	-.34	.00	.70	.19	-.07	.39	.19	-.40	.63	-.14	.50
Capable	.35	.16	.00	.24	.14	-.01	.10	.29	-.27	-.16	.79	.07
Artistic	.06	.16	.08	.28	.09	-.10	.07	.38	-.06	-.18	.10	.02
Stands up under pressure	.38	-.22	-.19	.25	.03	-.40	.12	-.01	-.42	-.06	.21	-.03
Tough-minded	.29	.18	-.15	.11	.38	-.16	-.21	.09	-.26	-.31	.47	-.12
Compassionate	.19	-.17	-.27	.32	.11	-.21	-.09	.10	-.01	.01	-.08	.38
Decides easily	.41	.01	.03	.09	.12	-.38	-.17	.16	.30	-.22	.79	.03
Tender	.44	-.22	-.13	.50	.05	.16	-.08	-.14	.09	.19	-.07	.84
Assertive	.13	.38	.03	.39	.37	-.28	.02	.26	.46	-.31	.75	.00
Likable	.23	-.11	-.30	.49	.09	-.18	.23	-.09	-.05	.15	.01	.83
Generous	.69	.04	-.01	.08	-.14	-.43	.37	.04	-.08	.38	-.06	.54
Affectionate	.74	-.04	-.07	.26	-.18	-.13	.41	.03	-.20	.33	-.14	.65
Warm	.60	-.36	.17	.37	.07	.09	.29	.00	-.07	.32	-.19	.82
Soothes hurt feelings	.37	-.24	.39	.26	-.07	.11	.26	.01	.06	.40	-.37	.50
Feels good about self	-.04	-.06	.13	.33	.07	.00	.38	.47	.21	-.18	.19	-.19
Loves children	.68	-.16	-.16	.31	.01	.38	-.24	.14	.12	.27	-.18	.01
Friendly	.28	-.13	.03	.63	-.02	.27	.01	-.08	.08	.75	-.21	.26

(Continued)

| | Females | | | | | | Males | | | | | |
| | 14-year-olds n = 32 | | | 18-year-olds n = 34 | | | 14-year-olds n = 35 | | | 18-year-olds n = 41 | | |
	1	2	3	1	2	3	1	2	3	1	2	3
Hardworking	.22	.44	-.25	.19	.32	.17	-.01	-.02	.23	.01	.37	.18
Tries to do one's best	.32	.06	-.34	.24	-.05	-.04	.13	.03	-.03	.41	-.12	.14
Never gives up	.53	.06	-.39	.05	-.09	-.18	.22	.09	-.01	.47	.12	.26
Active	.36	.51	-.37	.34	.01	-.11	.11	.18	-.06	.00	.49	-.06
Loyal	.25	.18	-.76	.37	-.07	.08	.26	.10	-.11	.33	.04	.27
Doesn't show feelings	-.09	.14	.03	.00	.39	.43	-.09	-.33	.12	-.48	.20	-.07
Quiet	-.27	.27	-.15	.11	.65	.12	-.04	.03	.14	-.30	.01	-.08
Lively	-.08	.18	-.04	.54	.25	-.16	-.34	.16	-.10	-.25	.46	-.13
Devotes self to others	-.26	.10	.01	.09	.57	.24	-.12	.09	.73	.09	.05	.10
Whiny	-.07	.44	.15	-.12	.15	.22	-.02	.02	.82	-.52	.30	-.24
Humorous	-.04	.16	-.46	.64	.03	.03	-.02	-.03	-.20	.20	.04	.41
Fun	.14	.15	-.37	.86	.24	-.02	-.05	-.03	-.08	.28	-.01	.53
Shy	0.09	.22	-.53	.01	.32	.76	.13	-.14	.67	-.04	.12	-.16
% of Variance	28.3	14.9	8.2	29.0	17.0	10.6	34.6	17.2	10.1	30.1	16.3	8.6
		51.5			56.7			61.9			55.1	
Factor Correlations												
1												
2		-.07			.11			.00			-.26	
3		-.06	-.10		.04	.12		-.04	.05		.18	-.13

APPENDIX VII

Factor Analyses of Importance Ratings of Most Girls by American Respondents

	Females								Males							
	14-year-olds n = 35				18-year-olds n = 30				14-year-olds n = 34				18-year-olds n = 39			
	1	2	3	4	1	2	3	4	1	2	3	4	1	2	3	4
Helpful	.61	-.11	.03		-.04	.84	.23	.30	.35	.19	-.12		-.19	.20	-.25	.05
Tall	-.34	.50	-.20		.94	-.10	.00	.19	-.09	.10	.15		.68	.16	.10	.14
Acts as leader	-.02	.03	-.61		.77	-.21	.26	.35	-.23	-.29	.35		.58	.35	.17	.10
Gentle	.40	-.31	-.19		-.07	-.85	.30	.19	.38	-.11	-.35		-.11	.26	.09	.55
Straight hair	-.15	.55	.06		.91	-.19	.07	.12	-.35	.11	.23		.81	-.02	-.27	.21
Socially adept	-.08	-.23	.35		.40	-.21	.51	.26	.13	.15	-.29		.69	.05	.01	.21
Competitive	-.11	.46	.51		.73	-.40	.45	.44	-.11	-.01	.73		.29	.22	.39	.07
Patriotic	-.26	-.55	-.37		.54	-.12	.19	.56	.25	.01	-.29		.42	.07	-.20	-.14
Kind	.59	-.20	.39		-.33	-.65	-.06	.23	.39	-.10	-.18		-.18	.15	-.06	.06
Insecure	-.11	.35	.57		.85	-.18	-.09	.31	-.13	.49	.53		.42	.06	-.33	.34
Aware of feelings of others	.26	-.39	-.41		-.57	.31	.47	.04	.55	.18	-.16		-.25	-.74	.32	-.01
Good looking	.22	.18	.19		-.41	.55	.46	-.45	.05	.32	-.18		.82	-.44	-.23	.40
Good person	.60	-.11	.21		-.09	-.30	.61	.22	.41	.42	.21		.14	-.14	.04	.29
Popular	.30	.43	-.10		-.10	.65	-.04	-.13	.18	.61	-.18		.90	-.23	-.03	.14
Sincere	.23	.01	.39		-.75	.41	.04	-.16	.24	.11	-.22		-.09	-.84	.10	.03
Liberated	.20	-.41	-.33		.37	-.71	-.03	.51	.21	.25	.23		.27	-.07	-.15	.14
Blue eyes	.12	.08	-.17		.88	-.20	.20	.28	.11	.49	-.16		.80	-.08	-.22	.27
Has leadership qualities	.00	.18	-.51		-.26	.65	.05	.26	-.02	.03	.03		.40	-.53	.17	.08
Creative	.15	.21	-.13		.61	-.51	-.06	.34	.25	.20	.29		.26	.59	.11	.26
Aggressive	.10	.28	-.15		.26	-.18	.05	.11	.09	.87	.23		.31	.27	-.27	-.03
Dominant	-.10	.88	.49		.45	.21	.06	.21	-.04	.10	.33		.49	-.24	-.15	-.19
Willing to take a stand	.25	-.46	.59		.32	-.41	.41	.45	.55	.06	-.22		-.10	.22	-.21	-.05
Subordinates self to others	-.21	.18	.29		.43	-.19	-.08	.32	-.10	.63	.48		.30	.17	-.42	-.04

(Continued)

227

	Females									Males							
	14-year-olds n = 35			18-year-olds n = 30						14-year-olds n = 34			18-year-olds n = 39			
	1	2	3	1	2	3	4			1	2	3	1	2	3	4
Strong	.08	.41	.45	-.14	.37	.01	.26			.30	.51	-.25	.15	-.86	.11	-.02
Emotional	.35	-.23	-.30	.08	.36	.29	-.27			.71	-.10	.03	.75	.05	-.20	.24
Strong personality	.28	-.25	-.39	.37	.26	.20	.21			.42	.15	-.28	.28	-.21	-.13	.33
Self confident	.29	.18	-.17	.12	-.16	.02	.77			.38	.49	.22	.01	-.29	-.12	.24
Athletic	.35	.68	.10	.63	.11	.01	.48			.23	.47	.01	.74	-.18	.00	.45
Self-esteem	.45	.20	.31	-.36	.80	.11	.02			.10	.65	.34	.19	-.86	-.02	.05
Cooperative	.15	-.18	.01	.15	.41	.32	-.02			.35	.15	-.26	.27	.08	.04	.30
Capable	.65	.24	-.10	-.13	.91	.47	-.21			.50	.33	-.15	-.24	.02	.41	.17
Artistic	.35	.10	.20	.78	.04	.20	.09			.75	.20	-.28	.26	.10	.69	.15
Stands up under pressure	.25	-.38	-.08	.15	-.04	.22	.14			.33	.15	.38	.01	-.13	.30	-.13
Tough-minded	.51	.30	-.06	.74	-.06	.23	.37			.52	.12	.08	.35	.18	.40	.24
Compassionate	.35	-.06	.61	.00	.03	.80	-.33			.39	.10	-.10	-.06	-.16	.80	.15
Decides easily	.18	-.23	.08	-.14	.50	.02	.06			.53	.10	.10	.19	-.80	-.05	.09
Tender	.73	-.20	.10	.07	.02	.06	-.31			.76	.10	.12	.36	-.22	-.18	.71
Assertive	.27	.24	.12	.38	.16	.09	.52			.15	.69	.10	.06	.04	.56	.01
Likable	.69	-.22	-.31	.37	.22	-.10	.18			.55	.30	-.10	.41	-.10	-.59	.45
Generous	.41	-.20	-.49	.36	.11	.26	.23			.86	-.03	.12	.16	-.81	.08	.49
Affectionate	.79	-.31	.30	.28	.00	.82	-.27			.91	-.10	-.17	-.13	.11	.86	.09
Warm	.65	-.22	-.24	-.29	.43	-.06	-.06			.83	.06	.12	.07	-.28	.13	.42
Soothes hurt feelings	.53	.08	.22	.63	.14	.33	-.43			.42	-.08	-.09	.41	-.20	.01	.68
Feels good about self	.48	-.11	.23	.22	-.07	.87	.16			.41	.40	.21	-.33	-.18	.86	-.10
Loves children	.32	-.13	-.24	.61	-.06	.44	.07			.15	.06	.08	.40	-.18	-.10	.74
Friendly	.49	.06	.67	.37	-.23	.61	.08			.38	.10	-.23	.22	-.15	.14	.17

(Continued)

	Females							Males						
	14-year-olds n = 35			18-year-olds n = 30				14-year-olds n = 34			18-year-olds n = 39			
	1	2	3	1	2	3	4	1	2	3	1	2	3	4
Hardworking	.50	.17	.10	.20	.63	.09	.58	.08	-.25	.51	.28	-.69	-.16	-.05
Tries to do one's best	.32	-.24	-.14	.29	-.01	.12	.55	.18	-.29	.28	.09	.15	-.13	.08
Never gives up	.29	-.08	-.12	.13	.14	.63	.21	.17	-.40	.55	.06	.15	.62	-.13
Active	.35	.10	.08	.32	.00	.32	.53	.23	.05	.93	.50	.09	-.48	.10
Loyal	.41	-.61	.31	-.54	-.18	.32	.19	.18	-.25	.43	-.36	.02	.30	-.31
Doesn't show feelings	-.28	.35	.27	.46	-.50	-.10	.08	-.30	.06	.85	.06	.45	-.66	.14
Quiet	.15	.19	-.10	.56	-.12	.42	.12	-.02	.03	.51	.22	.33	.24	.04
Lively	.31	.10	.20	.19	-.26	.10	-.07	.18	-.15	.23	.11	.30	-.53	.49
Devotes self to others	.12	.03	-.08	-.05	-.60	-.29	-.07	.06	.30	.58	-.11	.40	-.42	.09
Whiny	.14	.24	.31	.75	-.08	.39	.04	-.01	.28	.83	.27	.31	.45	-.13
Humorous	.35	-.33	-.38	.42	-.13	.15	.15	-.08	.01	.40	.34	-.03	.10	.71
Fun	.37	-.13	-.15	-.19	-.58	-.07	.10	-.16	-.03	.10	-.15	.29	-.13	.38
Shy	.08	.10	-.09	.90	.09	.04	.16	-.23	-.08	.85	.46	-.13	.00	.15
% of Variance	25.2	16.8	10.9	35.2	18.3	10.9	9.1	27.5	13.8	11.2	24.8	16.9	15.3	10.6
		52.9			73.6				52.5			67.6		
Factor Correlations														
1		-.12	.21		-.12	.04	.12		-.10	.16		-.05	-.12	.21
2			-.03			.01	-.14			-.05			-.08	-.03
3							.03							-.08

229

APPENDIX VIII

*Factor Analyses of Importance Ratings
of Most Boys by American Respondents*

	Females									Males							
	14-year-olds n = 32			18-year-olds n = 46						14-year-olds n = 41			18-year-olds n = 44			
	1	2	3	1	2	3	4	5		1	2	3	1	2	3	4
Helpful	.83	-.05	.08	.88	-.23	.29	-.09	.38		.38	.06	.79	-.27	.83	.23	.08
Tall	-.12	.81	-.06	.27	.13	-.37	-.33	.80		-.13	.25	.12	.42	.15	.08	-.12
Acts as leader	-.08	.58	.29	.33	.11	-.07	-.09	.84		.06	.95	.19	-.15	.20	.19	.93
Gentle	.78	-.22	-.15	.86	-.09	.19	-.13	.33		.29	.01	.33	.27	.33	.58	.43
Straight hair	-.31	.15	-.12	.28	.08	-.53	-.26	.74		-.06	.24	.05	.31	.08	-.25	.15
Socially adept	-.04	.18	.12	.30	-.05	.20	-.04	.57		.29	.16	-.18	.65	-.18	.04	.04
Competitive	-.27	.61	-.03	.44	.05	.24	-.60	.29		.18	.73	.23	.17	.25	.21	-.07
Patriotic	.17	-.19	-.06	.61	-.13	.46	-.28	.18		.43	-.06	.62	.11	.65	-.13	.34
Kind	.73	-.13	-.22	.85	-.18	-.02	.18	.22		.41	-.13	.08	.48	.10	.49	.02
Insecure	-.14	-.06	.15	.63	-.11	-.23	.13	.46		-.15	-.08	-.12	.25	-.13	-.24	-.24
Aware of feelings of others	.48	-.08	-.08	.86	-.10	.03	.02	.15		.65	.09	-.22	.26	.23	.10	-.03
Good looking	.06	.83	-.32	-.85	-.30	.11	.25	-.16		.25	.26	-.61	.14	-.67	-.22	-.15
Good person	.31	-.08	.31	-.38	.28	.14	.70	-.56		.43	.21	-.63	.11	-.59	.67	-.34
Popular	.01	.36	.13	.34	.04	.06	-.24	.89		.31	.27	-.14	.12	-.16	.11	-.26
Sincere	.33	-.06	-.08	-.28	.00	.15	.40	-.20		.71	.00	-.25	.88	-.27	.32	.17
Liberated	.19	.14	.06	-.82	.00	.01	.46	-.47		.62	.10	-.75	.20	-.73	.01	-.28
Blue eyes	-.07	.27	-.08	.50	-.07	-.30	-.10	.71		-.02	.14	-.20	.61	-.21	.16	-.10
Has leadership qualities	-.28	.71	.19	.58	-.16	.43	-.25	.54		-.03	.85	-.41	.51	-.42	.11	.18
Creative	-.06	-.14	.90	-.62	.45	.13	.57	-.05		.53	.12	-.91	.32	-.93	.02	-.23
Aggressive	-.22	.21	.25	.51	-.11	-.10	-.23	.53		-.15	.20	.45	.46	.47	.12	.19
Dominant	-.06	-.02	-.13	.25	.21	-.01	-.24	.45		.06	.46	-.16	.61	-.18	-.08	.00
Willing to take a stand	.19	-.06	.41	-.57	.31	.32	.38	-.30		.63	.10	-.65	.46	-.62	-.07	-.20
Subordinates self to others	-.17	.03	-.19	.38	-.26	.31	.13	.35		-.14	-.08	-.03	.34	-.05	.04	.16

(Continued)

231

	Females								Males							
	14-year-olds n = 32			18-year-olds n = 46					14-year-olds n = 41			18-year-olds n = 44			
	1	2	3	1	2	3	4	5	1	2	3	1	2	3	4
Strong	.13	.59	-.49	-.17	.12	-.35	-.48	.54	-.09	.53	-.32	.83	-.33	.01	-.20
Emotional	.65	-.12	.18	-.10	.08	.19	.93	-.24	.68	-.10	-.87	.32	-.89	-.01	-.15
Strong personality	.40	.21	.49	-.15	-.14	.36	.44	.10	.65	.10	-.25	.86	-.27	.31	-.08
Self confident	.37	.08	.54	.10	-.91	-.12	-.07	-.25	.26	.28	.18	-.05	.20	.81	.46
Athletic	-.16	.61	-.43	.10	-.43	-.75	-.12	.21	.14	.45	-.85	.18	-.89	.17	-.22
Self-esteem	.14	-.07	.51	.28	-.28	-.17	.28	.18	.38	.13	-.51	.33	-.54	.51	-.11
Cooperative	.58	-.13	.00	-.50	.29	-.10	.65	-.43	.85	-.08	-.63	.16	-.68	.22	-.43
Capable	.37	.16	-.13	.60	-.05	-.01	-.24	.64	.55	.20	-.10	.48	-.12	.42	.04
Artistic	.27	.68	-.31	.47	-.11	.17	-.11	.24	.53	.18	.38	-.06	.36	.15	.78
Stands up under pressure	.24	.09	.45	.05	-.01	.14	-.29	.24	.67	-.10	.14	-.07	.15	.02	.98
Tough-minded	.08	.69	.03	.00	-.37	.13	-.66	.04	.32	.79	.13	-.07	.15	-.17	.21
Compassionate	.38	.08	.06	.93	-.17	.24	-.09	.27	.61	.30	.27	.09	.26	.24	.71
Decides easily	.68	-.04	.26	.17	-.12	.19	.07	.36	.26	.35	.28	-.40	.30	.40	.61
Tender	.77	.12	-.03	-.07	-.13	-.17	.36	-.77	.31	.14	-.49	.26	-.52	.36	-.47
Assertive	.19	-.02	.32	.17	-.60	.32	-.02	-.02	.03	.31	.03	.47	.04	.08	-.18
Likable	.66	.08	.10	.25	-.32	.82	-.02	.03	.46	.09	.05	-.15	.06	.12	.87
Generous	.46	.21	.15	.05	-.65	-.18	.38	-.12	.65	-.03	-.38	.57	-.43	.21	-.38
Affectionate	.67	.02	-.09	.20	-.86	-.20	.09	-.08	.56	.10	-.21	.37	-.23	.34	-.08
Warm	.51	.24	-.12	.72	-.44	.13	-.02	.20	.42	-.08	.64	-.21	.66	.40	.64
Soothes hurt feelings	.37	.01	.02	-.33	-.77	.03	.04	-.16	.54	.00	-.01	.08	-.03	.41	-.08
Feels good about self	.08	-.07	.45	-.12	-.83	.01	-.14	-.27	.55	.06	-.15	.57	-.13	.43	.02
Loves children	.31	-.08	.06	.52	-.17	.52	-.23	.26	.30	-.13	.23	-.32	.25	.24	.61
Friendly	.47	.16	.08	.24	.00	.57	.09	.17	.57	-.04	.16	.15	.18	.87	.03

(*Continued*)

232

| | Females | | | | | | | | Males | | | | | | |
| | 14-year-olds n = 32 | | | 18-year-olds n = 46 | | | | | 14-year-olds n = 41 | | | 18-year-olds n = 44 | | | |
	1	2	3	1	2	3	4	5	1	2	3	1	2	3	4
Hardworking	.35	-.09	-.10	.34	-.03	.32	-.52	.13	.39	-.07	.12	.28	.10	.38	.11
Tries to do one's best	.14	-.25	.16	-.10	-.09	.07	-.20	-.75	.55	-.23	-.14	.10	-.12	.08	-.39
Never gives up	.53	.03	.19	.26	.03	.19	-.35	-.11	.58	-.20	-.28	.80	-.23	-.32	-.26
Active	.12	-.05	-.12	.17	.06	.70	-.36	.13	.13	.15	.36	-.26	.35	.03	.81
Loyal	.02	.02	-.55	.27	-.11	.04	.05	.12	.65	-.14	-.16	.89	-.14	.18	-.03
Doesn't show feelings	-.06	.27	-.13	-.05	.35	-.13	-.20	.06	-.08	-.27	.30	-.08	.32	-.45	.10
Quiet	-.07	-.22	.12	.50	-.33	-.26	-.30	.09	.08	-.12	.25	.65	.23	.07	-.25
Lively	.24	.55	.27	.10	-.79	.20	-.22	.20	.09	.08	.55	-.42	.51	.24	.42
Devotes self to others	-.13	.08	.34	.67	-.10	-.19	.04	.41	.01	-.03	-.08	.79	-.06	.00	-.18
Whiny	-.10	.10	-.05	.35	-.32	-.23	.03	.16	.08	.07	.34	.39	.31	-.10	.04
Humorous	.65	-.10	.17	.30	-.01	.47	-.07	.47	.48	-.24	.48	-.46	.49	.22	.60
Fun	.57	.00	.14	.36	-.14	.18	.40	.27	.68	-.25	.05	-.06	.02	.76	.08
Shy	.15	-.08	-.19	.63	.10	.03	-.21	.34	-.15	.18	-.01	.25	-.03	.01	.02
% of Variance	31.2	16.1	11.0	36.9	13.1	11.7	9.5	7.8	37.1	15.1	9.3	29.9	20.7	13.3	8.9
		58.3			79.0					61.5			72.7		
Factor Correlations															
1															
2		-.03			-.07					.05			-.19		
3		-.06	-.08		.07	-.01				-.03	-.02		.03	.01	
4					-.11	.01	.03						-.11	.22	.12
5					.22	.06	-.05	-.14							

233

APPENDIX IX

Factor Analyses of Importance Ratings of Most Women by American Respondents

	Females							Males							
	14-year-olds n = 38			18-year-olds n = 46				14-year-olds n = 38				18-year-olds n = 49			
	1	2	3	1	2	3	4	1	2	3	4	1	2	3	4
Helpful	.33	.10	.29	.42	-.29	.24	.40	.46	.10	.12	.79	-.15	.11	.16	.80
Tall	-.31	.42	.17	-.57	.15	-.02	-.43	-.26	.22	.18	.10	.16	-.28	-.14	.12
Acts as leader	-.18	.73	.24	-.42	.09	.23	-.61	-.08	.39	-.01	.51	-.25	-.36	.40	.53
Gentle	.32	.22	.57	.23	.09	-.04	.91	.73	-.06	-.22	.53	.39	.22	.31	.56
Straight Hair	-.16	.41	.10	-.51	.16	-.10	-.45	-.08	.29	.35	-.06	.00	-.67	.00	-.07
Socially adept	.25	.31	.77	.21	.12	.14	.03	.49	.09	-.41	.31	.22	-.08	.08	.30
Competitive	-.05	.55	.57	.03	.10	.64	-.40	.49	.55	-.06	.28	.07	-.42	-.33	.33
Patriotic	.20	-.10	.91	.47	.18	.28	-.19	.33	-.15	-.06	.18	-.27	-.44	.58	.20
Kind	.35	.31	.39	.23	.04	.49	.60	.91	.05	-.21	-.07	.01	-.35	-.03	-.03
Insecure	-.08	.23	-.04	-.21	-.08	-.02	.19	-.08	.30	-.09	-.17	.18	-.71	-.10	-.14
Aware of feelings of others	.36	-.11	.55	.76	.00	.14	.33	.34	-.15	-.21	.21	.23	.17	-.12	.30
Good looking	.11	.91	.12	.16	-.12	-.02	.11	.02	.18	.32	-.11	.09	-.22	.46	-.10
Good person	.08	-.01	.47	.42	-.01	.10	.11	.19	-.08	-.23	.18	.58	.70	-.30	.20
Popular	-.02	.90	.09	.07	-.24	.13	-.18	.05	.36	.67	.15	.59	.12	-.26	.14
Sincere	.04	-.01	.14	.43	.35	.13	.45	.41	-.08	.06	-.10	.37	.07	.24	-.08
Liberated	-.05	.03	.58	.05	-.08	-.03	-.07	.80	.10	-.13	.25	.52	.15	.00	.27
Blue eyes	-.05	.47	.17	.02	.10	-.15	-.23	-.23	-.13	.80	-.13	.62	.26	-.40	-.15
Has leadership qualities	.01	.19	.47	.28	.40	.72	.13	.29	.00	-.15	-.08	.79	.15	-.13	-.05
Creative	.08	-.29	-.03	.16	.68	.15	-.06	.33	.34	-.12	-.01	.70	-.06	.23	-.03
Aggressive	-.08	.45	-.08	-.04	.42	-.28	.38	-.16	.55	.05	-.41	.77	.29	-.27	-.39
Dominant	-.13	.08	.20	-.12	.27	.08	-.10	-.04	-.11	.10	-.18	.39	-.58	.00	-.16
Willing to take a stand	.29	-.06	.06	.27	.91	.24	.10	.24	.14	.18	-.33	.70	.16	-.16	-.29
Subordinates self to others	.31	.54	.09	-.11	.67	.02	.15	-.22	.24	.42	-.35	.49	-.55	.20	-.33

(Continued)

	Females							Males							
	14-year-olds n = 38			18-year-olds n = 46				14-year-olds n = 38				18-year-olds n = 49			
	1	2	3	1	2	3	4	1	2	3	4	1	2	3	4
Strong	-.08	.24	-.40	.09	.22	.17	.00	.06	.08	-.15	-.06	.24	-.26	-.40	-.01
Emotional	.21	-.14	.16	.46	.19	-.01	.41	.22	-.15	.23	-.03	.79	.35	.08	-.05
Strong personality	.55	.18	.10	.26	.54	.35	.00	.04	-.24	.11	-.01	.69	.21	-.09	-.02
Self confident	.65	.31	.35	.46	.57	.70	.00	.22	-.01	.23	.36	.02	.08	-.23	.38
Athletic	.22	.20	.14	-.23	.55	.25	-.36	.06	.17	.41	-.10	.35	-.09	-.18	-.01
Self-esteem	.15	-.05	.20	.11	.34	.53	-.23	.33	-.08	.11	.78	.15	.01	-.10	.75
Cooperative	.58	-.08	.10	.54	.00	.07	.23	.53	-.22	.18	-.11	.52	.75	-.24	-.08
Capable	.50	.00	-.31	.68	.42	.55	.15	.11	.18	.81	.14	.11	-.09	.09	.12
Artistic	.11	.21	.00	.02	.00	.10	-.04	.26	.10	-.11	.38	.38	.39	.63	.36
Stands up under pressure	.41	-.13	.18	.14	-.01	.38	-.41	.23	-.08	.06	.18	-.11	.03	.85	.16
Tough-minded	.15	.28	.18	.39	.27	.39	-.01	.19	-.18	-.31	.01	.21	.09	-.12	.00
Compassionate	.36	-.07	.18	.63	.02	.13	.76	.46	.12	-.09	.15	-.02	.15	.89	.13
Decides easily	.73	-.27	.24	.49	-.10	-.03	.13	.29	.14	.05	.53	-.22	-.19	.54	.49
Tender	.85	-.12	.07	.61	.23	-.16	.38	.32	-.21	-.12	.11	.48	.70	.14	.09
Assertive	.16	.09	.14	.41	.55	.58	.13	-.13	-.01	-.15	-.23	.29	-.40	-.39	-.26
Likable	.75	.15	.48	.55	-.01	.02	.16	.19	.03	-.06	.08	-.25	.06	.89	.10
Generous	.79	.20	.26	.24	.54	.28	-.02	.31	.01	-.22	.06	.53	-.14	-.30	.10
Affectionate	.44	.15	.46	.63	.41	-.01	.32	.47	.07	-.41	-.10	.32	.18	.21	-.12
Warm	.85	.19	.02	.62	-.11	-.02	.48	.73	.10	-.05	.59	-.49	.08	.60	.57
Soothes hurt feelings	.74	.03	.18	.34	.23	-.24	.28	.71	-.06	.20	.08	.51	.79	-.23	.09
Feels good about self	.17	-.11	.02	.53	.48	.58	.16	.20	.11	.53	.06	.31	.21	.27	.08
Loves children	.51	-.06	.32	.58	-.26	.13	.29	.66	.08	-.12	.12	-.20	.33	.69	.10
Friendly	.40	-.06	.11	.79	.26	.46	.34	.53	-.13	-.03	.18	.06	-.01	.07	.20

(Continued)

236

| | Females | | | | | | | Males | | | | | | | |
| | 14-year-olds n = 38 | | | 18-year-olds n = 46 | | | | 14-year-olds n = 38 | | | | 18-year-olds n = 49 | | | |
	1	2	3	1	2	3	4	1	2	3	4	1	2	3	4
Hardworking	.31	.24	-.05	.22	-.01	.85	-.06	.01	.06	.24	.69	-.12	-.06	-.01	.67
Tries to do one's best	.39	-.26	.15	.28	.31	.86	.04	.27	-.14	.00	.18	.20	.34	-.28	.15
Never gives up	.50	-.08	-.07	.13	.30	.77	-.25	.32	-.14	.00	-.20	.16	-.37	-.34	-.15
Active	.43	.23	-.08	.45	-.15	.58	.33	.45	.01	.06	.00	-.36	-.27	.72	-.02
Loyal	.48	-.16	.07	.34	.33	.20	.38	.57	.15	-.08	.01	.07	.32	.09	.10
Doesn't show feelings	-.12	.05	-.06	-.12	-.17	.00	.02	.02	.85	-.15	-.05	-.06	-.12	-.08	-.03
Quiet	.01	.35	.09	-.55	.35	-.13	-.20	.17	.73	.05	-.10	.05	-.68	-.35	-.04
Lively	.38	.23	-.16	-.39	-.07	-.17	-.19	.38	.45	.14	.55	-.51	-.09	.30	.52
Devotes self to others	.22	-.06	.08	-.49	.47	-.12	-.04	.01	.67	.33	-.06	.31	-.22	-.17	-.02
Whiny	-.18	.44	.31	-.41	.50	.07	-.17	-.07	.95	.11	.12	.20	-.76	-.15	.14
Humorous	.24	.15	-.06	.32	.19	.08	.15	.31	-.28	.01	.43	-.49	.04	.61	.44
Fun	.33	.06	-.35	.47	.58	.34	.24	.29	-.38	.10	.73	-.01	.06	.02	.77
Shy	.10	-.03	.20	-.51	.25	-.10	-.02	-.33	.11	.17	.08	.42	-.25	.12	.10

(Continued)

	Females								Males							
	14-year-olds n = 38				18-year-olds n = 46				14-year-olds n = 38				18-year-olds n = 49			
	1	2	3	4	1	2	3	4	1	2	3	4	1	2	3	4
% of Variance	32.1	17.2	13.6		33.0	16.5	14.1	8.5	32.5	15.2	11.0	8.8	31.4	18.7	12.9	8.6
		62.9				72.1				67.4				71.7		
Factor Correlations																
1		.06	.11			.08	.22	.25		.10	.11	.12		.15	-.06	-.09
2			.10				.19	.00			.13	.01			-.03	.04
3								-.06				-.02				.11

238

APPENDIX X

*Factor Analyses of Importance Ratings
of Most Men by American Respondents*

| | Females | | | | | | | | | | | Males | | | | | | | | | | | |
| | 14-year-olds n = 36 | | | 18-year-olds n = 49 | | | | 14-year-olds n = 36 | | | 18-year-olds n = 49 | | | | 14-year-olds n = 38 | | | 18-year-olds n = 46 | | | |
	1	2	3	1	2	3	4	1	2	3	1	2	3	4
Helpful	.19	-.10	-.19	.31	.24	-.38	-.40	.25	.29	-.21	-.22	.26	.35	-.07
Tall	-.20	-.10	.20	-.13	-.40	-.12	.07	.05	.37	.18	.35	.01	.07	.15
Acts as leader	-.10	.79	.06	.00	.19	-.70	.30	-.15	.87	.11	.12	.36	-.11	.54
Gentle	.65	.13	-.40	.20	-.43	.36	-.33	.45	.19	-.40	.51	.71	.00	.03
Straight hair	-.21	.42	.13	-.10	-.27	.03	.15	-.08	.19	-.08	.36	.20	.72	-.01
Socially adept	.15	.06	-.15	.22	.07	-.24	.14	.22	.19	-.19	.48	.27	.12	.39
Competitive	.13	.20	-.32	-.11	.40	-.08	.30	.10	.51	-.16	.40	.51	.39	.36
Patriotic	.36	.00	-.59	-.12	.08	.19	.25	.25	.21	-.43	.46	.67	.35	.35
Kind	.79	-.14	-.50	.39	.04	-.05	-.52	.46	.29	-.38	.06	.52	.52	-.30
Insecure	-.16	.44	.23	-.50	.09	.60	-.19	.15	.09	.13	.21	.10	.84	.14
Aware of feelings of others	.49	.04	-.26	.04	.35	.20	.40	.25	.32	-.37	-.02	.11	-.13	-.23
Good looking	-.12	.51	.18	-.55	.46	-.26	.22	.03	.16	.19	-.66	-.39	-.01	-.35
Good person	-.06	.27	-.30	-.15	.51	-.53	-.04	.20	.79	-.16	-.71	.21	.15	-.22
Popular	.08	.52	-.07	-.51	.40	-.29	.48	.18	.75	.16	.24	.38	.75	-.08
Sincere	-.03	-.21	.05	-.06	.25	-.59	-.12	.33	.38	-.43	-.25	.53	-.09	.14
Liberated	-.06	.42	-.45	-.84	.43	-.27	.04	.08	.37	-.26	-.83	-.33	-.13	-.18
Blue eyes	.10	.51	-.15	-.24	-.22	.38	.32	-.27	.28	-.08	.19	.41	.63	-.19
Has leadership qualities	-.24	.91	-.21	-.21	.44	-.11	.54	-.06	.92	-.12	-.34	.34	.70	.05
Creative	-.17	-.10	-.11	-.08	.06	-.42	.10	-.08	.43	-.23	-.83	-.05	.28	-.27
Aggressive	-.33	.34	.18	.15	-.19	.52	.45	-.24	.36	.24	.72	.22	.33	.13
Dominant	-.12	.24	.43	-.14	.16	.19	.91	-.28	.69	.18	.55	.20	.52	.36
Willing to take a stand	.19	-.17	.18	-.45	.79	-.31	.19	.12	.12	-.48	-.76	.04	.40	-.15
Subordinates self to others	.06	.47	.23	-.38	.47	.55	.31	-.26	.23	.41	.14	-.29	.18	.18

(Continued)

	Females													Males											
	14-year-olds n = 36				18-year-olds n = 49					14-year-olds n = 38				18-year-olds n = 46			
	1	2	3		1	2	3	4		1	2	3		1	2	3	4
Strong	.03	.19	.32		-.28	.35	.06	.37		-.70	.24	.13		.30	.25	.24	.56
Emotional	.56	-.25	-.07		-.51	.71	-.10	-.41		-.37	.08	-.43		-.38	-.01	.02	-.16
Strong personality	.36	-.08	-.08		.00	.47	.03	.38		-.07	.16	-.31		-.01	.52	-.06	.33
Self confident	.27	.13	-.18		-.12	.79	-.40	.43		-.06	.12	-.21		-.43	.52	.23	.03
Athletic	.24	.20	.12		-.25	.18	.19	.30		-.05	.77	.12		.05	.21	.09	-.22
Self-esteem	.06	.13	-.19		-.32	.52	-.09	.36		-.03	.57	-.22		.09	.75	.39	-.21
Cooperative	.31	-.31	.06		-.50	.47	-.08	.02		.41	.21	-.41		-.87	-.01	-.25	-.20
Capable	.37	.18	.02		-.28	.20	.00	.11		.12	.39	-.29		.35	.14	-.08	.23
Artistic	.08	.19	.10		-.70	.12	.36	.35		.08	.40	-.07		-.38	.01	.77	-.41
Stands up under pressure	.40	-.23	-.24		.63	-.40	-.14	-.11		.14	-.03	-.44		-.01	.48	-.14	.48
Tough-minded	.41	.20	-.17		.37	.04	-.22	.21		-.23	.09	-.28		-.50	.08	.29	.16
Compassionate	.23	-.14	-.21		.09	.20	.27	-.21		-.19	.19	-.03		.51	.56	.27	-.08
Decides easily	.40	.03	.04		.04	.07	.01	-.09		-.16	.18	.28		.24	.23	-.34	.79
Tender	.45	-.26	-.15		.44	.20	-.27	-.48		-.10	-.16	.16		-.27	.52	-.25	.05
Assertive	.13	.40	-.06		-.31	-.62	-.09	.64		.03	.21	.40		.20	.00	.07	.95
Likable	.24	-.13	-.32		-.17	.85	-.03	.18		.25	-.13	-.08		-.08	.17	-.11	-.34
Generous	.72	.06	-.04		.30	-.22	-.17	-.32		.39	.08	-.04		-.06	.24	-.55	-.12
Affectionate	.70	-.06	-.09		-.21	.50	-.17	-.17		.43	.06	-.22		-.70	.04	.14	-.14
Warm	.64	-.38	.19		.40	-.10	-.19	-.59		.31	.05	-.05		.10	.20	.15	-.08
Soothes hurt feelings	.39	-.26	.38		-.30	.62	-.07	-.11		.27	.05	-.02		-.70	-.07	-.19	-.39
Feels good about self	-.07	-.04	.12		.10	.06	-.19	.07		.41	.45	.38		-.42	.54	.06	-.05
Loves children	.69	-.18	-.14		.68	-.34	-.10	-.13		-.28	.18	.08		-.41	.41	.23	.06
Friendly	.30	-.16	.00		.18	-.04	.09	-.31		.02	-.09	.06		.23	.76	.08	.10

(Continued)

241

| | Females | | | | | | | Males | | | | | | |
| | 14-year-olds n = 36 | | | 18-year-olds n = 49 | | | | 14-year-olds n = 38 | | | 18-year-olds n = 46 | | | |
	1	2	3	1	2	3	4	1	2	3	1	2	3	4
Hardworking	.24	.48	-.27	-.08	.28	.07	.10	-.03	-.04	.24	.01	.19	.19	.32
Tries to do one's best	.35	.08	-.37	-.31	.40	.26	.00	.15	.06	-.06	-.82	.09	.10	-.09
Never gives up	.55	.07	-.41	.18	.11	-.04	.07	.24	.10	-.03	.30	.65	.36	.40
Active	.40	.53	-.43	.73	-.27	-.27	-.25	.13	.19	-.08	.52	.44	.05	.60
Loyal	.28	.20	-.78	.48	.17	.07	-.13	.28	.12	-.08	.19	.91	-.04	.17
Doesn't show feelings	-.11	.17	.05	.03	-.51	.16	.05	-.11	-.36	.18	-.01	-.06	.04	.58
Quiet	-.29	.31	-.12	-.18	-.16	.85	.05	-.06	.05	.12	.65	.22	.44	.17
Lively	-.10	.17	-.08	.34	-.26	-.12	-.19	-.36	.15	-.08	.31	.17	.20	.39
Devotes self to others	-.27	.09	.09	.21	-.18	.82	.34	-.06	.10	.74	.30	.28	.58	-.01
Whiny	-.06	.41	.18	.10	-.10	.44	-.02	-.03	.00	.85	.41	.23	.35	.32
Humorous	-.03	.15	-.48	.88	-.23	-.21	-.16	-.01	.00	-.25	.37	.51	.07	-.05
Fun	.13	.15	-.37	-.18	.95	-.03	.15	.00	.00	-.01	.26	.09	-.38	.10
Shy	-.01	.28	-.49	-.35	-.20	.76	.03	.18	-.19	.71	.21	.20	.83	-.06
% of Variance	25.2	17.1	9.9	26.3	22.1	10.3	9.3	31.6	17.3	10.2	29.6	22.3	14.2	8.6
		52.2			68.0				59.1			74.6		
Factor Correlations														
1		-.08	-.05		-.23	-.01	-.12		.02	-.05		.14	.01	.13
2			-.03			-.16	-.13			.07			.18	.11
3							.02							-.06

242

APPENDIX XI

*Factor Analyses of Importance Ratings
of Self by Swedish Respondents*

| | Females | | | | | | | | | Males | | | | | | |
| | 14-year-olds n = 14 | | | | 18-year-olds n = 23 | | | | | 14-year-olds n = 33 | | | | 18-year-olds n = 41 | | |
	1	2	3	4	1	2	3	4	5	1	2	3	4	1	2	3
Helpful	.59	-.39	.01	.16	-.29	.40	.30	-.51	.11	.44	-.09	.13	.51	.22	.23	-.01
Tall	-.24	-.17	-.13	.29	.03	.07	.07	-.08	-.08	.11	-.20	.43	.35	.11	-.01	.32
Acts as leader	.22	.52	-.01	-.13	.25	-.56	.14	.02	.19	.05	.22	.79	.03	.27	-.08	.08
Gentle	.78	-.25	-.10	.17	.31	.11	-.30	.19	-.03	.43	.01	-.05	.30	.47	.02	.17
Straight hair	.25	-.35	.07	.36	-.36	.07	.07	-.21	.12	.05	-.09	-.07	-.05	.11	-.74	.14
Socially adept	.21	.12	-.31	-.03	.28	-.03	-.09	.00	.25	.32	.42	.09	.13	.31	.23	-.21
Competitive	.41	.23	.27	.24	.37	-.10	.19	-.13	-.12	.21	.27	.11	.25	.28	-.03	.15
Patriotic	.69	-.03	.08	.63	.02	.29	-.54	.26	.14	.22	.23	.16	.24	.61	.04	.33
Kind	.74	-.31	-.05	-.34	-.19	.30	-.10	.06	-.58	-.03	.21	-.12	.47	.24	.31	-.04
Insecure	.01	.16	.91	-.01	-.43	.21	.24	.19	.12	-.43	-.20	-.16	.06	-.22	-.08	.24
Aware of feelings of others	.78	-.26	.41	.09	-.05	.11	.15	.05	-.90	.19	.22	-.06	.23	.20	.16	.14
Good looking	.47	-.56	-.18	-.10	.05	.11	-.04	-.13	-.09	.26	-.20	-.06	.06	.30	.33	.22
Good person	.37	-.54	-.27	-.18	.13	-.03	-.20	-.12	.23	.16	.04	.00	.17	.62	.02	.22
Popular	.47	-.13	-.16	.12	.28	.04	-.28	-.20	-.11	.76	.02	.03	.37	.58	.06	.33
Sincere	.52	.02	.04	.10	-.01	-.27	.12	-.03	.20	.02	.69	-.12	.42	.86	.09	.06
Liberated	.48	.00	.43	.32	.29	.08	-.15	.13	.26	.38	.58	.11	.35	.32	-.09	.16
Blue eyes	.02	-.90	-.10	.08	.36	-.07	.12	-.05	.40	.01	.12	-.02	-.03	-.01	-.42	.14
Has leadership qualities	.48	.32	.16	.00	.44	-.42	.08	.03	.38	.10	.30	.83	.30	.58	-.05	.31
Creative	.08	.24	-.42	.37	.02	.06	-.06	.26	.13	.41	.24	.22	.31	.43	.01	.20
Aggressive	-.22	.76	.02	.01	-.37	-.14	.32	.20	.27	.15	.33	.45	.14	.14	-.15	.78
Dominant	.13	.44	.18	-.19	.07	-.45	.46	.11	-.05	.10	.19	.93	.03	.05	.19	-.02
Willing to take a stand	.34	.01	.32	.23	-.12	-.37	.10	.67	-.07	.31	.32	-.33	.28	.53	-.11	.31
Subordinates self to others	.41	-.24	.16	.07	-.54	.07	.17	-.27	.02	.16	.00	.45	.06	.04	.20	-.10

(Continued)

244

| | Females | | | | | | | | | Males | | | | | | | |
| | 14-year-olds n = 14 | | | | 18-year-olds n = 23 | | | | | 14-year-olds n = 33 | | | | 18-year-olds n = 41 | | |
	1	2	3	4	1	2	3	4	5	1	2	3	4	1	2	3
Strong	.42	.34	.48	.06	.36	.00	-.19	.67	-.32	-.05	-.31	.08	.33	.19	.11	-.03
Emotional	.77	-.08	.01	.17	-.07	.62	-.05	.17	-.19	.12	-.15	.08	.31	.71	.34	-.02
Strong personality	.62	-.07	.19	.02	.21	.03	-.20	.08	.03	.61	-.10	.08	.20	.83	.00	.11
Self confident	.50	-.45	-.05	-.46	.69	-.26	-.27	.10	.35	.59	.06	.17	.77	.45	.06	.38
Athletic	-.10	.06	.27	.00	.48	-.16	-.15	.07	-.28	.25	-.29	.21	-.04	.36	.29	-.06
Self-esteem	.21	-.08	.65	.25	.44	.01	-.52	.16	.23	.60	.13	.16	.29	.72	-.21	.26
Cooperative	.24	-.47	.37	.06	-.06	.22	-.34	.05	.13	.19	.02	.14	.86	.62	-.10	.00
Capable	.42	-.50	-.33	.02	.38	-.13	-.45	-.27	.18	.27	-.06	.19	.92	.35	-.06	-.23
Artistic	.30	-.17	.06	-.12	.16	.11	-.19	-.05	.11	.38	-.13	.51	.09	.49	.17	.11
Stands up under pressure	.58	-.01	.11	-.02	.25	.21	-.23	.52	-.17	.54	.06	-.10	.82	.28	-.09	.29
Tough-minded	.54	-.04	.29	-.17	.11	-.01	.22	.17	.01	.18	.10	.32	.63	.26	-.16	.63
Compassionate	.32	-.38	.63	.27	-.34	.25	.31	.01	-.19	.31	-.10	.12	.38	.40	.39	.01
Decides easily	.46	.20	.16	.22	-.01	-.40	.31	.35	.03	.22	.11	.07	.62	.42	.16	.02
Tender	.73	-.35	.14	.17	-.16	.36	.20	-.14	-.14	.58	-.04	-.08	.59	.48	.30	.15
Assertive	.56	-.08	.27	-.24	.26	.15	.03	.02	.27	.42	.11	.34	.01	.51	.00	.55
Likable	.53	-.48	-.03	-.34	-.20	.58	.05	-.10	-.41	.48	-.25	-.12	.41	.34	.23	.32
Generous	.86	-.26	.12	.08	.06	.42	-.23	.06	.01	.31	.06	-.01	.48	-.16	-.13	.58
Affectionate	.90	-.09	.16	.00	-.12	.89	-.04	.07	-.14	.47	-.27	.06	.46	.11	.36	.55
Warm	.63	.00	.19	.22	-.16	.92	-.02	.02	-.08	.23	-.08	.05	.84	.20	.31	.42
Soothes hurt feelings	.25	.04	.53	.33	-.33	.08	.39	-.07	-.43	.32	.18	.14	.26	.25	.68	.25
Feels good about self	.39	-.88	-.09	-.07	.36	-.09	-.23	.11	.29	.53	-.22	.38	.26	.20	.23	.59
Loves children	.37	-.40	.30	.38	-.40	.06	.13	-.20	-.25	.65	.24	.01	.28	.12	.82	-.15
Friendly	.63	-.33	-.11	.65	-.16	.15	-.28	-.14	-.51	.58	.03	-.06	.62	.34	.32	.16

(Continued)

245

	Females									Males						
	14-year-olds n = 14				18-year-olds n = 23					14-year-olds n = 33				18-year-olds n = 41		
	1	2	3	4	*1*	2	3	4	5	*1*	2	3	4	*1*	2	3
Hardworking	.59	−.21	−.20	.57	.05	−.08	.19	−.26	.54	.29	−.19	−.13	.36	.59	.26	.08
Tries to do one's best	.68	−.09	.21	.43	.00	−.52	.29	−.03	.16	.18	−.15	−.01	.46	.18	.14	.03
Never gives up	.57	.00	.36	.32	.10	.13	−.08	.70	.02	.41	.02	−.18	.41	.45	.36	.28
Active	.42	.08	.25	−.01	.17	.08	.09	.32	−.02	.25	−.10	−.03	.16	.50	.36	.23
Loyal	.33	.00	.68	.27	−.03	.34	.11	.65	.29	.28	.20	.04	.12	.32	−.02	.34
Doesn't show feelings	.12	−.04	.33	−.23	−.06	.17	.05	−.02	−.01	−.27	−.59	.05	.08	−.06	−.09	−.05
Quiet	−.14	−.33	−.16	.22	−.63	.24	−.05	−.26	−.10	−.20	−.86	−.23	.03	−.09	−.01	.20
Lively	.16	.39	.13	−.15	.37	−.22	.41	.28	.01	.56	.29	.00	.08	.07	.31	.04
Devotes self to others	.27	−.19	.03	−.19	−.18	.02	.54	−.07	.17	.00	−.25	.62	.22	−.10	−.04	.09
Whiny	−.19	.28	−.08	−.56	−.17	.09	.76	−.16	−.09	−.17	−.20	.04	−.34	−.09	.37	−.14
Humorous	.21	.04	−.25	.21	−.05	.34	−.02	.14	−.06	.47	.09	−.12	.47	.05	.07	−.19
Fun	.28	−.38	−.18	.00	.05	.09	.26	−.18	−.06	.40	.13	−.15	.33	.02	−.01	−.00
Shy	−.27	−.09	.05	.60	−.65	.13	.07	.00	.10	−.20	−.79	−.26	.24	−.23	.05	−.10
% of Variance	38.0	15.2	9.8	8.1	20.5	13.3	9.8	8.8	7.7	35.9	10.9	8.2	7.9	31.2	10.1	8.2
		71.27					10.1					8.2			49.6	
Factor Correlations																
1		−.19	.08	.09		−.13	−.17	.12	1.07		.13	.08	.20		.06	.12
2			.05	−.03		−.10	−.04	−.07				.02	−.01			−.04
3				.08			−.04	−.01					.06			
4								−.04								

APPENDIX XII

Factor Analyses of Importance Ratings of Self by American Respondents

	Females								Males							
	14-year-olds n = 38				18-year-olds n = 50				14-year-olds n = 38				18-year-olds n = 44			
	1	2	3	4	1	2	3	4	1	2	3	4	1	2	3	4
Helpful	.61	-.40	-.02	.15	.13	-.20	.00	-.35	.43	-.08	.12	.49	.79	-.14	-.37	-.18
Tall	-.23	-.19	-.11	.25	-.64	.07	.17	.16	.08	-.11	.31	.31	-.23	.23	-.33	.01
Acts as leader	.23	.54	-.03	-.11	.67	-.22	-.07	.08	.06	.21	.63	.03	-.28	.50	.27	-.09
Gentle	.81	-.27	-.12	.19	.18	-.12	-.33	-.31	.50	.02	-.06	.31	.03	.59	.04	-.17
Straight hair	.27	-.31	.09	.35	-.03	-.12	.20	-.05	.06	-.11	-.13	-.01	.22	.07	-.32	-.15
Socially adept	.22	.14	-.32	-.06	.02	.16	.57	-.13	.33	.41	.10	.15	-.33	.33	.45	.18
Competition	.45	.25	.28	.26	-.21	.91	.26	-.04	.23	.28	.10	.27	-.13	.28	.04	.22
Patriotic	.71	-.05	.10	.65	-.10	.15	.06	-.92	.23	.25	.16	.28	-.03	.05	-.23	.12
Kind	.76	-.33	-.08	-.37	-.07	.69	.12	.09	-.01	.20	-.08	.45	.32	.14	.36	.52
Insecure	.03	.18	.93	-.02	-.61	.05	.31	-.20	-.41	-.18	-.16	.08	.08	-.12	-.55	.02
Aware of feelings of others	.80	-.24	.43	.07	-.05	.24	.08	-.06	.17	.20	-.03	.21	-.30	.37	.59	.44
Good looking	.49	-.58	-.20	-.12	.17	.10	.03	.16	.25	-.18	-.01	.02	.52	-.10	-.22	-.50
Good person	.39	-.56	-.29	-.20	-.25	.78	.24	.24	.15	.00	.03	.16	.36	.04	.48	.09
Popular	.48	-.14	-.18	.14	-.13	.40	-.11	.01	.78	.00	.01	.39	.37	.32	-.34	-.41
Sincere	.55	.06	.08	.12	-.04	.44	.33	.48	.01	.70	-.10	.40	.29	.11	.38	.03
Liberated	.49	.03	.41	.38	-.35	.73	.31	.07	.39	.61	.11	.37	.58	-.39	-.39	-.13
Blue eyes	.00	-.88	-.11	.09	.04	-.25	.03	.17	.03	.13	-.02	-.06	.25	.24	-.04	.01
Has leadership qualities	.45	.30	.14	.03	.12	.07	-.02	-.30	.12	.32	.85	.31	.02	.09	.41	.21
Creative	.09	.26	-.44	.31	-.25	.42	.27	.04	.43	.26	.24	.35	.52	-.14	.02	-.27
Aggressive	-.20	.78	.03	.04	.23	-.61	-.05	-.50	.17	.35	.47	.16	-.43	.47	-.24	.00
Dominant	.11	.42	.16	-.17	.30	-.27	.06	-.03	.12	.23	.95	.06	-.17	.19	-.43	.06
Willing to take a stand	.30	.05	.32	.25	.29	.05	.28	.10	.32	.35	-.38	.29	.56	-.16	-.07	.10
Subordinates self to others	.43	-.26	.15	.11	-.02	-.32	.19	.29	.18	.01	.47	.08	.11	-.04	-.79	-.08

(Continued)

| | Females | | | | | | | | Males | | | | | | | |
| | 14-year-olds n = 38 | | | | 18-year-olds n = 50 | | | | 14-year-olds n = 38 | | | | 18-year-olds n = 44 | | | |
	1	2	3	4	1	2	3	4	1	2	3	4	1	2	3	4
Strong	.40	.36	.50	.08	-.06	.28	.45	.47	-.07	-.36	.09	.35	.01	.10	-.05	-.01
Emotional	.78	-.10	.03	.19	.05	.55	.36	.46	.13	-.16	.10	.32	.52	-.22	-.20	-.34
Strong personality	.65	-.09	.21	.04	.18	.41	.68	.29	.63	-.09	.08	.21	.55	.04	-.14	-.12
Self confident	.51	-.48	-.07	-.48	-.04	.30	.35	-.17	.61	.05	.16	.72	.88	.15	-.04	-.34
Athletic	-.12	.07	.29	.25	-.46	.19	.74	-.12	.23	-.19	.20	-.06	.21	.14	-.31	.21
Self–esteem	.23	-.10	.67	.23	-.43	.29	.37	-.34	.59	.12	.18	.30	.03	.67	.47	.00
Cooperative	.21	-.48	.31	.12	-.35	.70	.29	.02	.21	.01	.12	.88	.72	-.35	-.11	-.11
Capable	.43	-.53	-.31	.04	-.15	.14	.50	.04	.26	-.05	.18	.90	.08	.79	103	-.09
Artistic	.32	-.19	.05	-.10	.05	-.09	.52	-.26	.36	-.11	.49	.19	.74	.14	-.27	-.51
Stands up under pressure	.61	-.03	.13	-.06	.58	-.42	-.13	.08	.55	.05	-.12	.81	.12	.59	.03	-.65
Tough–minded	.63	-.07	.31	-.19	-.14	.20	.33	-.13	.16	.12	.33	.64	.72	-.24	-.35	-.18
Compassionate	.34	-.40	.65	.29	.86	-.48	-.10	-.02	.30	-.09	.11	.36	.21	.53	.00	-.57
Decides easily	.48	.25	.19	.19	.83	-.46	-.10	-.11	.20	.09	.08	.63	.17	.57	-.19	-.59
Tender	.75	-.38	.16	.15	.01	.47	.18	.07	.56	-.02	-.07	.61	.63	-.11	-.23	-.01
Assertive	.58	-.10	.29	-.26	-.17	.04	.39	-.65	.41	.09	.32	.00	-.05	-.07	-.27	-.02
Likable	.58	-.11	.26	-.23	.95	-.21	-.11	.15	.46	-.23	-.14	.40	.35	.27	.11	-.73
Generous	.76	-.32	-.08	-.09	-.63	.75	.30	.19	.30	.05	-.02	.46	.06	.02	.13	.29
Affectionate	.92	-.08	.15	-.01	.12	.43	.55	.26	.49	-.28	.03	.48	.76	.05	.15	-.26
Warm	.66	-.05	.13	.22	.80	-.35	-.11	.12	.35	-.09	.06	.87	.15	.41	.21	-.75
Soothes hurt feelings	.23	.05	.50	.27	.22	.31	.39	.48	.35	.20	.16	.32	.56	-.35	-.03	-.21
Feels good about self	.31	-.83	-.10	-.08	.09	.40	.39	-.12	.55	-.25	.40	.27	.78	.03	.24	-.04
Loves children	.35	-.42	.28	.29	.84	-.31	-.36	.14	.63	.25	.03	.29	.75	.17	-.13	-.42
Friendly	.61	-.31	-.18	.63	.35	.10	.73	.23	.65	.02	-.07	.63	-.02	.34	.43	-.15

(Continued)

	Females								Males							
	14-year-olds n = 38				18-year-olds n = 50				14-year-olds n = 38				18-year-olds n = 44			
	1	2	3	4	1	2	3	4	1	2	3	4	1	2	3	4
Hardworking	.63	-.24	-.25	.61	.71	-.23	.14	.11	.34	-.22	-.15	.38	.16	.56	.03	-.41
Tries to do one's best	.66	-.10	.25	.45	.30	.12	.23	.16	.20	-.17	-.03	.45	.86	-.17	-.02	-.25
Never gives up	.61	.03	.38	.31	.11	.13	.32	-.10	.43	.03	-.20	.43	.37	-.03	-.42	-.45
Active	.41	.10	.27	-.05	.84	-.45	-.06	-.03	.23	-.08	-.01	.15	.25	.23	-.36	.62
Loyal	.31	.01	.71	.26	-.35	.55	.06	.25	.26	.18	.06	.14	.34	.05	-.14	-.04
Doesn't show feelings	.13	-.06	.35	-.25	.09	-.08	-.10	-.22	-.29	-.61	.03	.05	.06	-.49	-.62	-.08
Quiet	-.16	-.38	-.18	.20	-.58	.08	.11	-.01	-.18	-.85	-.12	.08	-.45	.35	.44	.39
Lively	.16	.43	.08	-.19	.97	-.17	-.07	.25	.59	.32	.06	-.05	-.18	.65	.31	.12
Devotes self to others	.28	-.17	.05	-.16	-.45	.04	.12	.12	.03	-.28	.63	.28	-.15	.22	-.42	.58
Whiny	-.15	.26	-.03	-.58	-.35	-.14	.16	-.11	-.20	-.32	.05	-.36	-.14	.01	-.81	.09
Humorous	.26	.08	-.28	.24	.87	-.27	-.25	.20	.49	.10	-.22	.18	-.38	.34	.74	.13
Fun	.33	-.41	-.21	.03	.58	.04	.47	.06	.42	.15	-.18	.31	-.14	.77	.20	-.05
Shy	-.29	-.11	.08	.63	-.55	-.21	.09	-.07	-.22	-.80	-.28	.26	.42	.28	-.14	-.01
% of Variance	26.3	20.5	14.2	9.1	25.1	21.7	12.3	9.7	29.8	18.6	14.1	9.3	27.5	19.5	15.8	9.5
		70.1				68.9				71.8				72.4		
Factor Correlations																
1		-.18	.07	.08		-.28	-.11	.10		.12	.07	.17		-.07	-.06	-.20
2			.04	-.05			.23	.12			-.02	.00			.16	-.10
3				.03				.04				.02				.07

APPENDIX XIII

Factor Analyses of Importance Ratings of Ideal Self by Swedish Respondents

| | Females | | | | | | | Males | | | | |
| | 14-year-olds n = 30 | | | | 18-year-olds n = 24 | | | 14-year-olds n = 32 | | 18-year-olds n = 31 | | |
	1	2	3	4	1	2	3	1	2	1	2	3
Helpful	.34	-.22	-.07	-.03	.33	-.09	-.07	.70	.15	.32	-.05	.52
Tall	.22	.20	-.10	-.34	-.18	.29	.29	.12	.49	.01	.84	-.01
Acts as leader	.34	.10	-.10	-.32	.32	.73	-.20	.29	.63	.04	.89	-.06
Gentle	.04	.01	-.02	-.08	.79	-.01	-.06	.56	.23	.25	.07	.48
Straight hair	-.08	.69	.03	-.19	.01	.13	.22	.00	.74	-.22	.45	.10
Socially adept	.29	-.02	-.10	-.68	.29	.19	-.56	.36	.04	.37	.07	-.14
Competitive	.05	.14	.00	.06	-.11	.93	.05	.51	.58	.11	.25	.68
Patriotic	.26	-.10	.02	-.82	.81	-.17	-.29	.65	.00	.22	.01	.70
Kind	.13	-.03	-.08	-.08	.74	.09	-.04	.81	.12	.26	-.18	.85
Insecure	.10	.35	.65	-.15	-.39	-.03	.81	-.25	.32	-.33	.30	-.12
Aware of feelings of others	.08	-.25	-.11	-.21	.51	-.13	-.08	.34	-.12	.21	.00	.71
Good looking	.38	-.19	-.15	-.47	-.08	-.06	.09	.38	.47	.59	.19	.01
Good person	.39	.09	.07	-.14	.37	.07	-.07	.56	.23	.39	.14	.35
Popular	.40	.12	.20	-.15	-.06	.06	-.18	.34	.55	.53	.17	.24
Sincere	.40	-.07	.15	.01	.83	.07	.00	.82	.21	.57	-.02	.22
Liberated	.09	.01	.15	-.03	.39	.27	-.20	.57	.19	.61	.03	.10
Blue eyes	.07	.90	.07	.12	-.39	.35	.29	.16	.80	-.12	.33	-.01
Has leadership qualities	.14	.30	.01	-.01	.30	.60	-.45	.32	.40	.27	.63	.15
Creative	.20	-.01	-.18	-.75	.53	.34	-.22	.51	.24	.26	.32	.31
Aggressive	.12	.24	.24	-.26	-.18	.32	.40	.31	.68	.06	.31	.30
Dominant	.10	.51	.22	-.18	-.14	.44	.31	.16	.88	.06	.21	.21
Willing to take a stand	.33	-.34	-.18	-.23	.65	.06	-.01	.85	.16	.18	.06	.15
Subordinates self to others	.01	.53	.26	-.01	-.14	.71	.30	.13	.38	.00	.21	.23

(Continued)

| | Females | | | | | | | Males | | | | |
| | 14-year-olds n = 30 | | | | 18-year-olds n = 24 | | | 14-year-olds n = 32 | | 18-year-olds n = 31 | | |
	1	2	3	4	1	2	3	1	2	1	2	3
Strong	-.03	.22	-.32	.48	.25	.10	-.15	.48	.36	.24	.22	-.01
Emotional	.37	.03	-.07	-.14	.41	-.07	-.01	.57	.01	.37	-.26	.43
Strong personality	.73	-.20	-.10	-.38	.61	.06	-.19	.63	.22	.23	-.25	.34
Self confident	.53	-.18	-.03	-.45	.57	-.11	-.18	.50	.26	.21	-.14	.02
Athletic	-.06	.34	-.17	.28	.03	.69	-.19	.28	.20	.33	.24	.11
Self-esteem	.34	-.18	.04	-.23	.55	.14	.06	.55	.20	.47	.07	.06
Cooperative	.25	-.39	.01	-.20	.62	.09	-.04	.70	.24	.49	-.20	.22
Capable	.58	-.19	.12	-.29	.17	.26	-.01	.72	.35	.19	.19	-.25
Artistic	.11	.02	.15	-.41	.36	.57	-.35	.56	.23	.27	-.16	-.08
Stands up under pressure	.46	-.41	-.08	-.25	.46	.05	-.41	.47	-.10	.56	.02	-.04
Tough-minded	.18	.22	-.27	.10	.18	.58	-.14	.61	.29	.26	.18	.29
Compassionate	.61	-.03	.11	-.32	.34	.21	.04	.62	.09	.49	-.12	.16
Decides easily	.62	.00	-.29	-.21	.24	.51	-.23	.47	.12	.69	.13	.30
Tender	.71	-.09	-.18	-.08	.21	.33	-.01	.60	-.02	.76	-.04	.36
Assertive	.28	.21	-.01	.26	.16	.65	-.10	.21	.21	.20	.48	-.04
Likable	.41	-.01	.12	-.22	.36	.36	-.17	.45	-.03	.84	-.08	.25
Generous	.15	-.28	-.06	-.47	.64	.14	-.01	.52	.09	.72	.22	.05
Affectionate	.34	-.16	-.10	-.20	.67	.17	-.02	.60	.10	.91	-.05	.12
Warm	-.05	-.18	.11	.32	.24	.07	-.03	.73	.12	.69	-.10	.58
Soothes hurt feelings	.37	-.03	.10	.33	.40	.05	.08	.57	.02	.45	-.31	.35
Feels good about self	.32	.08	.18	-.22	.51	-.03	-.19	.42	.28	.03	.37	.22
Loves children	.83	.08	.12	-.07	-.08	.23	.24	.44	.12	.06	.03	-.01
Friendly	.91	.05	.08	-.19	.69	.14	-.09	.67	.11	.26	-.06	.22

(Continued)

	Females							Males				
	14-year-olds n = 30				18-year-olds n = 24			14-year-olds n = 32		18-year-olds n = 31		
	1	2	3	4	1	2	3	1	2	1	2	3
Hardworking	.91	.03	.07	-.22	.47	.15	.07	.81	.13	.33	.13	.32
Tries to do one's best	.92	-.12	-.13	-.35	.47	.20	-.33	.83	.12	.40	-.07	.10
Never gives up	.81	-.22	-.24	-.17	.31	.25	.30	.85	.22	.45	-.03	.20
Active	.54	-.34	-.20	-.27	.35	.09	-.13	.74	.23	.24	.13	.17
Loyal	.04	-.30	.15	-.50	.72	-.15	-.32	.05	-.07	.39	-.07	.05
Doesn't show feelings	-.11	-.02	.89	.17	-.26	-.15	.84	-.24	.30	-.24	.28	-.06
Quiet	-.02	.09	.80	.05	-.15	-.25	.80	-.19	.13	-.19	.25	.01
Lively	.17	-.40	.28	.11	.27	.33	.02	.17	-.11	-.14	.60	.20
Devotes self to others	.10	.00	.61	-.20	.06	-.03	.47	.02	.27	-.02	.16	-.09
Whiny	.09	.08	.89	-.06	-.04	.11	.88	-.14	.23	-.21	.14	-.10
Humorous	.46	-.47	-.09	-.08	.35	.45	-.42	.65	.12	.41	.13	.38
Fun	.45	-.45	.03	-.03	.30	.51	-.24	.78	.12	.38	.09	.78
Shy	-.15	.16	.30	.01	.05	.12	.75	-.07	.08	-.08	-.23	-.04
% of Variance	29.4	12.3	9.6	7.9	35.5	14.6	11.5	54.4	12.7	31.7	12.9	8.4
		59.2				61.6			67.1		53.0	
Factor Correlations												
1		-.05	-.03	-.21		.04	-.12		.15		-.05	.16
2			.06	.09			-.02					.04
3				.00								

AUTHOR INDEX

255

SUBJECT INDEX